WE INTERRUPT THIS NEWSCAST

Local television newscasts around the country look alike and are filled with crime, accidents, and disasters. Interviews with more than 2,000 TV journalists around the country demonstrate that news looks this way because of the ingrained belief that "eyeball grabbers" are the only way to build an audience. This book contradicts the conventional wisdom using empirical evidence drawn from a five-year content analysis of local news in more than 154 stations in 50 markets around the country. Correlating the content of local news with ratings success shows that news stories on a wide variety of substantive topics draw viewers and that audiences reward good journalism with high ratings. The book shows that "how" a story is reported is more important for building ratings than what the story is about. Local TV does not have to "bleed to lead." Instead, local journalists can succeed by putting in the effort to get good stories, finding and balancing sources, seeking out experts, and making stories relevant to the local audience.

Tom Rosenstiel designed the Project for Excellence in Journalism and directs its activities. He also serves as vice chairman of the Committee of Concerned Journalists. A journalist for more than 20 years, he is a former media critic for the *Los Angeles Times* and chief congressional correspondent for *Newsweek* magazine. Among his books, he is coauthor, with Bill Kovach, of *The Elements of Journalism: What Newspeople Should Know and the Public Should Expect* (2001).

Marion R. Just is Professor of Political Science at Wellesley College. She is a coauthor of *Crosstalk: Citizens, Candidates and the Media in a Presidential Campaign* (1996); *Common Knowledge: News and the Construction of Political Meaning* (1992); and *The Election of 1996* (1997).

Todd L. Belt is currently Assistant Professor of Political Science at the University of Hawai'i at Hilo. He has published articles in the *Journal of Health and Social Behavior*, the *Columbia Journalism Review*, and *Campaigns & Elections*. He also coauthored the book *Getting Involved: A Guide to Student Citizenship* (2000).

Atiba Pertilla is currently a MacCracken Fellow in the Department of History at New York University, pursuing a doctoral degree in U.S. history. As a research associate at the Project for Excellence in Journalism, he has published articles in the *Columbia Journalism Review* and *Electronic Media* (now *Television Week*).

Walter C. Dean is a 35-year broadcast news veteran who is a senior associate at the Project for Excellence in Journalism and director of broadcast training for the Committee of Concerned Journalists.

Dante Chinni is a senior researcher for the Project for Excellence in Journalism and a columnist for the *Christian Science Monitor*. He is a regular contributor to the *Washington Post Magazine* and has written for *The Economist*, the *New York Times Magazine*, the *Columbia Journalism Review*, *Salon*, and *ESPN the Magazine*, among others.

We Interrupt This Newscast

HOW TO IMPROVE LOCAL NEWS AND WIN RATINGS, TOO

Tom Rosenstiel
Project for Excellence in Journalism

Marion R. Just
Wellesley College

Todd L. Belt
University of Hawai'i at Hilo

Atiba Pertilla
New York University

Walter C. Dean
Project for Excellence in Journalism

Dante Chinni
Project for Excellence in Journalism

CAMBRIDGE
UNIVERSITY PRESS

CAMBRIDGE UNIVERSITY PRESS
Cambridge, New York, Melbourne, Madrid, Cape Town, Singapore, São Paulo

Cambridge University Press
32 Avenue of the Americas, New York, NY 10013-2473, USA

www.cambridge.org
Information on this title: www.cambridge.org/9780521871150

First published 2007

Printed in the United States of America

A catalog record for this publication is available from the British Library.

Library of Congress Cataloging in Publication Data

We interrupt this newscast: how to improve local news and win ratings, too
/ by Tom Rosenstiel . . . [[et al.]].
    p. cm.
Includes bibliographical references and index.
ISBN-13: 978-0-521-87115-0 (hardback)
ISBN-13: 978-0-521-69154-3 (pbk.)
1. Television broadcasting of news – United States. I. Rosenstiel, Tom
II. Title.
PN4888.T4W37 2007
070.4'33 – dc22   2006025896

ISBN 978-0-521-87115-0 hardback
ISBN 978-0-521-69154-3 paperback

Contents

Acknowledgments

This book is based on nearly a decade of research and teaching. That journey has involved dozens of researchers, scores of broadcast news managers, and hundreds of local TV journalists. It began with the Project for Excellence in Journalism's Five Year Local TV News Project, which was funded by the Pew Charitable Trusts. We cannot name everyone involved here, but many deserve special mention.

That a project of this magnitude was ever undertaken is due to the intellectual leadership and financial support of Rebecca Rimel and Don Kimelman.

The project itself was the idea of Tom Rosenstiel. Marion Just joined almost immediately as academic adviser and has helped shepherd things from early on. Todd Belt joined soon thereafter as statistician. Atiba Pertilla was with the project next in duration, first as a research associate, then later as project manager. Wally Dean came next, filling the role of TV news professional on the project, and finally, to help transform the work into a book, Dante Chinni joined as editor and coauthor.

Carl Gottleib, now at WCBS in New York City, helped supervise the Five Year Local TV News Project at the Project for Excellence in Journalism from 1998 to 2002, offering the experience of a local TV news veteran during the five years of initial data collection.

Several scholars contributed to the content analysis design, including Michael Robinson, Ph.D., formerly Professor, Department of Government, Georgetown University; Professor Ann Crigler, Chair of the Political Science Department of the University of Southern California; and Professor Sherri Mazingo, School of Journalism and Mass Communications, University of Minnesota.

Princeton Survey Research Associates carried out the content analysis coding under the creative and effective leadership of Lee Ann Brady. Lee Ann provided the first round of content analysis statistical results and helped prepare reports on the content published in the *Columbia Journalism Review*.

Tami Buhr of Harvard University gave us practical and sophisticated statistical advice in the analysis of the content analysis data.

Our News Directors Surveys relied on the dedication and persistence of Rosalind Levine to produce an excellent response rate. Kathleen Regan was the stalwart data manager of mountains of survey questionnaires. Both Rosalind and Kathleen contributed to the analysis of the surveys and to reports about the study published in the *Columbia Journalism Review*. In addition, several Wellesley College students worked on the data collection and statistical analysis of the news directors' surveys. We would like to thank in particular Christine Yi and Grace E. Kim. Wellesley College and the National Science Foundation Social Science Summer Research Grant program provided support for student assistants and partial funding for Marion Just's participation in the project.

The project received invaluable support from Unju Chi and Jeffrey Polachek at Nielsen Media Research. We are grateful to Bob Olson for teaching Todd Belt "everything he knows" about ratings and to Nicole Simmons of the University of California, Riverside, for research assistance.

In addition, a Design Team of news professionals helped develop the criteria and methods that were used in this analysis. The titles and affiliations of the Design Team members are listed in Appendix A. We are grateful to the Design Team for their work in the early stages of the project, but members of the team are not responsible for the interpretations of the data or the conclusions of this book.

Throughout the five years of the Local TV News Project study, the staff of the Project for Excellence in Journalism contributed their advice and energy, including Amy Mitchell, Nancy Anderson, Stacy Forster, and Chris Galdieri.

The newsroom teaching that further informed our research was made possible by a grant from the John S. and James L. Knight Foundation to support the Committee of Concerned Journalists' (CCJ's) "Traveling Curriculum." Hodding Carter spotted the potential in conducting an ongoing dialogue about the purposes of journalism, and Eric Newton directed Knight's journalism initiatives.

Bill Kovach, CCJ chair, provided his always-thoughtful guidance, as did Tom Avila and Carrie Brown. Deborah Potter, Scott Libin, Paul Friedman, John Martin, Deb Wenger, Brooks Jackson, Charles Beirbauer, Bill Damon, and the late Marty Haag worked with the CCJ staff to conduct the newsroom training sessions. Brett Mueller, who undertook an assessment of the project, gave valuable feedback. Jennifer Fimbres provided logistical support.

We especially want to thank the almost 100 news directors and general managers who invited the CCJ into their newsrooms. Lane Michaelsen, Scott Libin, John Cardenas, Kay Miller, Wayne Lynch, and Dan Weiser were news directors at the first group of stations visited.

Finally, we want to thank the many hundreds of broadcast journalists who spoke candidly with us about their work and beliefs. Like many others in journalism, they told us they got into the profession because they wanted to make a difference. Our greatest hope is that this book will help them do just that.

WE INTERRUPT THIS NEWSCAST

1   A Prologue: What This Book Is For

"When you go to the public rest room, is someone watching you?"

That's the question the Channel 13 news team is asking tonight to tease viewers to watch its 10 o'clock broadcast.

When the newscast begins seconds later, anchor Art Baron, a jut-jawed 30-something white male, explains: "It's called cruising, and *13 News* discovered it's going on right here in New Mexico."

Baron looks harder into the camera for emphasis: "Now this story is disturbing, but you'll want to know what we found going on behind the walls of those stalls."

The special report takes up not only one-third of the news hole on this night but also on the next night on *13 News at 10* as well, when it is introduced with animated gun-sight cross hairs with the words "13 Investigates" stamped over them, punctuated by pulsating musical accompaniment.

Despite the time and effort invested, however, "Behind the Walls of the Stalls," as the report is called, turns out to be an empty exercise. While it notes that a Web site listed 50 bathrooms around the state as places for men to meet, reporters visit only three of the bathrooms and find ... nothing. In addition, a search of police records by 13's investigative team yields nothing more than reports of two incidents – both in the same place – of indecent exposure in public rest rooms in the entire state.

Instead, the report falls back on several claims it cannot substantiate, some of which seem spurious at face value. Baron, the anchor, goes so far as to hint that the story will reveal pedophilia, telling parents they will want to pay particular attention: "Your children use rest rooms in public places all the time ... sometimes they even go in alone." The report, however, offers no evidence of pedophilia associated with the rest rooms

the station investigated or even the Web site that has identified 47 other
public rest rooms. The allusion to children is a phony stunt, a lure to get
alarmed parents to watch.

Tomorrow night, *13 News* promises: "What secret signals you could be
giving out inviting someone to approach you in a rest room."

Some people might say picking out "Behind the Walls of the Stalls" to
highlight in this way is unfair. The series is a particularly grievous
example of a phony exposé that can't substantiate its claims, that is
designed to scare and manipulate, and, as an added insult, that is on the
edge of bad taste. Egregious examples of hype and sensationalism in local
TV news, skeptics would argue, misrepresent the medium. Local TV news
is about more than that. Every day across the country there is superb
work being done in the medium. And that is true without question. The
reality, however, is that "the Stalls" is by no means out of the ordinary.
Stations around the country air pieces like "Cosmetic Surgery Catastrophes" at the local day spa, "Killer Bras" whose wires can poke, "Is
Your Frozen Yogurt Making You Sick?" because it contains bacteria, and
"Killer Power Lines" that may or may not maim you if you live near
them. All of these are real examples, and most of them ran on multiple
stations, often at the suggestion of news consultants.

The more pertinent question is: Why? Why waste so much time and
money, and threaten a station's reputation, by leading with a report so
thin on meaningful news? Isn't there a risk of promising the audience
something and not delivering it? In other words, what is the thinking
behind a series like "Behind the Walls of the Stalls"? While that series
may be an extreme example, the thinking behind it is representative of
something larger, something that begins to explain, in spite of all the
good work in local TV, why there is so much that is bad.

"Behind the Walls of the Stalls" aired in Albuquerque during a "sweeps
week" – that period four times a year when Nielsen Media Research
counts the audience for the nation's television programs and comes up
with the ratings used to determine the rates that will be charged to
advertisers for the next three months. Nielsen ratings decide the fate of
programs and staff. "Behind the Walls of the Stalls," in other words, was a
ploy to prop up the ratings and profits of local news. It was an attempt to
catch the audience's attention. The people at the station looked at all the
topics available and all the resources at their disposal and decided that
"Behind the Walls of the Stalls" would be a winner with viewers.

A couple of nights after airing "Walls," the same Albuquerque station
ran an exhaustively reported, five-minute piece on an important, but

much less sensational, topic: What happens when people become "Too Old to Drive?" The story showed examples of accidents involving older drivers, footage of a driving class for those 55 and over, statistics that compared the accident rates of older and teenage drivers, and even an interview with the director of the motor vehicles office who had to tell his mother she had become too elderly to continue to drive safely.

What happened when the station aired these two distinctly different stories? Did either of them attract viewers?

On the first night the highly promoted "Walls of the Stalls" aired, there was no viewership increase whatsoever. The newscast received a 6 rating, the same as the average of all four Mondays in the four-week ratings period.[1]

What about the "cover story" on drivers too old to drive? The night it aired, about 10 minutes into the broadcast on a Thursday night, the 10 P.M. news received a 9 rating, the highest (by 2 rating points) of any night during the sweeps and 50% better than the nightly, weekly, and monthly average rating of 6.[2]

How should general managers, news directors, and newscast producers interpret these "results"? And if "Too Old to Drive?" fared better than "Behind the Walls of the Stalls," why did the latter get so much promotion, and why do local stations continue to produce stories like it? The answers to these questions are crucial not just for news directors or local TV stations – Americans depend more on local TV news than any other news source. It attracts a bigger audience than cable or national TV news, according to surveys.[3] Local TV news is the main source of information for many Americans about what is happening in their neighborhood, their economy, and their culture. How well local news serves its audience matters not only for the station's bottom line but also for the bottom line of the democratic enterprise.

One reason stations continue to run stories like "Behind the Walls of the Stalls" is that they are not sure what audiences really want. Newsroom decision makers operate by a set of elaborate, long-held assumptions about what motivates viewers, reinforced by anecdote, inference, and corporate mandate. Those assumptions, in turn, are reinforced by limited resources, lack of time, lack of reporter expertise, and growing demand for more programming – all conditions that are on the increase. Added to these forces in many cases is research from consultants too often conducted on the cheap and generic in nature rather than market-specific.

What's more, this mindset has not grown ratings for local TV news in recent years. In 2002, five years after "Behind the Walls" and "Too Old to Drive?'' aired, we studied the Albuquerque market again. Though the number of homes using television had increased markedly as the region grew, the number of people watching this station remained unchanged. Five years later, the 10 P.M. news was still getting a 6 rating, while its share of viewers had dropped from a 13 to an 11.

So what does work? That is what this book answers.

The conclusions we offer, moreover, are not based on hunches, anecdotes, or even conventional quick market research. They are derived from the most extensive study ever conducted on local TV news. This research includes a content analysis of five years of local TV broadcasts in large, medium, and small markets. Those findings, in turn, were correlated with actual viewer behavior – ratings and share data over time – not merely public opinion polls or focus groups, which have their value but can be misused. The study also includes an annual survey of news directors, dozens of sessions in newsrooms around the country to gather data, and focus groups with viewers. A panel of veteran TV journalists helped guide its design.

The research group behind this book is a mix of local television professionals, academics, statisticians, print and broadcast journalists, and media observers. Everyone who worked on this project understands that TV news is different from (not better and not worse than) journalism in other media and that different strategies are needed to make it successful.

Based on all this work and with that mindset, this book reveals what kinds of content on local TV news can be statistically proven to build audience. It describes the kinds of content that drives viewers away. It shows how local TV newspeople make story decisions now and how they should craft stories differently so that more people will watch them. And based on hard data, it details how newspeople should go about covering major subjects, such as politics, crime, education, and health, to increase viewer loyalty. Perhaps most important, this book points out that many of the assumptions that govern local TV content are patently wrong. Many of the current newsroom conventions lead to the practices that annoy not only critics of TV news but viewers as well.

Let's also be clear about a few things that this book is not. It is not a moral screed about "good Journalism" with a capital J or the latest tome from the "shame on you police." Nor is it the work of a group of academics or critics with little connection to or understanding of how newsrooms really work and why. This book is the result of five years of gathering data from 1,200 hours of newscasts from 154 stations – more than 33,000 stories – followed by three years of analysis. It draws from our work with more than 2,000 local TV newspeople at more than 40 stations around the country.

Our results show that there are elements that can be incorporated into TV news stories that make them credible and interesting to the audience – and that will get good ratings. We call these elements "The Magic Formula." But there is nothing mysterious about them. They come from what veteran TV journalists tell us makes good local news. They are the goals of news directors around the country, and they are taught in journalism schools. The real mystery is why they have such a bad rap in newsroom practice.

Is there a hidden agenda in this book? No. There is no "do good for goodness sake" thought process behind its creation. When we began this research in 1998 we had no idea where it would take us. Frankly, our best guess was that news content would make little difference in ratings. We figured the countless other factors affecting viewership – everything from anchor chemistry to program lead-ins to set design to viewer loyalty – would make it virtually impossible to find any correlation between certain kinds of content or approaches to the news and ratings success. We hoped to find evidence that a story doesn't have to "bleed to lead." This would be significant, we imagined. It would mean local TV news had a choice. When we looked at the data, however, they revealed far more than we anticipated. By cross-referencing our content research with audience data, we discovered a road map to better ratings. And in many cases, that formula is about better reporting. In these pages we share what the data revealed.

In Chapter 2, we show in detail how we did our work. We discuss the stations, the markets, the ratings, and the other sources of information we used to understand what is on local TV news today (The Knowledge Base).

In Chapter 3, we examine the current landscape of local TV news and demonstrate that, as many people observe, local newscasts often do look alike wherever you go (The Reality of Local TV News). In Chapter 4, we expose the myths that govern local TV news and give it that uniform feel; and we reveal how those myths hurt ratings, not help them. We prove, for instance, that many of the best-known bits of conventional wisdom are demonstrably false – the idea that it is more important to "hook and hold" an audience than to cultivate one, the reliance on yellow police tape to "grab eyeballs," and the belief that TV can't do idea stories well (The Myths of Local TV News).

Most important, we analyze the data to show what actually does work with viewers, and we offer specific ideas and strategies for doing better stories that get better ratings. In Chapter 5 we look at what approaches work – everything from the number of sources to the amount and type of enterprise and balance. We explain how longer stories aren't always the answer, and by analyzing the data we show how, and when, devoting more time to a story is a good idea and when a few quick moments of video are probably enough (The Magic Formula).

In Chapter 6, we take up particular story topics – crime, government, health, and education – and show what makes them resonate with audiences. We explain when viewers particularly want expert sources and when providing divergent viewpoints is crucial (Steps to Better Coverage).

And in Chapter 7 we take news professionals through specific strategies for implementing these new approaches in the newsroom. We suggest how to get past the old habits that die hard and how to assess the job a station is doing (Putting It All into Action). We offer checklists for news directors about how to motivate and produce news that viewers want to watch.

In the final chapter, we look to the future and the emerging technologies that are changing the way people get information. We show how the kinds of recommendations that we offer based on our results constitute a formula for facing the future as well.

Ultimately, our findings are crucial because they are about more than doing journalism right. They show how good journalism means more ratings points that can translate into tens of thousands or even hundreds of thousands of dollars to local stations. They are practical and bottom-line in an industry that demands bottom-line results.

We prove that doing certain kinds of journalism – using what we call "The Magic Formula" – really works. Although our content audit shows that there isn't a lot of high-quality/high-rating content on local TV, explaining why that is the case is not the principal point of this book. We describe in detail what is actually on local TV news and who watches it, and we offer insight into how those decisions are made. But besides the myths that govern local news, we recognize that there are several other factors that affect content and we touch on them briefly.

In part, local TV news looks the way it does because station owners expect 40% profit margins – about four times that of most U.S. industries. To make that kind of profit general managers often focus on the weekly profit and loss statement rather than thinking about the best way to do the news. This book shows, however, that profits and what most would term "quality" should not be considered mutually exclusive.

Our surveys tell us that consultants also play a role in determining the content of local TV news. This is not an anti-consultant book, but we have come to believe that the research many of them provide is often too shallow and too focused on the wrong questions to do much good. In fact, by steering stations wrong about their audiences' desires, consultants may do inadvertent harm. There is, and probably always will be, a place for consultants in the TV news business, but the limits of their research should be better understood.

On the whole, if there are any broad lessons from all the data we have examined they might be boiled down to this: The audience is discriminating and cares about how news is reported. The consistent message that comes through all of our research is that viewers reward stations that do a good job of gathering information and telling stories. Audiences recognize when a story is short on information or is being embellished. They tune out. They also know how to read coverage. If a station gives short shrift to a serious topic, they won't watch. And there is evidence that the audience is getting wise to the "flash and trash" approach taken by many stations.

Inside the industry there is concern. The days of growing audiences and appeal for the medium may be gone. Local TV news is still the most trusted, most used news source according to public polls, but its numbers are slipping. Its ratings overall are falling. And despite all the gimmicks and all the "Behind the Walls of the Stalls" reports, the efforts to hook and hold viewers seem to be having less and less impact.

The question for stations and news departments is: What now?

We think we have an answer. We cannot emphasize enough how much our recommendations face up to the real world – they are as good for the bottom line as for the soul. What if doing well and doing good could lead down same path? We think they do. Let us show you how.

2 The Knowledge Base

Much of what you will read in this book may startle you. If you are a news professional, it may counter what you have been taught in school or learned on the job. It may even seem to contradict what you assume from watching local TV news yourself. Why are our conclusions so dramatically different from the accepted truths about local TV news? It is important to consider from where the received wisdom of local TV news comes. Much of it is supported by anecdotes or practices handed down from bosses. Some of the conventions that are accepted truisms may be correct, but some may just be the way things "always" have been done. So from this point on, take all those things you "know" about TV news and put them aside. What you are reading uses hard data to reach an entirely new set of conclusions about news production and audience response. Among them:

- Local stations that take the trouble to produce higher-quality newscasts attract more viewers than other stations, even taking into account other factors that increase ratings, such as the lead-in program, time slot, station size, and network affiliation.
- Higher-quality news also attracts the demographic groups that advertisers seek.
- Many newsroom decisions that are made in the name of efficiency actually drive viewers away.
- Story topic, on which most audience research is based, is a poor indicator of ratings success.
- Newscasts that run longer, more detailed lead stories attract larger audiences.
- Flashing lights, yellow police tape, and so-called eyeball-grabbing visuals do not by themselves attract viewers.

What is the basis for our unconventional findings? Copious research in and out of newsrooms, unprecedented analyses of news content, and ratings data provide the hard evidence.

For five years, from 1998 through 2002, we studied the content of local television news around the country. It is the largest research project ever conducted about local news. The study analyzed more than 33,000 news stories from 154 stations in 50 U.S. markets of all sizes and in all geographic regions. This content analysis was correlated with ratings for each station and was supplemented with annual surveys of news professionals at those stations and around the country. We analyzed the tapes of newscasts to see what kind of news content correlated with higher or lower audience ratings. Our quantitative content and ratings data were supplemented with qualitative insights from focus groups and face-to-face conversations with more than 2,000 news professionals in more than 40 local news organizations.

We started this project to answer a basic question: What kind of local news content attracts viewers? Are viewers getting the information they really want to watch? Or are other factors driving the kind of news we see on local TV? How much, for example, does the station's profit target dictate how the news is covered? Is it profit expectations or the real demands of the audience that shape the news product?

When we began the project, we asked, What kind of audience research do stations use to program local TV news? What kinds of information do commercial consulting firms offer stations? What do academic studies show about the correlation between news content and audience trends? The answer was that the market is flooded with information, but there's a lot less hard data out there than we expected. Most of the audience data came from surveys or focus groups.

RATINGS

Ratings data have become increasingly important to stations and considerably more sophisticated in recent years. Originally, ratings were used simply to measure the size of the news audience. Now, they are being used to determine the value of specific kinds of news content.

For many years, the Nielsen ratings were based almost exclusively on diaries in which a member of a selected household kept track of everyone's daily TV viewing over a one-month period. These ratings were cumbersome and imprecise, undertaken only four times a year, and were accurate at tracking only general viewership trends. As a research tool, stations ferreted out what they could – for example, how many viewers were in a certain county or whether the audience skewed young or old. From this ratings "research," a newsroom might conclude it should do more stories from county X or replace the older sports guy with someone younger.

The use of ratings as a story selection tool became more pronounced in the 1990s with the proliferation of Nielsen audience meters that record when a set is turned on and off, what channel it's tuned to, and when the channel is changed. When a household member sits down in front of the TV, he or she is expected to enter a personal code so that individual demographic information can be correlated to what is being watched.

In 1980, 4 of the 5 top TV markets were metered. Ten years later, there were meters in 17 of the top 20 markets. As of 2005, Nielsen meters were embedded in households in 56 of the nation's 210 television markets ranging in size from New York and Los Angeles to Tulsa and Fort Myers. In all, meters monitor TV households in two-thirds of the country (69.58%) and speak for the members of 75 million households (see http://www.nielsenmedia.com).

SIDEBAR 2.1

THE METER MONSTER

The impact of audience meters can be measured in any number of ways, from ad rates to the faces behind the anchor desk, but the impact might be best understood by looking at how those numbers can affect a single station or a single newscast.

In November 2003, Orlando's WESH-TV had made the decision to run a high-profile series of investigative reports on housing inspections. After much discussion, producers agreed to give a reporter four minutes of airtime, an almost unheard of length, for the latest installment of the series.

The following morning, when news director Ed Trauschke arrived in his office, in his e-mail were pages of data that composed the "overnights," the metered ratings of the previous evening's newscasts compiled by Nielsen Media Research from 450 households in the Orlando market.

Trauschke was anxious to see how viewers responded to the housing story. Before him were two pages of columns with times and numbers that composed a minute-by-minute breakdown of what viewers did when certain stories, anchors, or segments appeared. It indicated that not one viewer had changed channels or switched off the TV during the 240 seconds the housing inspection story was on, but no one tuned over to the newscast either. According to the overnights, the story was, if not a home run, also not a dog.

But why did the story get that result? The overnights don't tell you. And this illustrates the problem with using overnights and other common audience measurement data to make decisions about content. The ratings are aggregated using only one of the many components of viewership: topic. Yet we have found that among the many factors that account for ratings, topic is relatively unimportant.

In the absence of a better measurement, however, the overnights are the Holy Grail. Here's how a general manager described their use at a group-owned station where he was a sales executive. Every morning during the ratings "sweeps" period, station executives, including news, sales, and promotion managers, gathered in the general manager's office. In their hands were copies of the overnights, with breakdowns showing ratings for each segment of the previous evening's newscast. Also, each person had a sheet of paper on which appeared cumulative viewership totals, including the prime demographic audience, up to that point in the sweeps period.

If the station, for example, was running slightly behind a competitor in terms of women 18 to 49, the news director would be instructed to come up with a story that appealed to women. The promotions department, meantime, would be expected to quickly develop several "topicals" (i.e., promotional teases about the story) that would air throughout the day.

Asked what he thought of this process, in which metered data are used to choose content designed to appeal to a specific audience without regard to what else was happening in the community that day, the executive said he had come to believe that "Meters have ruined local news."

– Walter C. Dean

The meters allow newsroom decision makers to compare minute-by-minute ratings breakdowns from "overnight" reports. What usually results is a "this topic held viewers and this other topic did not" kind of conversation. In the highly competitive world of local TV news, these "lessons" are not soon forgotten. Topics that hold viewers are covered. Topics that are "tune-outs" are dismissed.

This dependence on minute-by-minute ratings – particularly analyzed each night in isolation – tends to focus newsroom discussions primarily on *what* worked rather than *why* a particular story or approach was successful.

SURVEYS AND FOCUS GROUPS

Survey research has also been used to attempt to measure what people want to see, but it often turns out to be too limited in the scope of what it studies and in the way in which it gathers data.

The survey research used in local TV tends to present a list of topics or questions to ask people what they might want to watch. Various TV consulting firms initially deployed these surveys, for which stations often pay tens of thousands of dollars. But actual behavior (what people *really* watch) and answering a survey (what they *say* they would watch) are two different things. What's more, the surveys local TV consultants usually use tend to focus on familiar topics and lead respondents toward the answers, asking: "Do you want to see more news about (topic A) or (topic B)?" And, of course, surveys can be biased by the way questions are worded, by the order of the questions, or by the representativeness of the sample of respondents. One TV station general manager, for example, told us about a question that was included in consultant research his station had recently purchased: "If a dangerous criminal was in your neighborhood, would you want to know about it?" Not surprisingly, people said they would want to know. The answer provided the rational for the consultant's recommendation that the newsroom produce a series of stories on "The Ten Most-Wanted" local criminals for an upcoming ratings period.

One weakness of most of the local TV research we saw – whether from surveys, ratings, or meters – is that it is cued to the topic of the story and does not tell us how stories should be put together to attract viewers. As you will learn later in this book, the distinction between story *topic* and story *telling* is crucial. It turns out that treatment, not topic, is what matters most.

In addition to relying on surveys, commercial TV consultants employ focus groups. These are gatherings of a dozen or so viewers who are shown material, perhaps TV stories, and then are asked to respond to it. Focus groups were designed in the 1940s as a research tool for brainstorming. If you want to get new ideas from consumers or the public about something, gather a few folks in a room and talk with them.

In other words, although focus groups are often legitimately used as a "pilot study" to guide subsequent research, focus groups are not a representative sample of the audience. Because focus groups are so small in size and are usually not randomly selected, they cannot be relied upon to show how a community might react to something.

The problem with focus groups today is that they are often employed as a cheap alternative to more expensive surveys or other kinds of research. The basic flaw is in using focus groups for testing whether audiences will like or dislike something – not gaining insight into why. To garner a statistically meaningful or representative sample of the audience requires a group of several hundred people, often as many as 1,200. Focus groups, in other words, are valuable tools, but they should be used properly, and in local TV often they are not.

Another research technique sometimes used is "dial groups" in which audiences are asked to watch TV and then turn the dial on an electronic device to indicate whether they like something or dislike it, and by how much. Although the technology is fun, it has many of the same limitations as focus groups. The people with the dials represent only themselves. What's more, that is not how people watch TV. The dials and the researchers create an artificial environment. The act of observing viewers actually changes the way those viewers watch TV.

ETHNOGRAPHIC RESEARCH

Ethnographic research is another technique used by consultants. It requires researchers to go to people's homes and observe how they actually watch TV. Like focus groups, ethnographic research does not supplant surveys or other tools. But it adds significantly to knowledge. For instance, when such work was done by John Carey, who worked for NBC, he found that people don't watch TV during certain times of day; they listen to it while doing other things, walking in and out of the room. That discovery dramatically alters how TV news stories might be put together, putting much less emphasis on pictures, and much more on sound, and on the substance of the stories – what those stories were actually saying and not how they looked, which is the primary focus of editors, producers, and reporters. Yet this research is little used by news professionals.

These various methods of research produced few common findings. One example of the mixed signals came from news consultants.

In the late 1990s one big TV consulting firm was pushing its clients to air more crime news to increase audiences. A rival consulting firm, however, was telling its customers just the opposite: Crime is a turnoff, especially to the audience you want most, that is, younger women; better to do more family friendly news. If the two biggest research and consulting firms in the business came to opposite conclusions about what audiences want, it is a sign that there are problems with their research. Solid methods stand up over time and place. Either the consultants were not using solid methods or their recommendations were not tailored to the markets they were advising.[1]

DEVELOPING THE CRITERIA

Our interviews with news professionals, who helped us design our research, indicated that the flood of conflicting research has led to confusion about what works and what doesn't in local TV news. Newspeople told us over and over that lots of things go into ratings success: Who are your anchors, and what kind of chemistry do they have together? What is your lead-in, the show that precedes you, and what kind of audience does it attract? How good are your promos, your set, your lighting, your weather team? In some markets, especially in the South, there was evidence that loyalty was a big factor: The station in the market that had had its license the longest was often Number 1. News professionals, we were told, had instincts about what people wanted, based on their experience and personal taste. One might have had success with a certain style of news in one market. Another gravitated to a different style. But, as one executive put it, "Most of us aren't sure. It's a matter of our own personal values, our own taste, and our own experience."

In sum, we found a knowledge gap that focused on two basic questions:

1. Does the content of the news actually make a difference in audience response?
2. If so, does the audience prefer quality content – however you define it – or something else?

To answer those questions, we turned to research tools that had rarely been applied to local TV: content analysis that examines what local TV news looks like and statistical modeling that correlates actual viewership with the content.

A study that combined content analysis correlated with audience response is complicated, expensive, and difficult for a lone researcher to conduct. To make such a study possible we needed a large team. We consulted both news professionals and academics to be part of it.

One principle of the research was that whatever definition of quality we arrived at should come from news professionals themselves. They are the ones who are experts in the news business. If the findings of our study were going to have credibility with news professionals, the practitioners – not outsiders or academics – would have to come up with the standards.

The second principle was that the definition of market success, or measuring audience response, had to be realistic. The study would be authoritative if it depended on the kinds of measures that news professionals actually use.

To determine the standards of quality television news, we assembled a team of news professionals who commanded the respect of their peers. This "Design Team" would brainstorm the criteria for what a newscast *should* provide to its community. In time, we could test whether audiences and other news professionals agreed, using surveys of professionals and other research instruments (see Appendix A for a list of Design Team members).

We began by asking the TV news experts some basic questions:

- What do you think are the most important characteristics of a high-quality local TV news program?
- What do you think should be the key responsibilities of a TV newsroom to the community it serves?
- What does local TV news do well, and where does it fall down on the job? Given the typical newsroom's resources, what topics should receive more coverage, and what topics should be covered less?
- How much do news ratings depend on the content of a newscast?

The Design Team's answers to our questionnaire highlighted the following criteria for quality local news:

- Make the news local
- Cover the whole community
- Present significant and substantive stories
- Demonstrate enterprise and courage
- Produce fair, balanced, and accurate stories
- Be authoritative
- Employ high standards of presentation
- Avoid sensationalism

The Design Team said we should study local news in a variety of markets, from big cities to small towns, and that we should try as much as possible to study multiple time slots. The Team had a good deal to say about each of the criteria, and we used their descriptions to guide our coding of local news content. Then we sat down for a day during the Radio and Television News Directors Association annual convention in New Orleans in September 1997 to discuss these questions more deeply.

SIDEBAR 2.2

DEFINING QUALITY

By Randy Covington

Just what is good TV news?

It's a tough question with a lot of different answers. So how could a room full of professionals, many of whom barely knew each other, agree on a comprehensive definition in just one day? That was what I was wondering as I walked into a meeting room at the New Orleans Sheraton during the 1997 Radio and Television News Directors Association convention to be part of the Design Team for this study.

We certainly were a diverse group. We were from different parts of the country, different-size markets and different journalistic backgrounds. There were retired executives, like the late Jim Snyder of Post-Newsweek and John Corporon of the Tribune Company. There were then-current news directors like Gary Wordlaw of WJLA in Washington, D.C., Paula Pendarvis of WGNO in New Orleans, and Jose Rios of KTTV in Los Angeles. There was an executive producer, Alice Main of WLS in Chicago, and an anchor, Gordon Peterson, then of WUSA in Washington, D.C.

There were decades of experience in that room and certainly many different perspectives. In the next few hours, we were supposed to reach a consensus on what good local TV news should be, a definition from which benchmarks or models of quality could be derived. Oh yes, they were to be grounded in reality, market success, and the tenets of sound journalism.

In advance of the meeting, the Project for Excellence in Journalism had asked the Design Team to fill out questionnaires. Among our concerns:

- Too much crime
- Too much live for the sake of live
- Too much preoccupation with celebrity

According to the survey responses, we very much agreed on the key responsibilities of local television news. More than anything else, we felt a good local newscast should reflect its community. But what does that mean? The Design Team discussed several points of concern:

- The short tenure of so many general managers and news directors as well as the transitory nature of the business, as anchors, reporters, and producers migrate around the country without realizing they live in communities instead of TV markets.
- The commitment of station owners to provide the resources – reporters, photographers, live trucks, etc. – necessary to be competitive and get the job done.
- The role of consultants – who usually live somewhere else – in determining news priorities and shaping coverage, often using templates from someplace else.

The group decided that good community coverage equals a range of topics, neighborhoods, and ethnicities. But couldn't even a station with good community coverage potentially be pulled down in the ratings by other factors, such as bad anchor chemistry, an ugly set, or a weak lead-in? After all, one of the premises for this initiative was to tie newscast quality to market success.

How would the researchers be able to differentiate the cause of ratings woes or success among these factors? There were many questions we could not answer, forcing us to make a leap of faith that the academics would be able to answer them.

In that pre-meeting survey, the Design Team agreed that, in order of importance after good community coverage, local news should be informative, cover significant issues, be accurate, be fair, and offer depth and balance. All are traditional journalistic values. So perhaps it was not surprising that we had embraced them.

Sensationalism bothered us. We had little stomach for gratuitous video of blood on the sidewalk. But what about the grocery store owner who died trying to stop a robber? Would a tight shot of the gun in his lifeless hand be an example of sensationalism? Several of us did not think so.

Local TV news has always been a conflicted medium that combines journalism and show business, two fields that are not always compatible. As a result, there is an ongoing tug of war between content and production values. Sometimes they complement each other. Sometimes they contradict each other.

On that day in September 1997, the members of the Design Team learned that we had been pulling our newsrooms in the same direction.

SIDEBAR 2.2 (continued)

Now the question was: Could we pull other stations as well? If the study were successful, it would encourage stations to do more original reporting, seek out additional sources, and offer greater depth.

I remember walking out into the New Orleans dusk pleased by the day of discussion but puzzled about how the things we had discussed could be quantified. And there was one other thing on my mind and I suspect on the minds of others as well – what would happen if my station were rated?

Randy Covington, director of the Ifra Newsplex at the University of South Carolina and an assistant professor in the USC School of Journalism and Mass Communications, was a local TV news director for 16 years.

By the end of that meeting, we had isolated seven basic values that our team of professionals thought local newscasts should include – a set of minimum requirements for quality local news. The next step was to identify how those values are expressed in a newscast. We employed what the academic community calls content analysis. The analysis involves taping newscasts and then having trained personnel "code" what they see and hear, itemizing or breaking down stories and newscasts into clearly defined categories that represent the Design Team values (see Appendix B for a full delineation of Quality Grading Criteria and Value Codes; see Appendix C for Intercoder Reliability Analyses). Here are those basic values and the means of measuring them.

MAKE THE NEWS LOCAL

Almost every member of the Design Team believed that local TV news should provide service to the community. In a questionnaire, one member summed up the key responsibilities of a TV newsroom: "To unite a community through the sharing of information about local happenings, including legislation, education, jobs ... through the analysis of the impact national and international events have on our community, through the sharing of joy and angst, triumph and tragedy, of our neighbors."[2] Another person noted that a high-quality newscast should encompass "the entire viewing area – not just downtown."

We created a measure to assess this aspect of local TV news.

Relevance To capture the concept of emphasizing local news, our coders would evalvate the local connection of each story. This didn't mean stories had to be merely local, but the local relevance of a story, be it international or national, had to be made clear to the audience. Did the story affect citizens in the whole area, important institutions in the area, major demographic or geographic groups in the area, or smaller sub-groups? Or was it interesting but with no direct connection to the community? These local connections were critical to meeting the Design Team's specification that local TV news should cover the community.

Cover the Whole Community

Every member of the Design Team said it was of preeminent importance that a newscast should cover and reflect the community in its totality. No topic should be considered off limits, they said, and no topic was more important or less important than another. Crime, for instance, was not less important than government. They saw the main problem with local news as what was not covered.

Many members argued that local TV news failed to provide perspective on the wide range of events happening in the community; in particular, a common complaint was that coverage of crime precluded attention to other institutions and phenomena of life. A response to our questionnaire linked these two ideas together by noting, "We cover too much aberrant behavior at the expense of covering the struggles of 'average' kids and adults ... News should reflect the needs, concerns of the majority, not just the minority – i.e., good kids, not just bad." Another member suggested that the responsibility of a newsroom is "to give the community a good hard look at itself ... its schools and churches, its courts and its governments ... its rock bands and gospel choirs." We developed an elaborate set of codes for story topic, so that we could precisely measure the nature of the coverage.

Topic To measure whether a newscast covered the whole community, we noted the topic of every story so that we could precisely gauge the nature of the coverage. We looked at the politics, economics, and social life of the community – and scores of other categories – and noted whether stories with a national focus identified the relevance to the local community.

Present Significant and Substantive Stories

The second most highly noted value was that newscasts should be significant and informative – as well as interesting. Many Design Team

members saw an inability to "make what is important interesting" as one
of local TV news' principal shortcomings. They also felt that it was crucial
to do certain stories to give viewers some idea of larger events in the
community. "There are some stories you do because you educate
people ... They're not done always to be what people choose to want
to watch, because you're doing an important job." The Design Team
members indicated a variety of ways in which local TV news could
provide a better service to its viewers. "Examine area trends," wrote one.
Others noted that local news could do a much better job at covering
public policy, and that everyday incidents could be covered less "unless
there's a bigger story associated with the isolated incident and/or the
story is put into perspective."

> *Focus:* To assess whether a story was significant and provided substantive
> information, we developed a way to measure the "focus" of the story.
> This variable analyzes the degree to which each story touched on
> underlying themes, ideas, trends, or issues raised by the event or incident.
> Did the story examine an underlying idea? Or was it limited to the inci-
> dent itself? Was the story about a major event? Or did it focus on a rather
> common, everyday incident, without drawing out its larger significance?
>
> The focus of the story was scored on a scale from high to low sig-
> nificance. Issues of public affairs, for example, were considered more
> important than stories about celebrities. At the top of the scale were
> stories about ideas, issues, trends, or public malfeasance, followed by
> major events, civic institutions or actors, then trends, and unusual
> events. Lower down on the scale were political strategy stories,
> breaking events, everyday incidents, and everyday crime. At the lower
> end of the scale, which had 10 levels in all, were human interest,
> followed by celebrity gossip, and scandal or sensation.

Demonstrate Enterprise and Courage

The Design Team told us that newscasts should not only be local and
informative, but they should also be "gutsy" and "enterprising," provide
"context and depth," and show "initiative." As one Design Team
member put it, most local TV news could be divided into "mandatory" or
"discretionary." Mandatory news means coverage of the day's breaking
news, such as a mayoral resignation. On the other hand, he explained,
"In the discretionary coverage, you have your opportunity to distinguish
yourself ... [to] send those reporters and crews available to you to go out

and do things." The effort put into reporting transforms run-of-the-mill coverage into significant reporting.

One member of the team declared that enterprise reporting – going out and finding original stories – is a critical job for the TV newsroom: "It's ... just to tell people, 'We know something that you ought to know, and here it is, and you judge whether it's important.'" The Design Team members consistently pointed out that local news is excellent at providing live coverage of the events, but many found enterprise coverage lacking. "It needs improvement in explaining *why* things happen: i.e., better follow-up," one member wrote. Another Design Team member suggested that local news should cover fewer "press conferences."

> *Enterprise:* To capture the concept of initiative in reporting, we developed an index of journalistic enterprise. This variable measured how much effort went into creating the story. Was it a station-initiated investigation, interview, or series? If not, was the station responding to a spontaneous event? Or was it a pre-arranged staged event, the sort listed in the daybook (a daily listing of upcoming events)? Did the station send a reporter to the event, or just a camera? Was the story simply taken from the news wire or a video feed from another source, or was it based on rumors or gossip? The variable listed all of these levels of enterprise on a scale. The more enterprise demonstrated, the higher the score. In our analysis we looked not only at the total level of enterprise, but at the kind of effort to see what audiences specifically appreciated.

Produce Fair, Balanced, and Accurate Stories

Many members of the Design Team discussed accuracy and fairness as indistinguishable from each other. Eventually, though, we divided them into separate concepts: source balance and viewpoint balance. Our Design Team believed "presenting diverse viewpoints" was an important responsibility, particularly in stories dealing with complicated issues. As one participant put it, "I find that on a lot of things, I've got more than two contending sides ... I also think you have to say, if there are significant ones out there, then whatever it takes, you have to include them."

The Design Team suggested using the number of sources included in a news story as a way of gauging accuracy. As one member put it, "Sometimes I don't understand the story. It will go by too fast, or it will be too one-sided." One member noted that it's better "if somebody took the time to interview three or four different people rather than just one." Including multiple sources, as our Design Team saw it, is a way to ensure that viewers are given the chance to judge conflicting interpretations of a story for themselves.

> *Sourcing and Viewpoints:* To assess these qualities, the academic team decided to employ two straightforward measurements of sourcing. First, we counted how many sources were cited in each story on the premise that a story with more sources was more likely to be accurate and fair. Second, the study counted how many points of view were contained in any story that involved a dispute or controversy – just one, mostly one, or a mix of more than one point of view. Stories presented as undisputed (a fire happened) were noted separately. Together, the number of sources and the number of points of view provided a measure of fairness, balance, and accuracy.

Be Authoritative

An important gauge of quality according to the news professionals was that stories should be authoritative. In other words, it wasn't enough that stories be interesting and about important topics, but the information should be reliable and believable. This was related, obviously, to the accuracy and fairness of a story. The authority of a story, the professionals told us, depended on where the information came from, the sourcing.

One person noted that in his newsroom it was common practice to watch the same story as reported by all the competing stations in the market and to determine "if they had more detail, if one of their facts was better than our facts ... Then we go back and try to adjust what we do," to match or exceed the standard set by the competition.

Using person-on-the-street interviews was a practice that some Design Team members viewed favorably and others disagreed with. "People tell us in research: 'I want to hear what my fellow citizens have to say. I want to know what's on their minds,'" one member argued. On the other hand, another member cautioned, "You can't just take the first three people you see and toss it in."

> *Source Expertise* To assess this authoritativeness, the study examined the level of expertise of each source cited in the story. Expertise differed given the topic of the story. A qualified brain surgeon would be

a credentialed expert on a story about brain surgery. But a person on the street would be a qualified expert on a story about public reaction the President's latest speech. This credibility variable notes whether the source on the given topic was a credentialed expert, impartial data, the major actor in the story, an unnamed source, or, finally, whether no source was cited at all.

Coherence

Although they ranked low in the hierarchy offered by the news professionals we spoke with, two other criteria mentioned by the Design Team were included by the academic team. One was whether the basic presentation of the story was coherent and adhered to high professional standards, or whether it was truncated, choppy, or simply illogical. Only a fraction of stories were rated as difficult to follow, so this variable had little impact on overall quality scores.

Sensationalism

Finally, the study noted whether stories were sensational, which was defined as replaying video, graphics, or sound beyond the point that added new information. Still pictures or video of gore, violence, or thrilling action were also considered sensational. Stories without those features were considered neutral, whereas stories that contained many gory or violent references or repeated visuals were considered sensational.

ADDITIONAL THOUGHTS ON QUALITY

The Design Team did not think all stories should be alike. A story about big ideas, such as the issues in a local election, was considered more significant than one about a commonplace event, such as a robbery, but any story done well scored high. What didn't count toward quality of content is notable. Topic was considered neutral. A crime story might score as high as a science piece. Length was not considered by itself a good. Production techniques (other than sensationalism) were considered tools and were not rated separately for quality. The only standard of production that was employed was coherence, whether production failures interfered with communicating the point of the story. The study avoided rating qualities such as tone or negativity.

The Design Team's criteria and the coding that assessed those values covered the basics of broadcast journalism. But to find out what kind of content builds ratings, we are not wedded to this definition of quality.

The approach advocated in this book simply describes whether the specific characteristics of stories – however they are valued – correlate to higher ratings. The results could show that slash-and-burn techniques work (as it turns out, they do not). Our research did not prejudge the answer. We looked at how news stories are put together (how many sources are used, the amount of enterprise, the length of stories, etc.) independently and without value judgments. The correlation between journalism techniques and audience ratings is the principal product of this study.

Because the specific characteristics of news stories are our major concern, we wanted to make sure that the criteria developed by the 15 veteran news professionals could be appreciated by the audience. To find out, we conducted focus groups in two cities, Atlanta and Tucson, to see whether members of the public could recognize the aspects of news stories identified by the Design Team. Although focus groups have their limits, this was an appropriate use to verify the assumptions of the Design Team. Could the public distinguish between what news professionals considered good and not so good ways to tell stories?

The answer, it turns out, is yes. In every focus group, people independently raised the issue of covering the whole community. Many said they wanted to see a broader range of subjects in their newscasts, disdaining too much "repetitiveness." The typical newscast, as one man said, was "murders, murders, murders." People also thought multiple points of view were important and noticed when stations didn't give them both sides of the story. One participant said "slanting to one position" was likely to make him turn off a TV news program.

When our groups were shown two versions of a particular story and asked to rank them, they did so while citing reasons that sounded a lot like those of our news professionals. One person preferred a particular story because it featured "attorneys for each side … It's unbiased in terms of it giving the different arguments of that story." Viewers also told the focus group moderator that it was important for expert sources to be identified. After watching one story, a participant noted: "They say 'experts agree' and then they interview an expert, I don't even think they put his name up or said who he was. Who is this guy and why is he an expert?"

When it came to making stories significant, one person said, when asked about crime coverage, "They need to get a little detail and a little more focused on how to prevent it." In the Tucson focus group, several participants spoke out against sensationalism, noting with ire the use of pictures from a multiple homicide at a local fast-food restaurant: "They keep bringing that up ... We don't need to keep getting bombarded with [murder] every day, 24 hours a day, every time you turn the news on."

The local news viewers also noticed enterprise reporting, and they noticed when it was absent. In Atlanta, one person liked a segment called "The Whistle Blower," declaring "I love finding out what's going on in the government. Where the waste is. And I think they need to do more of that." A Tucson viewer criticized newsroom reliance on the police scanner: "They get a police readout and then you go, 'Oh, we've got a news break here,' and they're reading right off the police sheet."

A story about allegations of discrimination in Atlanta schools bothered one participant who felt that it demonstrated a lack of initiative on the part of reporters who were responding to complaints by a local organization rather than independently pursuing the story. "The squeaky wheel gets the news," said one person.

The focus group participants also preferred stories with good sourcing to stories with only passing references to a particular source. One viewer said that a particular story on a local environmental controversy was better because "you had more feedback from different individuals to give you a better perspective of what the issue was." A participant recalled a story on tainted meat that had been aired recently and expressed frustration that the station hadn't provided a complete list of the products affected: "There was a lot more information in that story than what I saw on the news." As one person put it, "I don't think they are doing a good job covering [health news] ... It's like let's either scare the hell out of them or just say it in passing just because we have a spot to fill and they don't find the facts out first."

We concluded from our focus group research that viewers do indeed hold opinions about the content of newscasts and can recognize the qualities that the Design Team pointed out and that we coded in our content analysis. It is important to emphasize that our analysis of audience response to newscasts is based on ratings and not focus groups. We used the focus groups to demonstrate that our criteria are recognizable and important to the audience. People can, indeed, make the distinctions that we attribute to them in our analysis of the ratings.

To further test whether our criteria of quality made sense broadly to the television news community, we surveyed more than 100 news directors in 2001 and 2002 to see if they agreed with our Design Team. We simply asked them what they thought went into a good newscast that would build ratings. Many news directors spoke of using new promotional campaigns and better "branding." But others were putting the basics of journalism into practice, and their ideas reinforced the values identified by our Design Team: "Solid story telling with an emphasis on issues affecting the community," wrote one news director, adding "Our previous management got away from that and our ratings took a turn for the worse." A top-10 market news director wrote that her station was doing "investigative [reporting] throughout the year," rather than confining it to sweeps periods as a stunt to entice viewers. One Florida news director wrote that his station focused on "hard news and relevance," adding "We ... work hard to make sure the voice of the public is heard in the process of setting public policy. We hold the powerful accountable." Another news director's plan was to "present stories that accurately reflect the issues."

Our measurements of quality, in other words, coincide with what the audience does with its remote controls (as explained to us by focus groups) and with the tactics that many news professionals believe are essential to making their programs successful.

HOW THE STUDY WAS CARRIED OUT

With our criteria set, we selected a stratified random sample of approximately 20 markets each year for five years from 1998 to 2002 (all but a few of the stations were affiliates of the three major broadcast networks). The sampling window for the content analysis included two weeks each year: the last week of February (during the Nielsen sweeps period) – when ratings are taken – and the first week of March (not a sweeps period). The reason for selecting both sweeps and nonsweeps weeks is that stations are infamous for "stunting"– that is airing stories that are full of hype and that are especially dramatic – during sweeps periods to drive up ratings (Ehrlich 1995; Hickey 2003; Moritz 1989; Potter 2001). We wanted to be sure that sweeps did not distort the analysis, but we also wanted to include the stories that stations chose to showcase in a given year. We included a nonsweeps week to represent ordinary programming. Taken together these two kinds of weeks represent the "news diet" that local audiences typically consume.

We studied a random sample of markets rather than individual stations, so that we could compare a station's content against the others in the same market. We could be sure that a station's scores were not dictated by the particular characteristics of the market, region, or time slot. Because stations in larger media markets have significantly greater resources for producing news than stations in smaller markets, we took a stratified sample of markets that would ensure adequate representation of communities of different sizes, from super-urban markets to tiny rural stations. Without a stratified sample, there was a danger that larger markets would be under-represented in the sample. Accordingly, the total list of local news markets was broken into groups by market size, each reflecting one-quarter of the total U.S. household audience. (see Appendix D for a list of stations sampled).[3]

Markets across the country air local TV newscasts at varying times, usually corresponding to their time zone. To maintain consistency, the Design Team suggested that the newscasts we sampled be based on the highest cumulatively rated local TV news half hour in a given market. The Design Team emphasized that we should be rating the time period that most viewers watched. Stations airing a local newscast during that half hour were selected into the sample. Only half-hour newscasts were chosen to maintain comparability across the sample. Using the standard of "most watched program in the market," more late-evening newscasts (10:00 or 11:00 P.M. start time) were selected than early evening (5:00 to 6:30 P.M. start time) newscasts: 70.7% were late and 29.3% were early due to the greater popularity of late news in so many markets.

The audience measures for each newscast were obtained from the A. C. Nielsen Media Research Corporation. Nielsen's results come in two measures – rating and share. Rating refers to the *percentage of total households* in the market that are watching a program at a given time. Share refers to the *percentage of just those households watching television* that are viewing a program at a given time.[4] In addition to households, ratings can be estimated for people belonging to different demographic groups. As household ratings for local TV news began to fall in the 1990s, news directors scrambled to make the best of the shrinking market. To that end, they began targeting the news to the demographic subgroups most desirable to advertisers to make up lost revenue (Bennett 2003). Generally, the most sought-after demographics are men and women 18 to 49 years of age. But news generally draws an older crowd, so the demographic window of men and women 25 to 54 years of age is also important.

Another concern in measuring commercial success is known as the "inheritance effect"– the extent to which a program retains the audience from the previous program, known as the lead-in (see Boemer 1987; Davis and Walker 1990; Tiedge and Ksobiech 1986). If a newscast is building on the lead-in audience, or doing a better job than the competition at retaining its lead-in audience, then that newscast is doing well commercially. Additionally, the inclusion of retention as a component of commercial success acts as a control, by accounting for the tendency of newscasts with popular lead-in programs to get better ratings than those following less popular programs.

To satisfy these considerations we obtained and calculated ratings for eight aspects of commercial success:

Household Rating
Household Share
Rating among Women 18–49
Rating among Men 18–49
Rating among Women 25–54
Rating among Men 25–54
Lead-in Rating Retention
Lead-in Share Retention

It should be noted that beyond market size and (hypothetically) news quality, many factors can influence the ratings that a newscast receives. Network affiliation and time slot also affect ratings, specifically through their relationship to the popularity of the lead-in program. Late newscasts generally benefit from following popular, primetime lead-in programs. Additionally, certain networks have more popular programming following the news. Therefore, we took network affiliation into account in measuring commercial success.

We also take seriously an argument that academics and newspeople themselves made about the disappointing quality of local news. The argument is that the greater the competition in a market, the less stations invest in quality reporting. Some observers even think that more competition invariably results in a "race to the bottom." To be fair to the most competitive markets, our analysis also controls for the level of ratings competition.

Because local TV newscasts suffered ratings declines during the period of the study, we also noted which year we assessed a particular station. In later chapters when we report that a particular kind of news was more commercially successful than another, our statistical models take into account ("control for") all of these factors: market size, competition, network affiliation, time slot (early or late evening news), and year of the study. When we say some practice works to increase ratings, we mean it works not only in large and small markets but also in highly competitive and less competitive markets.

The goal of the study was to compare content and approach – what was news and how it was covered and presented – with commercial success.

The headline is a simple one: *Newscasts that exhibited the high-quality television journalism defined by our news professionals do well. Stations that produce higher-quality broadcasts have higher ratings, higher share numbers, and more attractive demographics than stations that produce lower-quality newscasts. What's more, this is true to a degree that is statistically significant. The quality-success story is not a finding that might accidentally appear because of the particular stations we studied. Stations with higher-quality newscasts do better commercially than other stations even taking into account network affiliation, time slot, and the size and competitiveness of the market.*

INSIDE QUALITY

On its face, the idea that quality sells is happy news for any citizen who cares about his or her society or for any journalist who wants to do good work. And our findings spell out what news professionals can do to improve ratings while serving their local communities. We describe a Magic Formula that specifies what kinds of practices and story attributes are associated with greater commercial success.

In general, hard work pays off. So, especially, does enterprise. Stories that are hard to get, that require more effort, that involve talking to more people, going to more places, doing more research, taking more time to tell the story, do well with viewers. Viewers appreciate these qualities, and the ratings show it.

The "easy-to-get" stories – the "drive-by journalism" in which the cameraman sprays the scene and the reporter gets all the information from a single interview – don't win viewers and sometimes even turn them off. Unfortunately, The Magic Formula doesn't seem to be in use in much of local TV news and that, we argue, is one of the reasons for audience declines. "Live, local, and late breaking," continues to be the most popular brand around the country. In fact, if you look at local newscasts you find not only identical brands but also similar approaches to covering the news. In the next chapter we turn to what that stock approach to news looks like.

3 "I-Teams" and "Eye Candy": The Reality of Local TV News

Chicago is the broad-shouldered, bustling capital of the Midwest. It's an ethnically diverse metropolis of nearly three million people and the nation's third largest city. And its grand skyline rising high above the shores of Lake Michigan serves notice that it is a major center for commerce. By day its commodity markets draw the attention and money of investors from around the world. And by night its clubs play host to some of the best blues and jazz musicians in the country.

Of course, not everything is perfect in the Windy City. Traffic can be a nightmare, and the streets can be mean. More than 10% of the population lives in poverty. And in 2004 there were more than 400 murders, placing the city in the top 25 in terms of per-capita murder rates in the United States.

All these things, good and bad, make Chicago what it is. They define the city's image and its reality. They make it unlikely that people would confuse Chicago with, say, Sioux Falls, South Dakota.

With a population of about 130,000 that is 90% white, Sioux Falls doesn't make the list of the 150 largest cities in the United States. Its hilly skyline on the banks of the Big Sioux River is defined more by church steeples than skyscrapers. Two Interstate highways run through the area, but traffic is not a great concern. And although violent crime happens there as it does everywhere, it's not common. The city's homicide rate is extremely low – barely in the top 300.

One might think that the two cities, more than 500 miles apart and light years away from each other in culture, history, size, and ethnic make-up, would focus on very different kinds of news.

But if you tuned into the local TV news in each city you would find broadcasts that are strikingly similar. There are differences to be sure but not as many as you might expect, considering the tremendous differences in the two locales. Indeed, look closely and you will find the same kinds of stories and the same topics, often in the same order.

Consider two newscasts from May 1, 2002, a night the Project for Excellence in Journalism recorded newscasts in both cities. CBS's WBBM in Chicago, and KSFY, an ABC affiliate in Sioux Falls, both opened with crime stories and also featured reports on a trial or arraignment.[1] Both later tucked in another law enforcement story, and also another crime piece, and each had a health story. Neither carried any news about either government or education.

In fact, over the two weeks in early 2002 when the Project for Excellence in Journalism studied newscasts on six stations in the two cities (three stations in each), we found remarkable similarities. In each city newscasts opened with crime or disaster stories about 45% of the time, and overall about one out of every five stories concerned crime. Accidents made up 5% of the Chicago story count and 4% of the stories in Sioux Falls. In Chicago, business stories were 6% of the total, and 7% in Sioux Falls. Human interest stories were 8% in Chicago and 9% in Sioux Falls.

These similarities aren't a peculiarity of those two locales. Indeed, if you travel to many cities in the United States you'll see much the same thing. In five years of research, the study found some very good newscasts and some very bad ones. But the vast majority occupied the middle ground, and those newscasts were so similar they sometimes almost seemed interchangeable.

That finding also holds true today. A subsequent study of 50 local TV newscasts in 10 different cities from around the country in early 2005 found the same kinds of similarities.[2] Crime, accidents, and mayhem ruled even more of the airwaves, accounting for half (49.9%) of all news stories and three-quarters (77%) of newscast leads. "Civic" news – stories about social issues, politics, business, and foreign events – amounted to almost one-quarter (24.0%) of all stories. "Soft" human-interest pieces, news about religion and pop culture, and health news made up another one-fourth of stories (22.6%). In other words, the patterns that we saw growing from 1998 to 2002 appear to be continuing. These findings are further supported by the training we have done in newsrooms since 2002.

Turn down the volume, and surf the channels from the coasts to the plains to the mountains, and you'll see "eyewitness" newscasts that are "live, local, and late breaking" – largely predictable and surprisingly homogeneous. This is true across early and late broadcasts in markets large and small.[3]

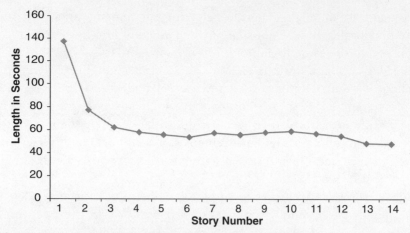

Figure 3.1. Average story length by story placement.

This chapter examines this surprisingly uniform landscape and explores what it means to the whole of local TV news – everything from content to story length to enterprise reporting. Understanding local TV news today begins with understanding what it looks like.

THE AVERAGE NEWSCAST AND THE X-STRUCTURE

The average local TV newscast contains 14 stories – most broadcasts average between 10 and 18. There are 6 short stories (less than 30 seconds), 4 stories between 30 seconds and one minute, 2 stories between one and two minutes, and 2 stories more than two minutes in length. The shortest stories – those less than 30 seconds – make up just 15% of the news hole, whereas longer reports – more than two minutes – command nearly half (46%) of all news time.

Those long reports are concentrated at the beginning of the broadcast and usually focus on public safety news such as a violent crime or a bad accident. The average lead story runs two minutes, 18 seconds, and the first 3 stories in a typical 14-story newscast consume a total of five minutes or about one-third (32%) of the average news hole. After those first stories the average length of a news item drops precipitously. The 11 other stories must compete for the remaining nine minutes (see Figure 3.1).

What's in those 11 remaining stories after the lead block? Again, there is a remarkably consistent pattern. Generally, pieces that do not fit the profile of crime, accidents, or disasters end up in the middle of the broadcast as short anchor-read "tell" stories that are thinly sourced and lack much narrative punch or even information. This middle is a

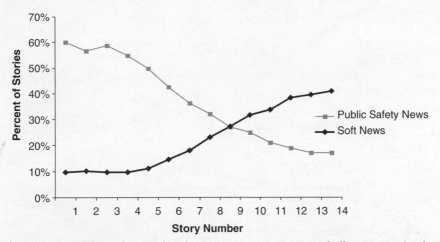

Figure 3.2. Public safety and soft news as a percentage of all news stories by placement within newscast.

"ghetto" where much of the important, but less breathless, news of the day is relegated. At the end of the broadcast come soft, human-interest stories that are "teased" relentlessly to keep people watching.

This pattern – mayhem at the top, teasable soft features at the end, and the rest of the day's news in the middle, creates the easily recognizable standard story order illustrated in Figure 3.2.

The "book-ending" of broadcasts by public safety and soft news emphasizes the violent and unusual and de-emphasizes everything else, from government to social issues to transportation to jobs and economy to defense and foreign affairs. Stories placed in the middle of the newscast are among the shortest. They receive the least promotion and teasing. They have fewer resources allocated to them (see Figure 3.3).

Figures 3.1 to 3.3 illustrate the X-Structure of local newscasts. The impact of the X-structure extends well beyond how stories are "stacked" in a broadcast. It touches nearly all elements of the newscast. It has become the standard for judging what is and is not newsworthy.

The "Hook and Hold"

This X-Structure is built on what might best be described as a "hook-and-hold" approach. Grab viewers with sensational news, often an alarming "late development," and keep them tuned in by holding out the hope of a soft story that is useful or interesting. In between are topics that are thought to lack immediacy or such dramatic visuals as flashing lights and

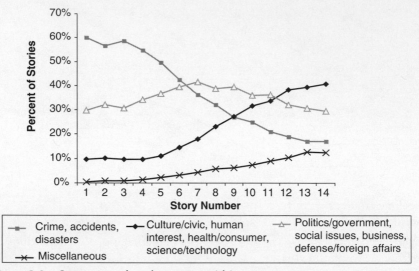

Figure 3.3. Story types by placement within newscasts.

yellow police tape. The nongrabbing, nonholding stories have little chance of breaking into the lineup before the fourth story, which is often the beginning of the second block of the newscast.

The hook-and-hold pattern dominated local news throughout our study, across more than 2,400 newscasts. Sixty-one percent of newscasts, almost two-thirds, led with crime, accident, or disaster stories. And it wasn't just one story. Thirteen percent of the newscasts – that's 1 in 8 – began with *three* crime stories in a row. And in nearly one-third (30%) of the broadcasts, the first *three* items were drawn from these three very similar categories of news – crime, accidents, and disasters. In contrast with the more than 60% of newscasts that led with crime, government or politics stories attained lead status just once in every 12 broadcasts, education once in every 41 shows, and health once in every 67 newscasts.

The X-Structure applied across all categories of local TV news (morning, early evening, and late evening) through all five years of the study, with the exception of defense/foreign affairs. In spring 2001, stories about the detention of an American spy plane in China and the sinking of a Japanese fishing boat by an American submarine pushed defense news to the top of the hierarchy.[4]

What Gets Lost

In the bipolar world of the X-Structure, where crime, accidents, and disasters lead the broadcast and soft news concludes the program, what

Table 3.1. Topic distribution on local TV news

| | Timeslot | | |
Category	Early%	Late%	All%
Crime	25	24	24
Human interest	10	10	10
Politics	12	9	10
Social issues	11	8	8
Business	9	7	7
Culture/civilization	6	7	7
Disasters	7	6	6
Health/consumer	4	7	6
Accidents	6	6	6
Miscellaneous	2	7	6
Foreign affairs	3	6	5
Science/tech	3	4	4

Note: Columns may not sum to 100% due to rounding.

remains is easily lost. Only after the sixth story in an average local news broadcast does civic news (politics/government, social issues, science/technology, etc.) surpass crime, accidents, and disasters and become the most likely topic to appear. And when civic stories are aired, these often complex issues are largely brushed over. (See Table 3.1.)

The aspect of newscast content that is most affected by the X-Structure is time. Whereas 30% of crime, accident, and disaster stories are a minute or longer, nearly three-quarters (73%) of the stories about government policy are less than a minute, and more than one-third (39%) are less than 30 seconds. Likewise, three out of five stories about social issues (61.2%) are less than a minute long. Even health and consumer news, which are thought to be popular subjects with viewers, can't buck the trend. Sixty percent of the health stories are less than one minute, and nearly two-thirds of those (37% of all health stories) are less than 30 seconds.

The obvious consequence of having less time for a story is that it must be told in shorthand. Sourcing usually deteriorates dramatically as the newscast progresses and stories become progressively shorter. Forty-two percent of all stories with three or more sources fall within the first three news items. And, not coincidentally, half of those lead-block stories are about public safety. After the first story, however, the frequency of multi-sourced stories drops steadily, while the number of items based on a single source or just a passing reference to any source increases.

SIDEBAR 3.1

"BREAKING NEWS RIGHT NOW"

A common refrain heard at local TV stations is that to be successful a newsroom must "win breaking news."

But we found that being able to go live to the scene of an event is a double-edged sword. Why? One reason is "the fog of war" effect. Covering late-breaking events pushes stories that had completed the editorial process off the air to make room for what is often no more than hearsay. Verified information, in other words, is replaced by rumor, speculation, and hyperbole.

Take the example of New York City's WCBS-TV, which opened its March 6, 2002, 11 P.M. broadcast with anchors Ernie Anastos and Angela Ray alerting viewers to "breaking news right now: a hostage drama in Valley Stream [Long Island]." Veteran New York news personality Penny Crone immediately appears on a large screen next to the anchor desk. "This is very, very tense," the gravely voiced Crone informs viewers. "What's going on here right now – apparently four men, heavily armed, are holding hostages, some employees, some customers, at a Staples store down the street." There is no sign of the store or much else, because all around Crone it is pitch black.

"This entire street is blocked off," she says. "We went with our live truck towards the store and some police officers ran up and said, 'Don't get anywhere near there, they're heavily armed and they could even shoot you.'" Crone turns to a man who says his 18-year-old son is inside the store. He explains that the teen had called his girlfriend, who told her mother, who called the man's wife, who had in turn called him to report that, "It was a robbery that went bad." After wishing the family "the best of luck," Crone throws it back to the studio. "We're here, we're live, and we'll let you know what's going on."

A second update a few minutes later: "This is a very tense situation," Crone begins. She repeats that there are thought to be four gunmen in the store and adds new information that there are "six or seven hostages." Crone then turns to the man she had interviewed a few minutes earlier, the father of one of the hostages. "Now I know you probably want to look at the camera and say something if you can to the men with guns in there," she informed him. The man, looking somewhat perplexed, pauses for a moment and then says, "Well, you might as well give it up because you're surrounded." After again explaining that, "We can't get anywhere near the store," Crone reports that a hostage negotiating team is talking by phone with one of the gunmen. She wraps up by telling viewers again, "This is a very, very tense situation ... If you live near here, don't go anywhere near here. It's very, very, dangerous."

A few minutes later, just before the weather, there is a third update: "And the drama continues," begins Crone. "We're on Sunrise and as you can see, there's nobody on the street." Wagging her finger at viewers she says, "Now we're going to tell you what's going on. There are at least six or seven employees of Staples that are being held hostage by about four men who police say are heavily armed. There were some customers inside the store. Staples didn't close until 10 and this happened at 9:15. As I said, these men are heavily, heavily armed. Police from the hostage negotiating team are talking with one of the suspects right now. We're going to have a lot more for you on our CBS morning show, the *CBS News 2 Morning Show*. We'll have more, more, more. We'll be here, we'll be watching it."

"Thanks Penny," said anchor Anastos, "we'll get back to you." And, at the end of the newscast, he does.

"Well, you know, I've covered a lot of stories and this is a very, very, tense story and one that I haven't covered," begins Crone. "It's very, very quiet here. I'm going to stop talking for just one second. [Silence] The only thing you hear right now and see are the police presence." Crone than repeats for the fourth time that she's standing in a street, that there are several gunmen and several hostages inside the store, and that darkness and the police make it impossible to see what's going on. "We cannot get any closer to show you anything more," she apologizes, "because of the situation, because these men are heavily armed and obviously we're going to hope and pray that everything works out fine."

Anchor Ernie Anastos: "Is there any sense they might be able to end this thing peacefully?"

Crone: "That's what they're trying to do, Ernie. They're talking on the phone to a suspect and hopefully, we'll keep our fingers crossed, that this will end soon."

Several hours later, the botched robbery did end when 12 employees (there were no customers), some of whom had been held at gunpoint and others who had hidden in the store, emerged from the building unharmed. Police arrested four men and confiscated an

SIDEBAR 3.1 (continued)

unloaded .380-caliber Beretta handgun, a .45-caliber pellet gun, a tele-scopic baton, and pepper spray. Police theorize the crooks had intended to burgle the store after everyone left but were discovered hiding in the basement, according to an Associated Press report the next day.

Crone's four live reports consumed a total of five and one-half minutes, more than one-third (34%) of the 16 minutes of news time in the broadcast. And for all that, viewers went to bed knowing little of what happened.

What impact did WCBS's late-breaking coverage have on the content of its 11 o'clock news on this night?

Taking into account a 15-second voice-over about a man who was shot and wounded that afternoon on a midtown Manhattan sidewalk and a one-minute, 45-second reporter package about the bail hearing for a policeman convicted of abusing a suspect, almost half (47%) of WCBS-TV's newscast was devoted to crime. Add to this a story about a freak Long Island Expressway accident and the amount of public safety news rises to 55%. If an update on Mayor Guiliani's divorce and an item about comedian Jerry Seinfeld's dispute with neighbors over off-street parking are included, the amount of crime/bizarre accident/celebrity news came to 10 minutes and 15 seconds, or almost two-thirds (64%) of the broadcast's news hole.

– Walter C. Dean

The thinness of sourcing in the bottom half of the newscast reflects the presence of shorter stories – anchor-read wire copy or press-release material illustrated with cover footage. These stories, told in short bites, cannot document where the information comes from, and they do not have enough room for interviews that allow audiences to judge the source of information (see Figure 3.4).

It's a vicious circle: if a story isn't C-A-D – about Crime, Accidents, or Disasters – it won't make the first block. But because first-block stories are awarded more time and more resources, middle-block stories that include substantive news about policy or issues don't get the time and sourcing needed to make these less-disturbing subjects understandable, and interesting.

And as we show in the next chapter and beyond, beefing up certain topics, such as government and education, can turn them into ratings

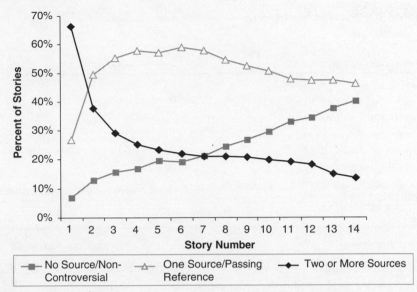

Figure 3.4. Quality of sourcing over the course of the newscast.

winners, whereas overfeeding crime, accident, and disaster stories actually turns viewers off.

Lead Stories

Another way of understanding the influence of the X-Structure is to take a more in-depth look at lead stories. The lead is not only a broadcast's single most important story, it is also an increasingly important marketing tool, a way to hook viewers from the preceding program and reel them into the newscast before they change channels or shut off the set.

What stories do newscast producers think will hook viewers? Almost two-thirds (61%) of the leads in the 2,400 newscasts we studied are about three topics that involve public safety:

- Thirty-nine percent are about crime.
- Thirteen percent are about natural disasters or other catastrophes, such as severe weather.
- Nine percent are about accidents.

More than half (56%) of the disaster leads were about unusual or severe local weather, which provides lots of exciting visuals. In fact, stories about severe weather or a major brush or forest fire (often related

Table 3.2. Specific topic matter of lead stories about disasters and catastrophes

Topic	Percentage
Weather, special prominence	34
Weather phenomena	22
Commonplace fire	21
Severe fire	13
Man-made disaster	5
Natural disaster	2
Geological phenomena	1
Other	2
TOTAL	100

to weather conditions) led nearly 1 of every 10 newscasts (9%). On the other hand, a blaze didn't necessarily have to be big to lead; "commonplace" fires made up about 3% of lead stories and 21% of all disaster and catastrophe stories. (See Table 3.2.)

What is especially notable about leads, in addition to the focus on crime and commotion, is that topics other the crime, accident, or natural disasters rarely get top billing. Fewer than 1 in 10 lead items (8.4%) are about politics or government affairs, though in 2000, when the presidential primary season occurred during our study weeks, stories about the campaigns boosted government/politics to more than 17% of leads. Another year when politics became a prominent lead story was in 1998, when the Clinton/Lewinsky saga was unfolding.

Over five years, defense/foreign affairs news averaged just less than 7% of lead stories, and in the two "political" years of the study, 1998 and 2000, international news dropped to less than 1% of leads. This was offset, however, by results in 2001 when two incidents involving the military (a U.S. spy plane in China and the sinking of a Japanese fishing boat) made headlines during our survey period and pushed foreign affairs/defense news to 18% of lead stories. In 2002, in the aftermath of 9/11 and with the war in Afghanistan underway, foreign affairs/defense were just over 10% of leads.

The lesson here is not so much that topics such as politics or foreign affairs are more likely to rise to lead story status in certain years. Rather, it's that crime and disaster stories are so constantly in the lead position. Crime stories, for example, are the topic of 42% of early news leads, though they make up only 25% of total stories in those same broadcasts.

Table 3.3. Topics of local lead stories	
Topic	Percentage
Crime	41
Disasters/catastrophes	14
Accidents/bizarre events	9
Politics	8
Social Issues	8
Business	6
Human interest	5
Foreign affairs/defense	3
Culture	3
Health/consumer	2
Science/tech.	1

On the late news, crime makes up 37% of leads from 24% of the stories. (See Table 3.3.)

The hook-and-hold approach relies on localism – the geographic proximity of events – to provide a degree of built-in relevancy for viewers. Crime news typifies localism. Fully three-quarters of crime news is local. Another way these stories are made relevant is by playing on emotional concerns about personal safety and welfare, a message often telegraphed by the visual images and hyperbolic anchor introductions in lead stories.

SENSATIONAL VIDEO

Lead stories are more likely to be illustrated with pictures that are sensational or unusual. In fact, the more dramatic the pictures, the higher the probability that a story will be used at the top of a broadcast. (see Figure 3.5). There are twice as many lead stories with visuals that are at least somewhat sensational than would be expected by chance.

In our study, though only 15.3% of all stories contain visuals that are *somewhat* or *mostly* sensational, these more dramatically illustrated stories compose nearly one-quarter (24.9%) of newscast leads, an approximately 60% difference.

Among the stories with *mostly* sensational visuals, the ratio was even higher, from 1.6% of all stories in newscasts to 3.1% of lead stories, a difference of approximately 89%. Among the three most popular lead

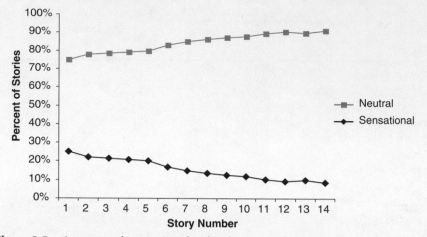

Figure 3.5. Amount of sensational video by story placement.

Table 3.4. Sensational footage in lead stories

Subject	Percentage with Sensational Video
Accidents/bizarre events	43
Crime	33
Miscellaneous	27
Disasters/catastrophes	25
Human interest	18
Foreign affairs/defense	17
Science/tech.	17
Social Issues	15
Health/consumer	14
Culture	14
Politics	7
Business	5

story topics, somewhat or mostly sensational visuals accompanied 33% of the crime stories, 25% of the disaster stories (weather stories made up one-third of this category), and 43% of the stories about accidents or bizarre events.

Topics that were less likely to appear as lead stories were, not coincidentally, significantly less visually compelling. For example, somewhat or mostly sensational visuals accompanied only 5% of the business stories and 7% of the political stories. (See Table 3.4.)

Besides being more likely to appear at or near the top of a newscast, stories with more dramatic video are more likely to be longer. Items with

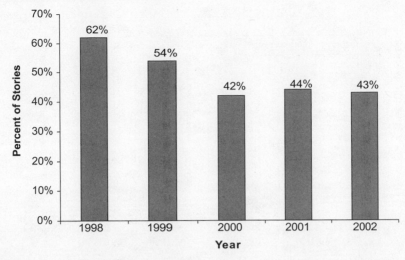

Figure 3.6. Stories with on-air reporters.

neutral graphics and footage averaged 61 seconds. Stories illustrated with pictures that were *somewhat* sensational were 1 minute, 7 seconds. Stories in which the pictures were *mostly* sensational – containing the most vivid video and often including elements such as gore or violence – were longest of all, at 1 minute, 22 seconds. Stories with no graphic element were shortest, with an average length of 25 seconds.

The Disappearing Reporter

Besides influencing *what* is covered, the X-Structure also affects *how* stories are assigned and treated. Indeed, the impact of the X-Structure has become even more apparent because of a recent trend: the disappearing reporter. Here's what the data reveal. First, the number of stories by on-air reporters has declined dramatically over time. Second, reporter appearances are increasingly concentrated in the first third of the newscast where crime, accidents, and disasters dominate. Third, stories *without* an on-air reporter get less airtime than stories with them. Not only does "flooding the zone" with first-block reporter packages on crime, accidents, and disasters raise the visibility of one kind of news – C-A-D – it often means there's no one left to cover the rest of the day's events.

Over the five years of our study, the number of stories typically presented by reporters dropped from 62% of all stories in 1998 to 43% of all stories in 2002 (see Figure 3.6). At the same time, all other content, including network-feed stories, anticipated events covered without a

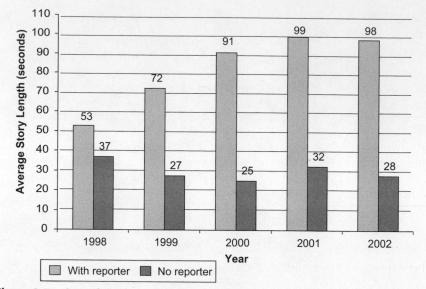

Figure 3.7. Story length in daybook reporting.

reporter, and anchor "tell" stories with no tape footage, increased from 38% to 57%.

The most striking decline in reporter appearances was not among high-profile first-block stories (most of which continue to be longer reporter packages) or in branded segments such as health tips or consumer reports – but in the second tier of news items based on pre-arranged events. Between the first and fifth years of our study, the number of these "daybook" stories (pre-scheduled events from press releases, agendas, etc.) in which reporters appeared declined almost by half from 35.9% to 18.6% of all stories. At the same time, the number of daybook stories delivered by anchors increased threefold, from 9.4% to 28.7% of all stories.

An examination of the content of 15 stations monitored in the first and last years of the project produced similar results. The proportion of daybook stories presented with and without a reporter flipped. In 1998, daybook stories were more likely to feature an on-scene reporter by a ratio of 3:2. By 2002, those same stories were more likely to *not* feature a reporter by a ratio of 3:1.

The decline of on-air reporting raises an important question. Are stories done by reporters necessarily better than those in which an editorial person is never seen? The answer is "yes" first and foremost because a story in which a reporter appears is more likely to be longer, better sourced, and convey more information (see Figure 3.7).

Table 3.5. Effect of having a reporter on the scene in coverage of daybook/pre-arranged events

Opinion Mix	Crime		Politics		Social Issues	
	With Reporter	Without Reporter	With Reporter	Without Reporter	With Reporter	Without Reporter
Mix of opinions	35%	15%	45%	25%	30%	13%
Mostly one opinion	10	5	10	6	9	5
One opinion	18	18	29	32	30	31
Undisputed/ Noncontroversial	36	62	16	37	31	51

So strong is this relationship that, for many topics, a reporter's appearance in the story is a predictor of quality. For example, a story about a pre-arranged event in which a reporter appears – whether it is to ask a question in a short interview clip or to narrate a longer package – is significantly more likely to contain a mix of opinions about a subject rather than just one point of view whether the story is about crime, politics, or social issues. (See Table 3.5.) (We go into this point in detail in Chapter 5.)

The decline in reporter appearances appears to indicate that newsrooms are assigning more "one-man bands" to daybook events, having photographers ask questions and take notes in addition to making pictures. However, it could also mean reporters are doing more assignments every day, writing "tell" stories for some broadcasts and appearing on-camera for others. Both things are probably occurring. Annual News Directors Surveys conducted as part of our research found that the number of daily stories for the average local TV reporter increased from 1.4 in 1998 to 1.8 in 2002, an increase of 29%.

Declining Enterprise

As might be expected, the decline in reporter appearances has been accompanied by a fall in enterprise generally. With the exception of a relatively small core of stories – news series and investigations – the need for material to fill newscasts means quantity, rather than quality, increasingly drives newsroom decision making.

We measured enterprise on a scale that noted the amount of effort put into a story. At the top was an original station investigation, exposé, or special series. At the bottom was airing a press release. In between, a

Walter C. Dean and Atiba Pertilla

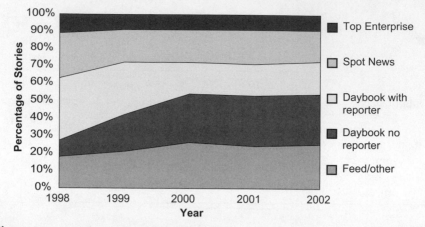

Figure 3.8. Levels of enterprise, 1998–2002.

story that showed a reporter on camera represented more effort than a story that simply aired pictures. An original local story demonstrated more effort than an item taken off a network feed.

We have already seen how the disappearing reporter affects the amount of enterprise in daybook news, which accounts for nearly half (47%) of newscast content. Much the same has happened to spot news – a category that includes "live and late-breaking" events. Many stations may advertise themselves as the place to turn for the latest news, but the evidence suggests this kind of coverage is actually declining. Over five years, spot news fell from 26% to 18% of stories, a drop of roughly one third. To cover spot news, a newsroom must have enough staffers on hand to chase breaking events without jeopardizing its coverage of other stories. Stations appear less able to do that than they were only a few years ago.

While the reporting of daybook stories and even spot news deteriorated, stations continued to invest people, time, and resources into investigative and special series that are a staple of the ratings "sweeps." Surprisingly this higher level of journalistic work – investigations, interview segments, and news series – held fairly steady over five years, at about 9% of stories (See Figure 3.8).[5]

Marquee segments aside, however, stations increasingly gravitated toward content that is readily found and efficiently harvested. And stations supplemented this easy-to-get news with stories that required no local reporting whatsoever. This was "feed" material from outside sources such as a network, affiliate cooperative, or independent

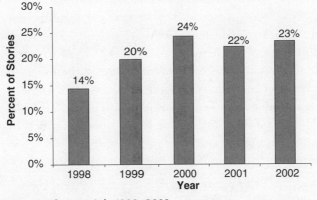

Figure 3.9. Feed material, 1998–2002.

syndicator, and it grew to account for almost one-quarter of all local stories. Indeed, during the course of the local TV news study the use of this outside material increased from 14.4% of stories in 1998 to 23.4% of stories in 2002 – an increase of 63%. On the 15 stations studied in both 1998 and 2002, the use of feeds nearly doubled, from 12% to 23.5% of all stories (see Figure 3.9).

SIDEBAR 3.2

HUMAN INTEREST – A MISSED OPPORTUNITY

Whether it's a "Wednesday's Child" profile of a youth seeking to be adopted, a seasonal opening of community swimming pools, or a July Fourth parade, human interest stories compose the second most popular topic on local TV news. They make up 10% of stories and, one might presume, showcase interesting characters or fascinating tales. Yet we found that most of the human-interest stories on local TV are more about events than about people.

Though storytelling is one of the strengths of television, there is surprisingly little of it applied to human-interest news. Stories that exhibit higher levels of enterprise – everything from investigations to interviews to news series – make up less than 9% of human-interest stories. As with crime news, human-interest stories tend toward the episodic. We see the ribbon cut, but we are told little about the vision or work that went into the project being launched. For example, 2 of every 10 (19%) human-interest stories focus on a parade or rally.

SIDEBAR 3.2 (continued)

These stories involve little reporting. Instead, they are "sprayed" in the lingo of the newsroom, that is they are shot by a photographer and written from a press release or a few bits of information picked up at the scene. What the viewer sees on the screen is often the extent of what the viewer gets in the way of information. In nearly 6 in 10 (57%) human-interest stories the information is not attributed to a source but is based instead on passing references or reports of what can be seen in video or is simply known to be true.

It's not surprising then that most human-interest stories are short – nearly three-quarters (72%) are 60 seconds or less. Most are from a daybook or press releases – more than half (57%) are from a pre-arranged event. Another one-quarter (24%) are based on feed material from a network or other secondary source.

As brief as they are, it's probably not surprising then that human-interest stories are rarely used as newscast leads. Only 35 of the 2,419 lead stories in our sample (or 1.4%) fall within the topic area of human-interest news.

When human-interest stories do feature a person as opposed to an event, it's often someone with a one-of-a-kind experience (17%). Human-interest items are the most likely of all stories to offer the perspective of the average person on the street (10%). Athletes are featured prominently (in 7% of stories) as is Mother Nature, so to speak. Stories about how people cope with the aftermath of bad weather or a natural disaster account for 7% of human-interest stories.

Yet despite their more personal focus, human-interest stories are not necessarily local. Though they might feature a local person, only 27% contain information that directly affects the local viewing audience. Indeed, news items with a national or international focus account for 13% of human-interest stories, indicating that most of these were taken from a network feed.

Given the broad appeal of human-interest news, it is too bad that stories covering other topics do not include a local focus on individual lives and concerns. Human-interest stories could be used to illuminate topics that are important to the local community such as unemployment, government services, education, housing, or transportation.

– Atiba Pertilla

Not only is feed material relatively cheap and plentiful, it complements the hook-and-hold formula. Newscast producers monitor the feeds, and they cherry-pick eye-catching video that is highly teasable or that can be used to fill gaps in the X-Structure. For example, if a producer wants to end the newscast on a light note and has no local "happy news," he or she simply pulls feed footage of a newborn panda cub at a faraway zoo. Local coverage can also be used to justify the airing of dramatic footage from somewhere else. Thus, a story about a local crime might be followed by helicopter footage of a spectacular police chase in another city.

CONCLUSION

Whether in Chicago, Sioux Falls, or most any other place in the country, the look of local news is one of form dictating content. At the beginning of broadcasts are the live, local, and late-breaking incidents producers believe will hook people into watching. At the end are the interesting or unusual stories to hold the audience through weather and sports. In many places, the X-Structure now defines what professionals think is newsworthy. Stories are either C-A-D – crime, accidents, or disasters – or they are "soft." Everything else becomes filler. To the degree that this formula governs the editorial process, and that degree admittedly differs from newsroom to newsroom, it influences what is covered, how it is reported, and the time and treatment it will receive on the air.

Critics might respond to our finding an X-Structure with: So what? If the flashing lights bring eyeballs to the screen, maybe the audience can then be fed the other news that is arguably more useful to them. There are two problems with this argument. First, the homogenization of the news distorts the reality of the local community. It makes Sioux Falls feel like Chicago, and viewers sense the loss of place. It is what makes local TV news feel like "the news from nowhere" (Epstein 1973). Second, the theory that the audience wants it this way is incorrect. In fact, this approach is pushing viewers away. And we can prove it.

Local TV viewers often tell researchers that news stations "all look alike." Broadcasters have trouble understanding this because when news people watch the news, as they do almost obsessively, they focus on the minutia – a garbled word here, a hair out of place there, or, when keeping score, who beat whom to the scene and by how many minutes. They have trouble seeing what the audience sees.

Stations spend untold millions of dollars promoting personalities and newscast brands in an attempt to differentiate themselves from the competition. Yet when it comes to what's on the air – the content of broadcasts and the structures in which that content is presented – the viewers have it right. A good deal is pretty much the same.

That this uniformity exists is especially noteworthy when one takes into account that there are 775 local TV newsrooms across the country that each day generate the content for newscasts carried on 950 stations. Or that thousands of individual reporters, producers, photographers, tape editors, writers, assignment editors, and technicians are engaged in this work.

How can it be that stations look so much alike? And how did it get to be this way? We'll answer these questions in the next chapter.

4 The Myths That Dominate Local TV News: The X-Structure and the Fallacy of the Hook-and-Hold Method of TV News

A series of myths dominates the world of local TV news. These myths are among the most influential forces in local TV. They are a set of long-held beliefs so ingrained that nearly every station operates by them unquestioningly. They explain why local TV is so similar from city to city, and why the "hook-and-hold" mentality and the X-Structure permeate local TV news. And they are manifestly, and provably, false.

Myth No. 1: It is more important not to lose audience than to attract one.

Myth No. 2: A newscast should emphasize stories that shock or amaze.

Myth No. 3: Immediacy is the most important value in local TV news.

Myth No. 4: Flashing police lights, yellow tape, and other "hot" visuals are "eyeball magnets."

Myth No. 5: TV is an emotional medium in which pictures are more important than words (or ideas).

Myth No. 6: Every lead story must have a live shot from the scene.

Myth No. 7: Viewers are voyeuristic and like to be titillated.

Myth No. 8: Viewers care only about local news.

Myth No. 9: Some stories are more important as promotion than as news.

Myth No. 10: Viewers won't watch long stories about issues.

In our five-year study of local TV news, we statistically catalogued the impact these myths have on the medium, as outlined in the previous chapter. In this chapter we will look at these 10 myths more closely – where they come from, how endemic they are – and take them apart.

MYTH NO. 1: IT IS MORE IMPORTANT NOT TO LOSE AUDIENCE THAN TO ATTRACT ONE

Ask a broadcast journalist to describe the typical viewer and chances are you'll hear about a short attention span and a finger on the remote control. Ask that same newsperson how this view of the audience influences the way news content is prioritized and the next thing you are likely to hear is the phrase "hook and hold." This idea arose in part out of the media environment in which local TV came of age – the late 1970s and '80s.

Until the emergence of cable TV in the 1980s, there were only three or four TV stations in most markets, and about the only thing to watch at 6:00, 10:00, or 11:00 P.M. was the local news. With the arrival of cable and satellite transmission, viewers suddenly had scores of alternative programs to watch instead. Now, in most places, subscribers can receive more than 100, even 200, programs or sporting events. Even households without cable or satellite may receive as many as a dozen over-the-air stations. Whatever the case, viewers have been exercising their prerogative not to watch the news – tuning out flagship early and late local newscasts at a rate of about 1% annually; these broadcasts have lost close to one-fifth of their audience over the past 10 years.[1]

Stations, in turn, have essentially given up trying to attract viewership to specific newscasts, opting instead to promote an overall brand and concentrate on retaining lead-in audiences inherited from the more highly viewed entertainment programming. The consulting firm Audience Research & Development, for example, found that when a newscast's first story is unappealing, 20% of local news viewers "often switched" and 40% "sometimes switched" channels.[2] This large pool of fickle viewers provides the margin a station needs to "win" a time period – that is, to receive the highest Nielsen rating in the market. Consistently winning the time period means a station can charge a greater amount for advertising than the next closest station. Because so many uncommitted viewers are "in play" every night, for a few precious seconds, every station in the market can be competitive.

To discourage switching, newsrooms employ a "hook" and "bait" it with a story that is new, local, and showcases the station's on-top-of-the-news reputation and state-of-the-art technology.

Table 4.1. Stories used in the newscast "stacking" exercise	
Hard News	
Anthrax	Suspicious white powder is found at a local post office.
Bomb hoax	An airplane lands after a suspicious note is found.
Mayor	Late night news conference about city hall security.
Body	A man dies at a home in an exclusive neighborhood.
Soft News	
Bobo	An elephant briefly escapes from his enclosure at the zoo.
Pain	Doctors have new ways to treat chronic pain.
Other	
Pakistan	Martial law declared after Pakistani official assassinated.
Schools	Funding cuts could prompt layoffs and school closings.
Streets	Budget shortfall could mean big cuts in street repairs.

This may not seem like too great a challenge. Yet coming up with a "live, local, and late-breaking" lead for every newscast every day is a daunting task. And stations, perhaps not surprisingly, tend to rely on bait that is easy to come by. Our content analysis of more than 2,400 newscasts found that almost two-thirds of the lead stories were about everyday public safety incidents.

The ubiquity of crime, accident, and disaster stories mirrored research we conducted with more than 2,000 local television reporters, photographers, editors, producers, anchors, assignment editors, and managers around the country as part of the Committee of Concerned Journalists' newsroom training called "The Traveling Curriculum." As part of the curriculum, we presented local TV news professionals with a list of stories to "stack" – to determine where they would place them in a broadcast and how.[3] (See Table 4.1.)

The list presents a busy news day, so busy that broadcast journalists must make hard choices that reveal priorities. A bomb hoax has forced an airplane to make an unscheduled landing. There's a report of a suspicious white powder at a post office. Police are removing a dead body from a mansion in an upscale neighborhood. The mayor has called a press conference on new city hall security measures. A leader in the Middle East is assassinated. Bobo the elephant is back in his enclosure at the zoo after an escape attempt and a short walk. Local school funding will be significantly cut this year, and money for the maintenance of city streets will also be reduced. Doctors have new ideas about how to manage chronic pain. (See Figure 4.1.)

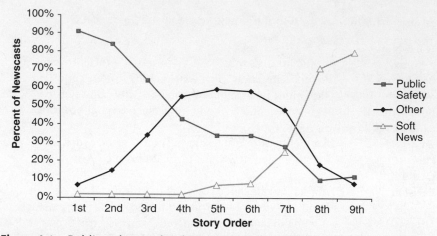

Figure 4.1. Public safety and soft news as percentage of newscasts stacked.

In the story-ordering exercise, two-thirds of the 250 small groups opened their hypothetical broadcasts with "Anthrax," a late-breaking story about a suspicious white powder discovered beneath a mail-sorting machine at a local post office. Though there was nothing to indicate the substance *was* anthrax, other than its appearance and existence, TV journalists jumped on the story. "You've got to do it," explained a news staffer from a North Carolina station, because the story will "hook 'em in." Why? "It's live, local, and late breaking," is the answer we consistently heard. From a station in the Midwest, "It's something they'll actually pay attention to." Said a participant in another group session, "It's captivating – hooks viewers." "Intensity," reported another group, "Happening right now, everybody gets mail and will possibly be affected." The overall reaction was summed up by the person who said, "Potential chaos, urgency, extraordinary – even though we've had a million anthrax scares, and most of them turned out to be nothing."

A small minority – typically one out of five people in each group – felt the anthrax story didn't warrant so much attention. One group that led with a live picture from the post office elected not to send a reporter. "We don't want to be too alarmist," said their spokesperson, "we don't know [if it's really anthrax] and we don't want to freak them [the audience] out until we know." Another person worried that by making a big deal out of something that was probably not, in fact, true, the newsroom might undermine its own credibility. "We don't report bomb threats," they noted, asking, "Should it even be covered?"

The next two stories that appeared most often in the composite newscast were also about public safety threats – the unscheduled landing of an airliner at a local airport some hours earlier because of a bomb threat (which had been already proved unfounded) and a live statement from a local mayor (who had scheduled his announcement to coincide with the beginning of the newscast) about new security measures being implemented at city hall.

About the bomb threat, which caused only minimal disruption to airport operations and no injuries, a person from one of the many groups that ran the story second explained, "It would perk up everybody's ears if you heard there was a bomb. It would pique their interest and keep them watching." That sentiment was echoed by people in other sessions: "If you don't do it, people will flip to someone else," and "They would go to cable to see it."

A staff member at a successful top-50 market station told us: "Our job is to draw people into the news and keep them there." A participant at a station in the Midwest explained: "In this day and age we've got to get it on the air. The other guy will put it on and [our] missing it would be noted."

"Viewers are more inclined to pay attention to the first three stories about security," said one person. "You need to put the most visual stuff on the top at eleven, need to keep the viewer engaged and need to be constantly moving to keep the viewer from shutting off and going to bed."

Reality Check

There are really two questions here. The first has to do with the audience. Do viewers really watch the news with a "trigger-finger"? And, more importantly, what prompts them to flex it? Research suggests the answers is yes, viewers flip around the dial, but not nearly to the degree that broadcast journalists assume. About three-quarters of the *news directors* (78%) polled by the Radio and Television News Directors Foundation (RTNDF) believed people switched stations at least twice during the last newscast they watched, and one-third of those (28%) believed viewers switched four or more times.

But when *viewers* were asked how much they switched, less than half (44%) said they "channel surfed" twice or more, and nearly half (46%) said they never switched at all.[4]

Moreover, broadcast journalists' angst over channel surfing fails to take into account the viewers who leave a newscast but eventually return to the program. The firm Audience Research & Development, for instance, found that 60% of those who left a favored local newscast at the beginning eventually flipped back.[5]

So what are people looking for? What kind of news are they more likely to watch? Is spot news, with its commotion and hyperbole, or other stories with a high degree of sensationalism, the best bait to hook and hold the audience? Or are there other, more effective, alternatives?

Our data suggest two fundamental preferences of local news viewers. First, people care most about things they feel are important or interesting, and second, they like that information to be presented in a well-rounded story. Spot news by its very nature – it just occurred – doesn't lend itself to this kind of coverage. But other news does.

In both early and late broadcasts, for example, our research shows that people watching the previous program are more likely to stay tuned for the news if the lead story focuses on something of widespread interest or lasting importance. Viewers stay with long lead stories (more than two minutes) that include authoritative sources. Lead stories focusing on scandal or sensationalism actually showed a tendency to get slightly (though not significantly) lower ratings. Other stories that failed to hook viewers were those that focused primarily on people, popular behavior and human interest, celebrities and entertainment, or the big "recurring" event of the day if there were no significant new developments.

On the other hand, lead stories that focus on issues or policy got one-quarter of a rating point and two-tenths of a prime demographic point more than celebrity news. In fact, these policy/issue stories – often thought of as boring institutional news – can win a station an additional 4.9% in ratings retention and an extra 4.5% in share retention compared with the celebrity stories.

Newsrooms have a choice when it comes to viewership. They can opt for a strategy that is primarily defensive, a "don't touch that dial" approach that relies on hype and hyperbole to frighten or trick people into watching. Or they can pursue what is arguably the more difficult, but provably more effective, strategy of building viewership on a foundation of good storytelling about important issues and events.

MYTH NO. 2: A NEWSCAST SHOULD EMPHASIZE STORIES THAT SHOCK OR AMAZE

This myth is a corollary of the hook-and-hold approach. A good story is either frighteningly "hard" or memorably "soft." The hard stuff – that which is new and often violent or threatening – goes on top. It's a case of "important stories versus urgent stories," one person told us. And "urgent stories are the attention grabbers and you have to grab their attention. CSI. Urgent trumps important."

The soft stuff – especially if it's unusual or outrageous – goes last, not because it is least memorable but because it is "teasable;" it can be foreshadowed with promotional teases mentioned throughout the broadcast to keep people watching.

Had Bobo the elephant left his enclosure and wandered around the zoo closer to news time, it would have been deemed breaking news and aired at the top of the broadcast. "If it stampedes, it leads," was how one newsperson put it. But because several hours had passed since Bobo's brief escape, the story had rapidly morphed from hard to soft, from urgent to merely unusual, and thus it went from the top to the bottom of most broadcasts. "It was probably the most memorable story, but not really that important," said someone who noted that, "before we even read it, we decided it was the kicker." Someone else in another city said, "It has all the elements of a great story – injury, video, reaction of witnesses. We like to scare the crap out of people." But because it was not new, it was no longer hard news. A colleague summed up what many people told us when she said that though it was "the best story, what people will talk about, it was not journalistically sound to lead with it. It's over."

Another participant said, "We have an anti-feature element in the newsroom," which was ironic because "one of our purposes is to show memorable news." "If I don't care about people watching, this would be important," said a newsman at one station. "Maybe it's our fault with not good storytelling. It's why I'm in counseling. There's no time to do it on our level."

The X-Structure, with live and late breaking at the top and soft at the bottom, means the broader news agenda is consigned to the editorial backwater of short voice-overs in the middle of the broadcast. The education and street repair stories often suffered this fate in our newscast stacking exercise, despite their potential effect on many viewers.

"Boring on paper and boring on TV," said the spokesman for one group about the street repair story. "No action, no video, no excitement, no elements," someone in another city told us. "We have no elements and can follow up tomorrow" was a common reaction.

"It is important, but not visual; complex and not immediately explainable. It's deadly by nature," another person said. "We need to have action and a reporter standing there [on a deteriorating street] won't do it."

Reality Check

In this myth we see the X-Structure at work. Stories that shock or amaze are considered the most memorable and are the "bookends" that hold broadcasts together.

How does this bipolar construct – this "professional" and presumably ratings-driven definition of news – compare with what viewers might consider news based on their own lives and concerns?

SIDEBAR 4.1

COMMUNITY CONCERNS – HOW PLUGGED IN IS LOCAL TV?

A common complaint about local TV news is that it focuses on the trivial and sensational at the expense of covering other important community news. News directors, however, say they're just giving people what they want. As proof, they cite consultant research and the ratings. Who's right?

We discovered that as our study of newscast content was taking place, other independent research into local issues was being undertaken in some of the markets we were monitoring. So we decided to compare the two sets of results. They revealed a wide gap between the issues citizens say matter most and the topics local TV news chose to cover.

In 1999, the John S. and James L. Knight Foundation conducted surveys in 26 communities around the United States where Knight-Ridder newspapers were published. That same year, the Five Year Local TV News Project study examined newscasts in four of those communities: Miami, Minneapolis-St. Paul, Philadelphia, and Wichita.

The Knight-Ridder surveys questioned residents about 12 specific concerns – for example, "the lack of affordable child care" – and asked them whether these issues were a "big problem," a "small problem," or "not a problem" in their community. Then, residents were asked to name the community's most important problem.

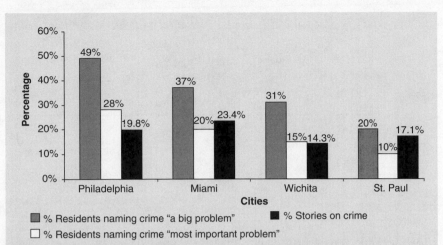

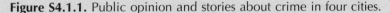

Figure S4.1.1. Public opinion and stories about crime in four cities.

Crime was commonly cited as a "big problem" by half of the Philadelphia residents (49%), and more than one-third (37%) of the respondents who lived in Miami. In Wichita, 31% saw crime as a big problem, whereas in St. Paul the number dropped to 20%.

Yet the Local TV News Project study data collected in these four cities indicate that there was little relationship between the amount of coverage given to crime and citizens' concern about the issue. The percentage of crime stories on the newscasts in the four markets was not as varied as one might imagine – from 14.3% of stories in Wichita to 23.4% of stories in Miami. (See Figure S4.1.1.)

It is not axiomatic that the number of stories or the amount of time devoted to a particular issue is indicative of the quality of the coverage. But with a finite news hole, the topics presented week in and week out telegraph the priorities and values of the news organization. And, at least in theory, newscast content reflects the measured judgment of the TV newsroom about what the public needs to see and hear.

It is hard to say whether there should have been even more crime coverage in Miami and Philadelphia or less crime coverage in St. Paul and Wichita. But based on what people in each community said was important, there was a disconnect between concerns and coverage.[6] The pattern in crime stories suggests that some topics may receive a certain amount of coverage (too much or too little) regardless of community concern.

SIDEBAR 4.1 (continued)

Table S4.1.1. Unemployment: Perception of the problem and amount of news coverage

	Miami	Philadelphia	St. Paul	Wichita
Percentage of residents naming unemployment "a big problem"	23%	35%	4%	7%
Percentage of stories addressing employment issues	0.50%	0.70%	2.90%	2.00%

At the same time, another issue on the minds of many citizens was ignored entirely. A significant number of respondents to the Knight survey in both Miami and Philadelphia said that unemployment was a big problem (23% and 35%, respectively), whereas in St. Paul and Wichita the unemployment issue was much less important. But the amount of coverage given to job-related issues (including everything from layoff announcements to strikes and slowdowns) was similar at all four stations. It was very low. In fact, stations in the St. Paul and Wichita markets actually covered *more* stories involving jobs (such as stories about strikes, layoffs, new plant openings, etc.) than the Miami and Philadelphia stations. (See Table S4.1.1.)

Another part of the community survey revealed a "hidden issue" on the minds of many citizens, but one that was almost completely invisible on local TV news: concern about unsupervised children and teenagers. The Knight surveys found that many people saw the issue as a big problem, with concern ranging from 25% in St. Paul to 47% in Philadelphia. In St. Paul and Wichita, supervision of children essentially tied with crime as the "most important problem" in the community. (See Table S4.1.2.)

Our study did not track issues related to children and young adults per se; however, by looking at whether parents, families, or children are being featured as the "main actor" in a story we tried to get a sense of how much coverage is being given to children's issues. And it turns out that the amount of coverage focused around children and families was minuscule, ranging from 2.6% of stories on St. Paul's TV stations to 5.7% in Philadelphia.

In other words, the news agenda is remarkably fixed in local news, regardless of the problems and concerns of the community it serves.

Table S4.1.2. Children's issues: Perception of the problem and amount of news coverage

	Miami	Philadelphia	St. Paul	Wichita
Percentage of residents naming "Too many unsupervised children and teenagers" a "big problem"	34%	47%	25%	34%
Percentage of stories with children, parents, or families as main actor	3.90%	5.70%	2.60%	5.00%

– Atiba Pertilla

We have already noted that the average newscast is so front-loaded with public safety news that 6 of every 10 broadcasts open with a story about a crime, accident, or disaster, which, in one-third of the broadcasts compose the first *three* stories.

Yet when we attempted to quantify the impact of this hard news on ratings, we were, frankly, surprised. Of the 2,419 newscasts in our study, 1,454 (60%) led with public safety stories. Yet in terms of ratings, newscasts that led with public safety got no better or worse ratings overall than stations that led with less "exciting" topics.

If the professional's definition of exciting news doesn't resonate with viewers, what does?

We found that when stations bucked conventional wisdom by adopting a broader definition of news and then committed the reporting resources to cover a variety of topics more completely, viewers noticed and approved.

Lead stories about health or political malfeasance were more popular than stories about everyday crime among the most sought-after demographics: men and women ages 18 to 49 and 25 to 54.[7] Economic lead stories that were specifically local in their perspective did 7% better than other stories in terms of retaining the rating and share performance of the lead-in program.[8]

Newscast producers should note that given the choice, viewers will opt for a "boring" topic such as stem-cell research over a "talker" about Paris Hilton – even younger viewers. Stories that focused on policy, in fact, get two-tenths of a prime demographic rating point more than celebrity stories. Policy stories are also better at holding audience, with a 4.7% rating retention and a 4.4% share retention over celebrity news.[9]

Beyond the ratings, there are other reasons why the X-Structure template for news is not an effective way to build audience. First, it tends to make all stations look alike. Second, although covering predominately one kind of news may certainly attract a part of the audience, it also risks turning away many other viewers – especially regular news viewers (Patterson 1994). Third, leading with sensational news fails to exploit the value of reporting and underutilizes a station's enormous financial investment in people and equipment.

This is not an argument to disregard spot news or unusual stories. In fact, our research shows that *any* topic – including topics such as crime or celebrity talkers – can be covered in ways that win viewers. The key, however, is that different kinds of news must be allowed to become lead stories or "stories everybody will talk about." And that won't happen unless the reporting process is allowed to work its magic on *all* kinds of stories.

MYTH NO. 3: IMMEDIACY IS THE MOST IMPORTANT VALUE

The fear of the channel-flipping audience combined with the technology to go live to the scene of an event is behind this third myth. Although spot news coverage actually dropped over the five years of our study (from 26 to 18% of all stories), judging from what we heard in our "Traveling Curriculum" sessions, this decline is due more to a shortage of reporters and photographers than anything else.

Local stations see themselves as competing against 24-hour news channels (even though most cable channels carry only national and international news) and the Internet, and that has increased the tendency to "report first and ask questions later."

It's not that newspeople have abandoned factual reporting. Rather it's that the existence of a few facts about something – isolated though they may be from history, context, or even common sense – now provide an excuse to air a story.

So intense is this pressure that late-breaking stories – simply because they are new – often undergo only the most cursory attempt at verification, let alone the reflection and debate that usually go into most editorial decision making. Fully half (49.7%) of all crime stories in our five-year study, for example, were based on the thinnest kind of attribution – sources mentioned only in passing, anonymous sources, or with no sources mentioned at all. In addition, one-quarter of all crime stories (24.3%) relied on only a single source – for example a police department's information officer. On the other hand, it's difficult to provide good sourcing for a story that is still being sorted out.

"We don't make assumptions in news, we have to cover the stories that are urgent at that hour," explained a journalist from a mid-Atlantic station about the anthrax scare. "It just happened and there must be something to it because Hazmat [hazardous materials] is there," said someone else.

In fact, many of those who participated in the newscast stacking exercise mentioned the anthrax story's "potential" importance and maintained that in the case of public safety incidents that present even a remote possibility for wider harm, they are more inclined to pass on information first and make judgments about its authenticity later. "Why does it have to be right, why does it have to be true?" said one TV staffer. "When it comes to the difference between not doing it versus doing it wrong, it's better to have it out there." But then, he added, "I'm not sure that's right." Someone in another city put it this way: "Just because it may not be real doesn't mean we should ignore it. We've got to do it to be competitive."

In another newsroom, a journalist questioned that line of reasoning, arguing that refusing to make a judgment about the story's newsworthiness abdicated the newsroom's responsibility to the public. "We can't be crying wolf. Part of our job is to be reliable. We need to be true to what we are and making it [anthrax] the lead hypes it." "We're not making it up," was the response, "the police and fire department are there and the potential for harm exists." Another person told us, "The mentality is that an 'emergency landing' drives coverage, even if it were one of those things that happen every day. It sounds worse than it is."

The possibility of a "big security announcement" by the mayor was the third story in the hypothetical newscast rankings. Groups had mixed feelings about the story. Some believed the mayor would not be so secretive if the announcement were not important, whereas others thought it was probably a publicity stunt. About 40% of the groups decided to switch live to the announcement despite a lack of details. Most said they played it high in the broadcast because "it fits with security" and "is happening now."

A Florida broadcaster put it this way: "Immediacy is so much a part of us that we don't even think about it. We know there's nothing to it [the post office anthrax scare], but you just have to be there. Our audience knows it's a potential threat and we cover events based on what the competition covers. We'll come in the next morning and ask, 'Did you see how [the other channels] did it?' 'Live, local and late breaking' is the mantra of what we do." A broadcaster from a station in the Southeast summed up a common theme: "Excitement – it's what people want to see and we're going to make the most of it."

Reality Check

Viewers seem a good deal less enamored with "live, local, and late breaking" news than the journalists who have bought into the immediacy myth. In fact, the live, local, and late-breaking genre does not deliver audience as well as other strategies. Indeed, we found that starting a newscast with a story about an unanticipated everyday crime or incident made zero difference in ratings.

It's not that viewers aren't interested in late-breaking news. The story, however, must be indisputably important for it to materially affect lead-in audience retention. We found, for instance, that a late-breaking story about a serious national disaster, say a plane crash or devastating tornado, even in another part of the country, is more likely than other stories to build an audience of younger viewers than a "live," but essentially empty, local story.[10] Yet that kind of late-breaking, big-news event is relatively rare. And in the absence of important "breaking" news, a station will hold or attract more viewers by airing a well-reported, enterprising story about an important, if less late-breaking, topic. Consider that the 8,198 crime stories on local news (24% of stories in our sample) got .08 *fewer* prime demographic ratings points than stories on other topics.[11] On the other hand, the 4,317 stories that dealt with ideas, issues, and policy (13% of stories) received .10 *more* prime demo points than other stories.[12]

Even the television consultants who helped perpetuate the immediacy myth are having second thoughts about its effectiveness. Frank Magid Associates, a major TV consulting firm, told clients in early 2004 that they might have to get more serious to survive. "Our research is saying that, for people to watch local news today, they want two things. One, it must be topical, right now. And it must have news value ... If you can't give me news, real news, I'm out of there," said Magid Vice President of Research Dick Haynes in an interview with trade magazine *Broadcasting & Cable*.[13] The problem with this is that relatively few stories meet both criteria each night. And given the choice of immediate or significant, most local TV news people still opt for immediate. The numbers show that that approach is misguided.

MYTH NO. 4: FLASHING POLICE LIGHTS, YELLOW TAPE, AND OTHER STIMULATING VISUALS ARE "EYEBALL MAGNETS"

There is no easy explanation about why TV newspeople are attracted to yellow police tape and the pulsating lights on emergency vehicles, but we found an almost universal appeal for these rather common pictures in both the TV newscasts we studied and in our trainings of news personnel. It may be that news professionals feel that television's visual pull overrides all other considerations or that these emergency visuals stir journalists' competitive instincts. In every session of the "Traveling Curriculum" we asked participants why they chose incident-based public-safety-threat stories as the top items in their hypothetical newscasts. And in every session we heard responses such as this: "Flashing lights and yellow police tape are eyeball grabbers."

The positive reasons for putting the anthrax and bomb hoax stories first included "good visuals, Hazmat, police tape, flashing lights, 'space suits,'" said participants in one city and "big police and fire presence, Hazmat suits, yellow police tape, flashing lights," said people in another. One participant exclaimed: "It's live, it's going on now, there's police tape, flashing lights, it's a crime scene, good pictures." A staffer at a Midwest station said, "It's exciting, visual, a great backdrop for a reporter with Hazmat, yellow tape, flashing lights." In another city we were told, "The reporter is in front of yellow tape – that's always good. People are always drawn to yellow tape and flashing lights. The commotion grabs the viewer's eye."

About the airport bomb hoax story, a news staffer in yet another city said: "If someone is flipping around on the dial, they will stay with it when they see the flashing lights and the [emergency escape] chutes deployed." "We aim for good content but often get caught up in the flash," a group at another station told us. "It's hard not to get caught up in the flash when there is such a significant emphasis placed on ratings," linking dramatic visuals with commercial success.

Reality Check

The notion that so-called action video, often referred to as "eye candy," is a never-fail technique to capture the attention of lead-in entertainment program viewers was what first piqued our interest in the myths of local TV news. The reason is that we heard this myth in *every* newsroom we visited. So we decided to determine if flashing lights and yellow police tape really do "grab eyeballs."

We first identified the lead stories in the 2,419 newscasts we studied and segregated the topic, focus, and visual elements. We then compared the lead stories with the viewership of each station on the night the story appeared, as well as with rating and share trends over time. Here is what we found:

First, there wasn't much video that could truly be called sensational. Of the 584 stories identified as spot news, only 22 stories contained pictures that were strikingly out of the ordinary. So we broadened our search to include stories in which the pictures were "somewhat sensational" and came up with 203 stories, or just more than 8% of the leads. Then we looked at the ratings for the lead stories with sensational video and those with more neutral images.

On the late news, where the concern over audience retention is highest, there is no statistically significant link between lead stories that typically feature flashing lights and yellow police tape and the ability of a newscast to retain lead-in audience. In fact, stories dealing with a response to a spontaneous event that contain mostly or somewhat sensational visuals lost .44 share points compared with those stories with neutral (less sensational) visuals.[14] Add to that the data showing that crime stories lacking information perform poorly – the kind of stories that feature mainly flashling lights and yellow tape – and there is no evidence here to support the fascination with these kinds of images.

MYTH NO. 5: TV IS AN EMOTIONAL MEDIUM IN WHICH PICTURES ARE MORE IMPORTANT THAN WORDS (OR IDEAS)

Newsrooms believe that stories with certain pictures attract viewers and stories without compelling visuals lose them. When broadcasters say, "TV is a visual medium," what they often mean is that the picture is the most important component of the TV viewing experience. A producer in one of our sessions explained it this way: "It's a passive medium, people aren't alert when they watch! Even people in the building can only remember one or two stories from the competition. Eye candy works; it's part of the changing times."

This helps explain why, among the 34,000 stories in the five-year Local TV News Project sample, there were twice as many easily photographed, everyday occurrences such as traffic accidents, house fires, and crimes

(41% of stories) or even ribbon cuttings than stories devoted to issues, which are more visually challenging. Or why the 15% of stories that contained somewhat or mostly sensational visuals made up nearly 25% of newscast leads.

The reasoning behind the myth could be heard in our newscast stacking sessions. Many groups believed the story about a reduction in education funds that would probably halt construction of a new middle school and high school would be "top of the mind for many people in the audience." But because it was also "more of a newspaper story," school funding ended up as the fourth story, which most groups placed in the middle of their model newscasts.

For most, in fact, the school-funding story was what one local television journalist called "another boring budget story. What are you going to see, kids with backpacks, classrooms?" "We can't lead with it because viewers will turn away. No video, not sexy, not visual," was how another summarized the case against schools. A member of another group said: "It is not as urgent, and the pictures are not as good [as anthrax, airliner, or mayor]. You see school pictures all the time." Another participant put it this way: "High impact, poor visual elements." Said another succinctly, "It's education and not breaking news." Another news staffer maintained that "ninety-five percent of the people who care about education are asleep. They probably heard about the story earlier. It's old news and has no compelling video."

The contrary opinion from a group that wanted to run the education story higher said, "It affected a lot of people. We could talk to students, parents, and teachers." "Young parents would be awake and would be interested in this," echoed another TV broadcaster, while another said, "It affects kids, quality of life, and almost every household." Yet these arguments were usually overruled by more medium-oriented thinking about a lack of immediacy, visuals, and urgency.

Ultimately, it was not *whether* to do the story but *how* to do it that concerned most participants in the exercise. "No schools are open, no teachers available. Lacks video and audio elements. Too many obstacles," summarized one person. "No time to report – can't pull it together," said a participant in another city. "Talking head, no details," somebody else told us. "Vague information," said spokespersons for several groups.

The story about a shortfall in street-repair money got the same rap. It was, in so many words, too difficult for TV.

These comments are revealing. The momentum behind the myth of TV as an emotional or visual medium rather than an intellectual one is not ultimately that TV cannot communicate ideas. The momentum is driven by something subtler. It is, instead, easier to rely on visuals to give stories their appeal than it is to do it though reporting, information, and storytelling. It takes less time. It takes less expertise. It takes less imagination. The most successful TV news program in history, financially and in appeal – *60 Minutes* – was built around stories driven by reporting ideas. But those stories are carefully selected, thoroughly researched, and extensively reported.

Reality Check

The data reveal, contrary to the myth, that if so-called newspaper stories are covered in ways that make them interesting to the television audience, these items actually attract and hold viewers better than other kinds of reporting.[15] As we found in the myth of sensational video, airing eye-catching visuals does not, by itself, lead to better audience retention.

Instead, doing stories about ideas, issues, and policy actually builds viewership. As we noted earlier, these stories about ideas are not only an effective way to lead a broadcast, they received .10 more ratings points among the coveted prime demographic than did other stories. And when we compare these stories with just crime news in a hypothetical trade-off during late news, they did even better among the young, female viewing audience by a margin of .35 demographic rating points.[16]

We found that given the choice between viewing a minute-and-one-half reporter package on a spot news crime story and a reporter-packaged piece of the same length about an event from the "daybook," viewers are more likely to watch the latter.

SIDEBAR 4.2

MAKING DECISIONS: SPOT NEWS OR ENTERPRISE?

It's 8:00 P.M. and the late news producer has a decision to make – right now.

A report of a shooting has just come over the scanner. Medics aren't at the scene yet, but the first police officers to arrive have called for backup and the crime scene guys. The producer knows that if the competition gets there first and captures some dramatic footage, those pictures will soon be in the promos that air throughout prime time.

The "Nightside" reporter and photographer are covering a dispute about a new shopping center. They've already taped "exteriors" of the site and made cover footage of a neighborhood meeting. But the best stuff, a presentation by the developers and the reaction of residents, hasn't happened yet. Should the reporter and photographer be pulled from the meeting and sent to the shooting?

The producer is confronted with a typical management dilemma: how to deploy limited resources to maximize profits, in this case ratings. Which story – the shooting or the zoning dispute – are viewers more likely to watch?

Because we are often asked this question in our work with local newsrooms, we decided to see what, if anything, the data would reveal.

We began by narrowing our search to stories that could actually be influenced – made more or less complete – by an investment of newsroom resources. Thus, we eliminated content from outside sources such as network feeds or syndicated news services. We focused instead on what the newsroom controlled – its reporters and photographers. Then we created a hierarchy of coverage wherein each level required a greater commitment of a newsroom's time, personnel, and technical resources.

- Level 1: The anchor-read "tell" story about a pre-arranged "daybook" event is at the lowest end of the scale. These are less than 60 seconds, contain only one source if they are sourced at all, and offer a single perspective.
- Level 2: If the same daybook-inspired, anchor-read story includes videotape – perhaps a sound bite from a press conference or cover footage of a person or place – it is ranked somewhat higher because, at minimum, the newsroom must dispatch a photographer to the event.
- Level 3: The stories in this category are brief, lasting from 30 to 60 seconds, and contain only one source or perspective, but the fact that a reporter either voices or appears in a story means the station has invested an "editorial" presence (as opposed to only a photojournalist) in the story.
- Level 4: A daybook-inspired story in which a reporter obtains comments or information from two or more sources requires somewhat more effort and, because it contains more opinion or information, is usually longer, for the purposes of our enterprise index, 45 seconds or more.

SIDEBAR 4.2 (continued)

- Level 5: Stories in which two or more sources offer a mix of opinions are indicative of a still higher level of enterprise. In addition to tracking down people with different views, this kind of story usually requires some research. Shooting one of these stories takes more time because the reporter and photographer must often go to more than one location. These stories run one and one-half minutes or more.
- Level 6: Original investigations or a story that is part of a news series represent the highest level of a station's commitment to enterprise. These stories are 90 seconds or longer, and they feature two or more sources with a mix of opinions. A reporter and photographer might spend many hours gathering the elements for one of these.

Using the elements of each story in our sample – was it an anchor read, did it have tape or include an interview, was it a spontaneous or scheduled event – we assigned a level of effort to each. We then compared each story, and the level of effort a newsroom would typically expend to cover it, with viewership data.

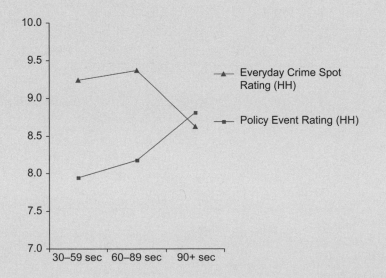

Figure S4.2.1. Length of everyday crime vs. policy event story household rating.

The first thing we discovered was that effort pays off. The formula is simple: more enterprise = better ratings. To the degree that *every* story – from the 30-second reader to the multipart investigative series piece – can be made more complete by more and better reporting, the audience will reward it with progressively greater viewership. For every notch up our hierarchy of enterprise (e.g., going from a level 4 to a level 5 story), there is a corresponding gain of .069 rating points, .150 share points, .037 demo rating points, .660% rating retention, and .627% share retention.

The second thing we found was that the relationship between enterprise and viewership is not limited to just a few topics – it occurs across the board. *How* a newsroom covers a story – the degree of thoroughness, the amount of enterprise and, ultimately, the investment of a newsroom's time, resources, and energy – has a greater influence on ratings than *what* the story is about. In other words, contrary to popular belief, *treatment* trumps *topic*.

When we applied our hierarchy of effort to the 34,000 stories in our sample, we also discovered that although enterprise helps all stories on all topics, it affected some more than others.

Spot news, for example, got better ratings when these items were short. Among stories between 30 seconds and one minute, viewers were more likely to watch an item about a spontaneous event such as a shooting, fire, or traffic accident than a story about an important policy or trend. As stories got longer, however, the equation began to change. After one minute, the viewership of spot news items starts to drop off, by some measures dramatically, while interest in policy and trend stories increases correspondingly. At one and one-half minutes, policy and trend stories equaled or exceeded spot news in every one of the rating measurements we applied: household rating and share, key demographics, and rating and share retention (see Figures S4.2.1 and S4.2.2).

When we compared policy-event stories to just late-breaking crime – the kind of spot news event that often bumps a daybook-inspired story from the air – the trends become even more pronounced (see Figure S4.2.3 and S4.2.4).

Among the two most desirable groups of viewers, the prime demographic 18- to 49-year-olds and the much sought after lead-in audience, the results are dramatic. From almost the moment an everyday crime story appears, the most-coveted viewers begin tuning out. The longer the story goes, the more people switch away.

SIDEBAR 4.2 (continued)

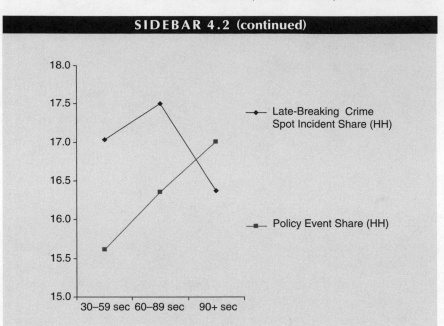

Figure S4.2.2. Length of late-breaking crime vs. policy event story by household share.

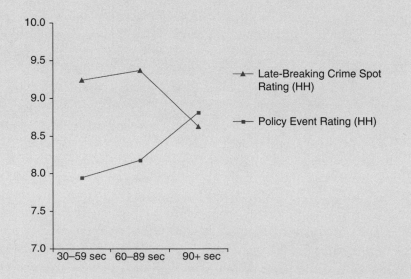

Figure S4.2.3. Length of late-breaking crime spot vs. policy event story by household rating.

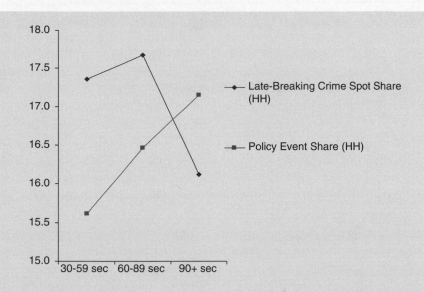

Figure S4.2.4. Length of late-breaking crime spot vs. policy event story by household share.

But notice what happens when an issue/trend daybook story airs. Not only do people stop switching, the newscast actually builds viewership (see Figure S4.2.5).

Looking at Figures S4.2.1 to S4.2.5, there's a temptation to engage in rule-making. One could argue, for instance, that every late-breaking crime should be covered with no more than 45 seconds of anchor-narrated tape and that every issue/policy story should consist of a minute-thirty reporter package. It's not quite that simple, however.

The larger lesson here is that storytelling helps all stories on all topics and that the absence of storytelling has the opposite effect. We believe this is why, at one and one-half minutes, everyday crime reports start to recoup lost viewership – there are fewer essentially hollow live shots or "this just in" tape – and more reporter packages that exhibit more reportorial effort. In other words, there's a point where these stories become meatier.

We also believe the issue of storytelling helps explain why, at one and one-half minutes, viewership for policy/event stories starts to drop off. Although the data show that viewers are indeed predisposed to hear about important policies or issues rather than late-breaking but everyday crime, their patience is not unlimited. Though the need

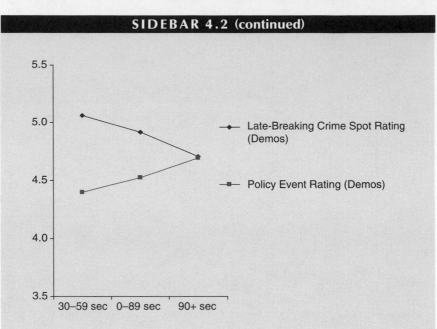

Figure S4.2.5. Length of late-breaking crime spot vs. policy event story by rating demographics.

for storytelling may be less immediate, even important stories at some point need the Magic Formula (see Figures S4.2.6 and S4.2.7).

So how might the hypothetical producer use these findings to decide whether to short-change the institutional zoning story to showcase a theoretically more compelling event such as a shooting?

Our analysis suggests that the course most likely to improve ratings would be to "spray" or simply tell the spot news story and keep the reporter/photographer team on the daybook event. Having a reporter package a policy/trend story clearly helps that kind of news. Having a reporter at the scene of a spot news incident does not necessarily help, and may in fact undermine, viewership of that story.

In addition, because much of the zoning story has already been researched and photographed, the reporter-photographer team has what amounts to money in the bank – the elements of a thorough report or good tale. There are few certainties with the shooting story, other than the likelihood that the station's competitors have dropped the enterprise stories they were working on and are heading out the door.

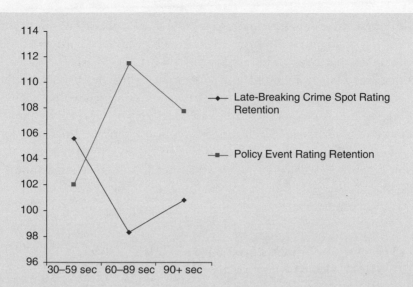

Figure S.4.2.6. Length of late-breaking crime spot vs. policy event story by rating retention.

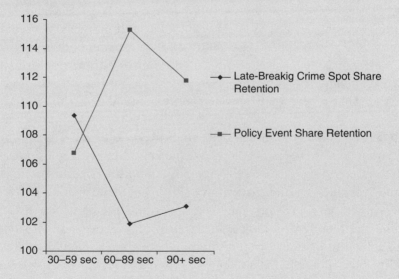

Figure S4.2.7. Length of late-breaking crime spot vs. policy event story by share retention.

– *Walter C. Dean, Atiba Pertilla, Todd L. Belt*

Moreover, doing longer, more complete stories about important local issues will build audience. Some of the coverage approaches most closely associated with more traditional print reporting – a special series of stories, reports on investigations (even by other news outlets), and interviews (on-camera in the case of TV) are all associated with higher ratings. These stories get more than half a share point (.574 share points) more than other stories. Their ratings are more than one-third of a point higher (.339 ratings points), and more than two-tenths of a demo rating point higher (.219 demo points) than stories that require less hustle and initiative.[17] We explore the impact of journalistic enterprise in more detail in the next chapter.

MYTH NO. 6: EVERY LEAD STORY MUST HAVE A LIVE SHOT FROM THE SCENE

"Live for the sake of live" is broadcast industry shorthand for the notion that every top story should be reported live from the scene. One might assume a live presence allows stations to get the latest available information on the air. But our conversations with newspeople indicate otherwise. Again it appears the ability to do it is paramount, along with the appearance that the newscast has the most up-to-date information and technology. Broadcast newspeople, in fact, are among the first to complain that reporting live is often more about showbiz than journalism.

In deciding that an anthrax scare at a local post office was the best lead from among nine stories in a newscast stacking exercise, a person from a station in the Midwest noted that the police and fire department activity would provide "an action-packed live shot." Someone at another station said, "It's an on-going story, could be something, there's action going on behind the reporter, flashing lights, yellow tape, space suits. It's better than going there tomorrow and standing before a blank building." Even lacking live action, placing a reporter in the proximity of where an event occurred that same day is considered the next best thing.

The prospect of being at a crime scene was also a factor in the judgments newspeople made about the story of a body being found at a home in an exclusive neighborhood. Despite concerns that it might be a suicide or accident, one group decided that, "Police are still out there and we can get live pictures." Another group concluded it "could be high profile" and assigned it a live shot even though, said one person, "We don't know anything and [the reporter on the scene] doesn't have enough to say to make it sound like we should be there." "Dead bodies don't affect a lot of people but the [exclusive neighborhood] location is a factor," said someone else. "There are good pictures and we got the most important shot [body being removed]. We can almost take viewers to the scene."

The story about the airplane bomb hoax was given first-segment billing by many groups because, "We have the elements [interviews and footage of flashing lights and passengers] and we can do it live." However, "By fronting it live," one person maintained, "you make people think it's more important than it is. Nobody was seriously hurt, it landed safely, there was no bomb – it is not a big deal."

Reality Check

Live for the sake of live doesn't work. We found that having a reporter live on the scene of a story was not a factor in retaining or building audience. Using stories reported live also showed no relationship with audience attention.[18]

This supports other research showing that there are distinctions in the drawing power of live-on-the-scene reporting. A study conducted for the research and training organization NewsLab found that only a small percentage of respondents knew which station in their respective markets went live more often than its competition or which was the first to cover a particular breaking news story. And very few said they based their viewing choices on such factors. "While most of the respondents said live reporting can enhance a station's coverage of a news story, many said they think live coverage is used when there is no true need for it. A majority of viewers in the sample seem to think that, at times, events get covered because they happen close to or during the news hour and reduce the time given to other, more important, stories." When asked for examples of meaningless live shots, viewers in the Newslab sample mentioned reporters standing in the rain in front of someone's house for no reason, standing on the side of a nondescript highway with traffic flowing normally behind them, reporters still on the scene of a shooting or court hearing hours after everyone else had gone home, and a live report from an empty sports arena to preview the next night's game. One person wrote: "Live reports have a place, but not when nothing is happening."[19]

A separate companion study by Newslab of 18- to 24-year-olds found that live reporting is not a factor in their choice of which local newscasts to watch. Seven out of 10 respondents said there are times when live reports are meaningless. And almost half said that local TV news operations often report live for no apparent reason other than because they can. Researchers concluded that, "Committing time and resources to stories with little news value but which lend themselves to live coverage may further erode viewer confidence ... rather than attract and retain a new wave of loyal watchers."[20]

And though local TV teases and promos might suggest something different, there isn't even that much live coverage to begin with. In our study of 34,000 stories, only 1.2% (422 stories) actually included live action happening at that very moment. In other words, most "live" shots are not really authentic. This, indeed, is at the crux of the myth. There isn't enough live, local, late-breaking news to fill the space. So producers use live shots to fake it. And viewers know the difference.

MYTH NO. 7: VIEWERS ARE BASICALLY VOYEURISTIC AND WANT TO BE TITILLATED

Behind the idea of the hook and hold, the emphasis on visuals and TV as an emotional medium is another myth about human nature – the idea that people, or at least TV audiences, are basically voyeuristic. They do not watch to be informed but to be entertained, and to look in on other people's misfortune.

In our newscast stacking exercise in one newsroom, for instance, the story about the discovery of a dead person at a home in an "exclusive" part of town led to a discussion about the merits of stories that appeal to the baser instincts of human nature. The situation had all the elements of live, local, and late-breaking coverage but was so thin on detail that some groups were reluctant to air anything because, as one person explained, "The guy could have had a heart attack and fallen on his head." Most groups thus ran it in the middle of the broadcast, despite having what were often described as "good body bag pictures." Several folks noted, "It could be big or it could be nothing." No matter which, as one participant put it, "It's a 'talker,'" meaning it will titillate. "It's got great potential and if we miss it, the competition might exploit that." Still, downplaying this story was a difficult decision for many newspeople because, as one local broadcaster put it, "Murder sells."

Another newsperson explained, "It's mysterious and there's a crime scene with yellow police tape. It's unsettling because it's a possible homicide. Viewers will be interested in a death. It's a Jerry Springer thing. We could shine a light on this neighborhood [to say that] bad things happen here, too." A broadcaster from a station in the Southwest said, "Although we don't know if it was an accident or a suicide, it feels right. It's interesting but its importance is uncertain."

Of the 8,198 stories in our sample that were about crime, the law, or the courts, 9 of 10 (7,229) aired as one of the first three stories. We don't know how many of these were "whodunits," but we know that three-quarters of crime stories (73%) were about local crime and that three-quarters (76%) of those stories were about *everyday* local crime.

Why so much emphasis on rather common, if unfortunate, events? Judging by what was said in our newscast stacking exercise, there is more at work here than keeping the public informed.

About the discovery of the dead man, one person called it "a 'gawker' story" where "the possibilities are probably more interesting than the truth. [These stories] grab you and hold your attention. People love to know other people's business, especially [when it could be a murder] in an exclusive neighborhood. Which story would you want your reporter to cover? These are sexy, exciting, and visual." Another local journalist said: "It's almost like a movie, it makes you want to watch." One news staffer told us, "This could happen anywhere, meaning, 'It could happen to you,' and we are educating viewers to 'watch your surroundings.' The story has emotion – if it bleeds it leads. The video is huge – the body being removed."

Not everyone in local TV feels this motivation as strongly. "I looked at what would affect more people. This doesn't affect everyone in our viewing area," explained one local news professional. Another news staffer concurred, saying that although the story "has potential and is late breaking, it could be nothing." In the same newsroom, a person whose team slotted the story sixth reported, "The only reason it's not higher is that it may not have been a murder. And if it's not a murder, we will look like idiots [for playing it up]."

"Every one of these [public safety] stories is playing on people's fears," said another person. "We have a responsibility not to scare people to death." Yet others liked public safety stories precisely because they *are* scary. A broadcaster in another city said of the anthrax story, "It likely is [harmless] white powder, but we can't go in thinking that way. In reporting scares, it's the 'What if?' that's important." Another person called the coverage "eye candy, style over substance."

"These stories ought to have a disclaimer," remarked someone from a station in the Southwest, 'This is anthrax or it's not. This is a murder or it's not.'"

Reality Check

The notion that showing pictures of a body bag and coroner's van parked in front of a house in an exclusive neighborhood somehow equates to a murder mystery worthy of *CSI* is, at best, an illusion. *CSI* and other popular crime dramas are based on carefully crafted scripts in which a plot unfolds, characters are developed, tensions ebb and flow, and the whole story is resolved in an hour-long episode. That's not the way it happens on local TV news.

To begin with, crime stories tend to be quite short – two in five (42.6%) are less than 30 seconds long; another 26.9% are between 30 seconds and one minute. Considering how short they are, it's not surprising there's little story-line development.

As far as major "actors," only one-quarter (26%) of crime stories have two or more. A criminal or suspect performs a role in nearly one-third of the stories (31.6%) but, unlike on *CSI*, viewers rarely get to meet him or her. Nor, because the plurality of stories are about person-to-person crimes and the victim is at the police station, the hospital, or the morgue and thus unavailable for comment, do viewers get to see that person. Instead, the audience hears the story second or third hand from police, relatives, or witnesses.

Unlike a crime drama, there is rarely a beginning or end to most crime news. Instead of a story, viewers see only the residue of an incident.

The absence of enterprise and the elements of effective storytelling may explain why incident-based crime news fails, by itself, to attract viewers. We found that titillation, such as flashing lights and yellow police tape, does not hold viewers or build audiences. This type of story counts for almost 12%, or one in eight, of all local TV news stories, but the data show it does nothing to improve viewership on any of the measures we examined.

As with other topics, however, the ratings for spot news improve if the story is more complete. A spot news story with three or more sources gets one-third more of a ratings point among households and one-quarter more of a ratings point among younger viewers than a spot news story based on anonymous sources or no sources at all.[21]

MYTH NO. 8: VIEWERS CARE ONLY ABOUT LOCAL NEWS

This myth grows from two sources. The first is long-standing audience research showing that viewers are most interested in news that is close to home. Add to this the presumption that people interested in a national or international story will see it on cable, and it's perhaps understandable why the farther away a story is, the less likely it will appear on the local TV news.

International news, for example, makes up just 2.7% of all stories, and half of these (49.5%) are shorter than 30 seconds. Events in the United States, but outside the viewing area, account for 18% of all stories. Again, half of these (49.8%) are less than 30 seconds long.

For the newscast-stacking exercise, we included a story set in Pakistan, where a top government leader had been assassinated, presumably by terrorists. We created this scenario and then ratcheted up the potential threat by pointedly noting that Pakistan possesses nuclear weapons. Most of the newspeople said the Pakistan story was simply not local enough to warrant more than a mention, if that. "It's international news and local is more important," said the spokesman for one group. "No one knows the place or the people," said another, "it's not local news and it won't stick with people." "People in double-wide trailers don't know where it is," said someone in another city. "Big deal, lot of impact, but needs to be local." At yet another station we were told, bluntly, "It doesn't pass the 'Who gives a shit?' test."

A small number of the newspeople, however, ranked the story high because, one of them told us, "It is part of the security theme and is important because this country has nuclear weapons. There's the nuclear war potential." "We will probably run a V/O [short voice-over story] on it tonight and then war will break out and it will be the lead story for the next two weeks," said another broadcaster. Nevertheless, tonight, "its impact is less direct to the community." A journalist from a different station worried that, "People don't know who or where this is, but this could shoot us in the butt" if it turned into a crisis. Nevertheless, said a person from the same newsroom, there's "not a lot of interest by our audience. They're probably watching CNN."

Someone in another city summed up the mixed views about the Pakistan story by saying: "It's not local but it does have the potential to start World War III." That group, nevertheless, made it a 30-second voice-over and slotted it as the fifth of nine stories in the hypothetical newscast.

Reality Check

It's a mistake to assume people don't care about events outside their community and to cede or even drive viewers to cable. Survey research, in fact, indicates local TV news audiences have almost as high an interest in national and international affairs as they have in local issues. The Pew Research Center for the People and the Press's June 2004 survey of media consumption found that among local TV news viewers, 29% said they followed local government "very closely," whereas 25% kept track of international affairs "very closely." Local TV news viewers were just as interested in national politics, with 28% saying they follow events in Washington, D.C., "very closely."[22](See also Rosenstiel and Iversen 2002.)

Our five-year local TV news analysis confirms that interest in national and international news is, at minimum, considerably more than local newspeople believe. To begin with, we found that leading a newscast with a national or international story that was new and important does not lose viewers. Moreover, national or international news about significant events, or late word about a major disaster in another part of the country, are topics that hold and even build audiences in late-news time periods. In fact, leading with a national story proved to be a way of increasing the ratings and share of the lead-in programming – it built on both lead-in ratings and lead-in share by 6.45%.[23]

Finally, we found that if a newsroom is able to explain how a national or international story might affect local viewers, ratings will improve even more. We will discuss the aspect of relevance at greater length in the next chapter.

The location of news is important. But it's less important than the character or nature of the individual story.

MYTH NO. 9: SOME STORIES ARE MORE IMPORTANT AS PROMOTION THAN AS NEWS

This myth goes along with the "hold" part of the hook and hold as well as being part of the rise of newscast branding. If a soft story is especially interesting or unusual, it is morphed into a promotional vehicle that can be placed at the end of the broadcast and promoted repeatedly throughout the show.

In the newscast stacking exercise, the "Coping with Pain" report was one of two stories that fell into this category. In 9 of 10 line-ups (93%) it was one of the last three stories, the most popular spot being next to last (54%).

Even though some newspeople saw the pain report as potentially a "dynamite health piece: hope, breakthrough, personalized, how you can get help," most thought it better to hold for the last half of the newscast. "Obviously a lot of interest in it," said the spokesman for one group, "but it couldn't compete with developing stories. It would feel out of place in the middle of hard stories. It is [however], a highly promotable story and would be a good vehicle to hold viewers." "It's a promotional vehicle to a certain extent," said a journalist from a station in the Southwest.

"This would never be in the A bloc [i.e., the first segment]," but if it was "highly promoted and teased, it will keep them watching," said another participant. "Very high viewer interest, teasable elements, will hold viewers, leaves an important last impression," said another person. "Our agenda is to hold viewers thru the first 15 minutes of the broadcast for ratings," said another person, "and as a viewer I would wait for this story." Someone else said, "We all hated it. There's more urgency in other stories. This was B-bloc news [i.e., second segment] and the only reason we ran it at all was because it had been promoted."

Promotion was also the key to the placement of the elephant story in our news stacking exercise. "Bobo" the elephant made a brief escape from his enclosure at the city zoo, terrifying onlookers but causing no serious damage or injury. The incident was captured in a few seconds of grainy home video that the station obtained. It's a fair bet that had the escape *just* occurred, Bobo would be at the top of the show. But by the time our model newscast was supposed to air, Bobo had been back in his grotto for several hours.

More than half of the small groups (56%) used Bobo as the final story and 8 of 10 groups (83%) put it in the latter third of the broadcast as one of the last three stories.

"Tease video into every break," said one person. "Would have shown this video several times," observed someone else. Another person called the Bobo incident, "a teasable story that can be carried through the newscast."

"Out of all these stories," someone told us, "this is what people will talk about. It's interesting – wild animals in a public place. Safety issues. How did it get out? Many people go to the zoo. Will it [the elephant] be put to sleep?"

Reality Check

The practice of including certain kinds of news primarily for its teasability ironically plays to the weaknesses rather than the strengths of a broadcast. It makes the program predictable, inviting some viewers to leave when it's clear the hard news is over. It surrenders valuable storytelling time to teases and promotions, which often undermine the story by giving away the best pictures or revealing the surprise that makes it interesting or unusual. And it assumes a hierarchy of news values viewers may not share.

Yet as the X-Structure illustrates, this is exactly what happens in most newscasts. Soft stories make up less than 10% of leads, but by the end of the newscast they account for more than 40% of stories. This raises three questions. Do viewers share the newsroom's definition of what is hard and soft? Should soft stories be lumped together at the end of the program? Does continually teasing these stories throughout the broadcast work?

Our study revealed that viewers define hard news quite differently than do broadcast journalists. The public sees the news as encompassing an infinite range of topics and interests, not just C-A-D – crime, accidents, and disasters. Not surprisingly then, the topic of a story has less impact on ratings than how it is reported and produced. This is so much so that "enterprise" is a statistically significant identifier of newscast leads that produce successful ratings among households and younger demographics.[24] That explains why well-done health stories (the "Coping with Pain" genre) were more effective in retaining late news lead-in audiences than violent, late-breaking but everyday crimes.

When stories are immediately labeled as soft (as happened to Bobo in our newscast stacking exercise) they don't get the time or reporting that would allow them to compete with hard topics for a higher spot in the rundown. On average, stories that appeared in the last 10% of newscasts were significantly less likely to have multiple sources or a balance of views, had less credibility in terms of the use of experts, and were an average 25 seconds shorter than first-block stories (64 vs. 39 seconds).

But doesn't it make sense to front-load the broadcast with the most "important" news – reporter packages with elements of urgency or action – and then end on a lighter note? Not necessarily. Paul Friedman, a former executive producer of the *Today Show* on NBC and *World News Tonight* on ABC, believes a successful newscast should look more like a mountain range than a boat ramp. Rather than automatically progressing from hard to the soft, from the intense to the sublime, Friedman thinks newscasts should have peaks and valleys. Breaking the routine provides a measure of serendipity. And placing a short, simple item after a long, complex story allows viewers to catch their breath and better digest the emotional or complicated news they just saw.

Academic research, moreover, has found that the common practice of creating "flow" by grouping together similar stories in "blocks" may actually confuse the audience. Nor does the news have to "bleed to succeed." We found that airing a C-A-D story instead of any other topic within the first three stories made no difference in ratings.

Regardless of how hard news is defined or the degree to which broadcasts should be "hard at the top, soft at the bottom," the appeal of soft news is often undercut by the very promotion that's supposed to draw attention to it.

As part of our local TV news study, the Project for Excellence in Journalism and NewsLab conducted four viewer focus groups, two each in Atlanta and Tucson, in 1999. The groups were made up of adults ages 25 to 54 who watched the local evening news at least three days a week. These viewers felt competition among stations to attract and hold audiences often caused newsrooms to engage in self-promotion and hype. One of their specific complaints was about the number of teases during a typical newscast.

Many were angry and frustrated with stations that promote a story throughout a newscast, only to have it turn out to be a throwaway. One participant said, "They make a big deal about something you want to hear, and it's like 30 seconds and there's nothing to it." Some viewers said they'd rather tune out than be strung along. Others, however, expressed a desire for newscasts with a more structured format, so they would know when to tune in for (or presumably tune away from) certain kinds of stories.[25]

We also found that the practice of "cherry picking" talker stories off the closed-circuit network affiliate feeds and then running a snippet of the tape in a local newscast does not help ratings. Often talkers are about celebrity gossip or are based on rumors from the tabloids. Yet we found that this is precisely the kind of story that audiences rejected. Stories about celebrities and other entertainment news resulted in lower household and demographic ratings, and they hurt a newscast's ability to hold lead-in rating and share.[26]

The myth that some stories are more valuable as promotion than as news is not merely flawed, it may rise to the level of injurious. It devalues potentially good stories, encourages the misuse of promotion, and spotlights news the public has little interest in.

MYTH NO. 10: VIEWERS WON'T WATCH LONG STORIES ABOUT ISSUES

If viewers are mostly interested in eye candy, it's only logical to assume they won't like long, issue stories that aren't inherently visual. Or so the reasoning goes. The street-repair story in our newscast stacking exercise was about a significant shortfall in the city budget that would severely reduce residential street repair, especially in low-income neighborhoods that had been complaining about discrimination in city services. Although most agreed it was an important story, they also felt it was "boring." That is why these "dry" stories get buried in the middle the newscast, tossed off as short tell stories. Overall, "Streets" ended up seventh in the composite newscast, where stories are usually shorter and often just voice-overs. People said much the same thing about the story of a shortfall in education funding, which was also relegated to the middle of the hypothetical newscast after being trumped by news that had more "immediacy."

We found the same pattern in our local TV news content study data: Newsrooms downplay stories about issues, ideas, or policy, both in terms of where these stories appear in newscasts and in the amount of time and resources they receive.

Only after the sixth story in an average local news broadcast does civic news (politics/government, social issues, science/technology, etc.) surpass public safety to become the most likely topic to appear. And when civic news does air, it is usually brief. A quarter of the stories that focus on important issues (27%) are less than 30 seconds long; more than half of all issue stories (53.3%) run 60 seconds or less. Fewer than 1 in 10 (8.6%) get more than three minutes.

"It's a newspaper story," several people told us about "city streets." "Just a fact story," was how another person characterized it. Many people noted that it lacked "video and sound." "No elements," was how several described it. "It's interchangeable with education," said someone else. "These stories are more about public interest and everybody cares about them. But they are not 'live, local and late-breaking,' and people are more concerned about public safety than about potholes. Safety is bigger news and more immediate."

Still, some TV newspeople felt these stories had potential. A group in one training session that proposed running the street story third in the composite newscast said that although they "didn't want to lead with it because it was in the newspaper, we're confident we could advance it. It affects more people in many ways. We could do a creative live shot with good story telling." Other groups during training similarly brainstormed about how to make these "important" stories more visual, but it was a challenge. One group said it "could show bad streets," whereas another news staffer suggested telling viewers "how it will affect everyone's commute." At one station, a group decided that, "We could have a crew with a live camera drive down a street full of potholes. Everybody drives, it evokes emotion, and people are angry about budget shortfalls. For competitive reasons we couldn't lead with it. But we could go to the weatherman to talk about how the weather affects potholes." Another group said, "It's important and affects a lot of people. How will this compare to the last cutbacks? It could be a live 'walk-and-talk' on a torn-up street. It doesn't have to be boring."

These groups, however, were in the minority, in our training sessions and in the real world of TV. "There is a lot of viewer impact," explained one TV news professional, "but if we are being realistic, it won't get the attention it deserves. It's really sad. It's immediacy; it's what's happening now that determines our agenda. We just throw up our hands and we give up." Another person noted that, "It would require the right reporter and photographer and unless we're willing to invest a lot of time and effort, the story won't be any good. This is a budget story and people don't care. The streets suck every winter. We assume people care, but do they really? They can't affect the outcome. The word 'budget' is a turnoff. All we'd have is meeting video and reporters talking above people's heads."

In other words, "important" or "significant" stories that aren't considered easy to make visual generally are buried because newspeople think they will bore audiences. Are they right?

Reality Check

At short lengths, we found spot news stories get almost the same ratings as stories about policy-focused events (the source of the typical "meeting video" story). But when we compared slightly longer stories, a fascinating trend appeared: As policy event stories grew longer, they became *more* likely to hold or increase their audience, while adding length to a spot news story did nothing to win more viewers. Looking just at stories over 90 seconds, we found the policy event stories hold 4% more share over their lead-ins than the spot stories (see Sidebar 4.2, "Making Decisions," earlier in this chapter).

In fact, we found that making stories longer generally led to better ratings. Adding 30 seconds onto a story builds the household rating by .042 points, the household share by .075, and the ratings among the most highly sought demos by .025 points. But as we shall see, length is only part of the equation – how a reporter uses that time matters most.[27]

Yet because newspeople believe viewers are not interested in long issue stories, airtime and news resources flow instead to so-called breaking news. Basically, newsrooms have it backward. Spot news doesn't need a lot of reporting. But issue stories do. When they get it, "boring institutional stuff" not only competes with "live, local, and late breaking," it wins.

What Do Newspeople Really Know

Despite the dominance of these myths in local TV, newspeople acknowledge frankly that their grasp of what audiences want is mostly received wisdom, not science.

"We talk about what's important to the viewers. But I get the feeling we're just guessing," one news professional confided during a training. "And no one in the newsroom spends much time talking to viewers. So no one really knows what they want or need." Said another, "The majority of our staff, especially those charged with the bulk of producing the newscasts, have no idea what viewers want," wrote a staff member at a number-one-ranked station in the Southwest. "We fixate on what's easy and cheap to cover, with no regard to viewers' wants or needs."

At the end of a newscast stacking exercise, after each small group's story order had been recorded on a flip chart and its members explained the reasons for their choices, we asked participants whether they saw any patterns in the rundowns. "Late-breaking, scary, public safety threats at the beginning, boring but important stories in the middle, interesting but not breaking news at the end," was their almost universal response.

How is it that more than 2,000 news professionals from more than 40 stations working in 250 small groups independently create newscast lineups that are nearly identical? A newsman in the Midwest confided that, "Our standard for success is to watch the other two stations to see what they have. Then, follow them around to get their story. We all look the same at the end of the day. The first station to turn off [the monitors and not watch] the other two wins."

The Public Already Knows

The real danger with these myths is that although newsrooms rely on them to decide what to cover and how to stack broadcasts, the viewing public has a different set of values. That is the ultimate finding of our data. Viewers see the myths as gimmickry and show business. And that leads to a larger problem.

There is a growing disconnect between broadcast newspeople and their audiences that may in some sense be rooted in their respective definitions of news. What the professionals consider most important – crime, accidents, and other misfortunes – are usually not the same things that affect the daily lives of the audience. In fact, our research suggests viewers have a much broader definition of news than the news professionals.

As the statements in this chapter illustrate, journalists themselves often feel trapped by the formulas that have come to dominate local TV news. They are uncomfortable about the choices they make, but that's what the rules dictate.

Now that we've shown that those rules are largely based on myths, the obvious question is: Do our data suggest strategies or formulas for putting together a different kind of newscast that can be more successful?

Yes. We present them in the next chapter.

SIDEBAR 4.3

THREE PRINCIPAL FACTORS BEHIND THE MYTHS

Where do the myths around local TV news come from and why do they persist? Their roots can be traced back to the beginning of the rise of the local news and three principal factors.

- The impact of portable cameras, videotape, and "live" technology
- The adoption of research-driven consulting
- The discovery that local newscasts could produce immense profits

Technology

Though immediacy had always been a foundation of broadcast journalism, actually doing TV live from anywhere but a studio was, until the 1970s, a laborious and expensive task.

Film cameras had become much more portable and were the standard of the 1960s, but film had to be carried back to a station and developed in a processor before being edited and aired. "Film at 11" was a catchphrase of the days when the timeliness of TV news was measured in hours rather than seconds.

In the 1970s, however, local TV newsrooms began investing in ENG – electronic news gathering. ENG combined two of TV's core strengths: immediacy and pictures. And its impact was felt quickly.

SIDEBAR 4.3 (continued)

On the afternoon of May 17, 1974, 400 law enforcement officers streamed into a south Los Angeles neighborhood and surrounded a house. They had received a tip that members of the radical Symbionese Liberation Army (SLA), which had murdered the superintendent of the Oakland public schools and kidnapped newspaper heiress Patty Hearst, were holed up inside. After unsuccessful attempts at negotiations, tear gas was fired and a gun battle erupted.

Equipped with a shoulder-held ENG camera and a portable microwave transmitter, a photographer from KNXT-TV sent live pictures of the gun battle back to Television City. KNXT broadcast the two-hour shoot-out live and made the coverage available to 50 other West Coast stations. When the gunfire was over police recovered the bodies of six SLA members.

Though the pictures had been jerky and the camera batteries gave out just as the confrontation reached its climax, an estimated 20 million television viewers watched the gun battle.[28] From the safety of their living rooms, viewers had become, in a way never before possible, eyewitnesses to history. The fact that so many people watched the story galvanized local newsrooms. As one general manager put it at the time, every newscast had an "election night kind of excitement." By 1979, a study by the Radio and Television News Directors Foundation found that the number of local TV newsrooms with ENG had reached 550 – 86% of all stations (Allen 2001, p. 164).

The reliance on newer technologies and on being able to broadcast live and first has only grown. More recent examples of this approach are news choppers and Doppler radar.

Consultants

From the early days of local television the Nielsen Company counted the size of audiences by tallying household diaries of TV watching. The Nielsen ratings told stations how many people were watching and when, but not why viewers tuned in. In the late 1960s and early 1970s, consultants McHugh & Hoffman and Frank Magid changed the game when they began using the techniques of qualitative research, using open-ended questions to get inside viewer's heads.

One of the first qualitative studies of TV news was commissioned by McHugh & Hoffman and was conducted in three cities two weeks after the November 22, 1963, assassination of President John Kennedy. Researchers found that people had been "glued" to their sets, with some able to recall the entire drama. Researchers also discovered that viewers had been especially drawn to CBS anchorman Walter Cronkite. Cronkite's impact was "off the charts" because at times during the marathon coverage he dropped his serious newscaster façade and came off like a member of the family' (Allen 2001, pp. 64–66).

Consultants who were beginning to conduct research in big local markets also discovered that many viewers said they would be more likely to watch TV news if relevant stories were explained in simple, conversational language, by anchors who were like the "friend next door," and if stories were presented with as much style and technical razzle-dazzle as possible. The result was the development of formats – really news philosophies – with names such as "Eyewitness" and "Action."[29]

The consultants also gained influence over the hiring and firing of anchors, reporters, producers, and news directors – local TV news' most influential leaders – contributing at least somewhat to their increasingly nomadic career paths. A 1992 Freedom Forum survey found that the typical local news anchor was 32 years old, had already held three jobs in three cities, and had not worked in any city for more than four years (Allen, 2001, pp. 204–205). In the 1990s, the typical news director had held his or her current job an average of just 2.8 years. Though in the profession between 14 and 19 years, he or she had already worked at five to eight other stations.[30] At least some of this extraordinary mobility could be attributed to "churning" generated by TV consultants.

Soon consultants were also helping choose the stories stations covered. In 1989, for example, Audience Research & Development's top-five rankings were, in terms of the level of audience interest: emergency weather, crime prevention, crime coverage, weather, and children's issues. That same year McHugh & Hoffman's top-five were: weather, local events, crime and corruption, national/international news, and business/economics.[31]

As the technology used by the consultants to probe and analyze the audience improved, the flow of survey information to broadcasters increased. The shift by the Nielsen Company from ratings diaries to meters not only provided more data, but it also delivered it the next day in what became known at the "overnights." By 2005, meters were

SIDEBAR 4.3 (continued)

collecting information from 25,000 households around the country every day of the year.[32] Ultimately, this information about "viewer preferences" finds its way to the desks of local TV news directors, assignment managers, and broadcast producers whose jobs depend more than ever on their ability to parlay this research into ratings and, ultimately, profit.

News for Profit

In 1969, network news ratings exceeded those for local news broadcasts. Just three years later, however, 15 to 20 million Americans who had never regularly watched TV news had become part of the local news audience, pushing affiliate news viewership well past the network evening news shows. This rapid ascension of local TV news to the country's most used and most trusted source of information led to a third phenomenon that has influenced news content: the newsroom as a profit center.

Newsrooms that make money are nothing new. For 200 years, the business model of American newspapers has been built on a foundation of news and information. But when the people who ran what was until this time primarily an entertainment medium, TV, discovered that news could be also be profitable, it's perhaps not surprising that they were predisposed to shape their journalism around values that emphasized attracting an audience by entertaining them.

Armed with research about what viewers wanted and advice from consultants about how to provide it, and with new eye-catching technologies to deliver the "product," local stations embarked on what eventually became a frenzy for audience and profits. Stations added more newscasts, paid record salaries to on-air stars, and pumped more money into satellite, weather, and graphics equipment. The cost of staffing, and of gathering and presenting the news, often totaled half of a station's annual operating budget, a figure that is even higher if one includes newscast-related services provided by the promotion, engineering, and production departments.

But considering the profits to be made, especially in larger markets, it was money well spent. The general manager of one top-10 market network affiliate estimated in early 2004 that in the biggest 15 TV markets, a network-affiliated station should probably have a return on sales of 50 to 60%; in markets 15 to 50, it would return 30 to 40%; and in markets below 50, the return on sales would be 20 to 30%.

Those targets, however, face new threats.

Technologies such as satellite, cable, the Internet, and wireless "news on demand" let viewers get the weather report or headlines whenever they desire. And there is now so much local news on the air that many markets have become saturated with information programming while newsroom staffs have been thinned out, further diluting the content of broadcasts.

Stations have already witnessed a decline in viewership. Since 1977, the share of available viewers commanded by local early evening newscasts around the country dropped 18%. The share for the late news – after prime time is over – dropped 16%.[33] As a result, newscast producers have received new marching orders. Rather than try to build viewership, the objective is not to lose any more of the audience.

– Walter C. Dean, Dante Chinni

5 The Magic Formula: How to Make TV That Viewers Will Watch

The previous chapter showed how a series of demonstrably false myths and conventions about what audiences want from local TV news governs the medium and severely limits its quality. So that's what doesn't work. The obvious question is what does work? If so many of the conventions of the medium are wrong, what is right? We address these questions in this chapter.

Let's start with three assumptions:

1. Newsrooms want to produce the best-quality news with the resources at hand.
2. Newscasts have to be commercially successful.
3. Newsrooms have lots of choices about what to cover in reconciling assumption #1 (quality) with assumption #2 (profit).

Our five-year study of local TV news shows that newsrooms can do good journalism and still build profits. Stations don't have to choose ratings over reporting.

Using a broad measure of commercial success, we have identified a set of practices that are associated with bigger audiences, regardless of the topic of the story. Because these practices can be applied to any kind of story, we call them "The Magic Formula." This Magic Formula of demonstrably successful journalistic practices consists of six steps. In brief, they are:

- Step 1. Cover Important News – and give it resources and emphasis
- Step 2. Invest in Enterprise – time and effort pay off
- Step 3. Make Sourcing Authoritative – use data and consult experts
- Step 4. Provide Perspective – get more sources and viewpoints into stories

- Step 5. Look for Local Relevance – viewers watch if they know how stories affect them
- Step 6. Make Important Stories Longer – but don't pad shallow ones

These recommendations aren't based on wishful thinking or our own agendas. They are derived by analyzing local news program content and comparing that with the actual audience trends for each broadcast, and then testing those relationships statistically to find what correlations are real and not simply random. Our recommendations are not based on what viewers say they want – for example, what people tell a pollster or a focus group. Instead, our conclusions about building audience are based on what viewers actually did with their remote controls.

SIDEBAR 5.1

RATINGS TERMINOLOGY

Throughout this chapter we discuss a number of ratings measurements we have used to study the relationship between news content and audience viewership. Here is a brief summary of what these measurements mean:

Ratings measures the size of the audience for a specific program as a percentage of all of the households in the market that have a television.

Share measures the size of the audience for a specific program as a percentage of all of the households that are using television in the market during the time period in which the specific program airs.

Ratings Retention measures the ratings of a program as a percentage of the ratings of the preceding program.

Share Retention measures the share of a program as a percentage of the share of the preceding program.

We used these measurements on the entire audience to determine the success of the newscasts we studied. However, because local stations have grown increasingly concerned with reaching younger audiences (considered the most "demographically desirable" by advertisers), we also used ratings among "key" demographic groups for news.

For entertainment programs, the most sought after demographics are Men and Women 18 to 34, but because news audiences tend to be older, Men and Women 18 to 49 and Men and Women 25 to 54 are considered key demographics for news. In all, then, we tracked how local TV news audiences respond to specific stories using eight separate audience statistics.

– Todd L. Belt, Marion R. Just

THE MAGIC FORMULA

The formula we outline in this chapter is not conditional on the particular circumstances a station faces. When we describe the effect of news content on ratings, we have taken into account factors that are beyond the newsroom's control – including the network affiliation, the size of the media market, the intensity of competition within the market, the time of day of the broadcasts, and the overall viewership for news that year. When we say something "works" to build the audience, our conclusions hold in spite of these "uncontrollable" factors. In other words, these strategies can be applied in any newsroom, in any market. With that in mind, here are the elements that make up The Magic Formula.

Step 1.   Cover Important News – and Give It Resources and Emphasis

A given newscast might contain a range of topics. It may begin with a late-breaking crime story, followed by a story that explores a change in K-12 education policy, followed by a fluff piece about a celebrity visiting town. Given the notable difference in the focus of these stories, we examined viewer ratings to find out what types of stories attracted and held audiences. Do viewers really prefer fluff to hard news? Will a story about education policy drive viewers away?

To get at the answers to these questions, we classified all of the stories in our sample in terms of their broad impact on viewers, or their *significance*. We rated stories that focused on ideas, issues, or policy as well as stories that reflected a focus on public malfeasance (the journalistic "watchdog" role) as having the highest level of significance. The scoring of significance then descended among the following categories: very significant/major events; public/private/civic institutions or actors; substantive trends; unusual events; stories about political strategies/gamesmanship; breaking events; everyday incidents; everyday crime; human interest stories; celebrities/entertainment; stories about sensationalized scandals; and at the very bottom: station personnel or network promotion (see Appendix C for coding). Then we compared the size of the audience for stories with different levels of overall significance. We discovered some intriguing things.

Imagine you are in charge of the newsroom. You have enough time left for one more story. Do you air a story about what's going on in a local

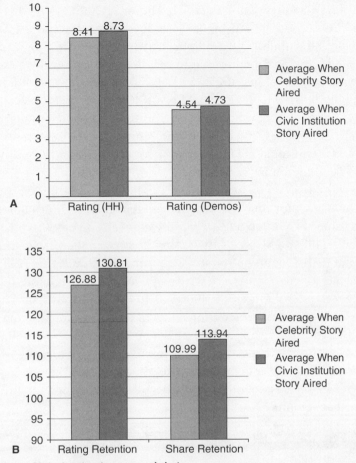

Figure 5.1. Civic institution vs. celebrity.

charitable organization, or do you choose a story about a celebrity's visit to your town? Which do you think the audience wants to see?

If you chose to go with the celebrity story instead of the story on the local charity, you just cost your station one-third of a rating point. Moreover, your audience will be 4% smaller than your lead-in program both in terms of rating and share. You will lose coveted younger viewers as well – at a rate of about one-fifth of a rating point among all four of the prized demographic groups.[1] Those differences may seem small, but over the range of stories and weeks of newscasts, they could add up to tens of thousands of dollars of advertising revenue, depending on the market.

In New York City, according to sales executives at two network affiliates, one ratings point is worth 73,000 households. In terms of households, a ratings point is worth about $1,000. Apply that to 16 "avails" (30-second advertising slots) × seven days a week × 52 weeks and the result equals $5.8 million. Because only 85% of avails are actually sold, the $5.8 million figure needs to be reduced by a factor of .85, yielding a total of just under $5 million per year in revenue for one rating point in just one newscast (11 P.M.). However, one sales executive said the figure is much higher when you look at prime demographics, which are valued at $1,700 to $1,800 per rating point. Plugging the larger figure into the formula means that an increase of one rating point could bring in $8.9 million more per year.

Even in mid-size and smaller markets, these small rating fluctuations can mean big money. In a market such as Denver, each household rating point is valued at $200 to $225. Over the course of a year, this adds up to about one million dollars. As the saying goes: A million here, a million there, and pretty soon you're talking real money (see Figure 5.1).

We came to these discoveries through a statistical technique called multiple regression analysis.[2] It allows us to hold constant several factors at once while concentrating on the effect of one factor in particular – the content of the news story. With this approach we can predict what happens to ratings when stations air low significance or high significance stories, while taking into account the time slot, market size, station affiliation, market competition, and the overall audience for the study year for that station.

SIDEBAR 5.2

HOW WE DID THE ANALYSIS

Because we taped and coded the most popular broadcast in each market, some of the newscasts we studied were in the early time slot and some in the later evening. Early and late news, however, have different goals and audiences. News directors often regard the early news as their newscast of record because it is primarily local, even though in many markets the late news has the largest audience.

The content of the late and early newscasts often reflects different missions. Early news precedes national news and is expected to carry the local brief. Late news, by contrast, is expected to devote some time to wrapping up important national news as well as reporting local stories. Late news audiences want to hear the late sports scores and are eager to know what the weather will be like tomorrow when they get out of bed. The whole mix of late news content must be accommodated in a rigid half-hour time slot.

Generally, late news does better than early news in terms of ratings – on average it gets four-tenths of a rating point more than early news and contains a significantly higher concentration of the "prized" demographics (Men and Women 18–49 and 25–54) than the early newscasts, although late news retains less of its prime time lead-in audience. The late newscasts average 1.2 rating points more among the female demographics than early newscasts, and they do a full rating point better than the early news among the male demographics. Our multiple regression analysis therefore holds time slots constant so that our findings about content are not skewed by when a particular type of story aired.[3] In large metropolitan areas, such as Los Angeles, New York, Chicago, or Boston, it may be difficult to define a story with broad "local" impact. People who live in Manhattan are not especially moved by problems with trash collection in Queens, and Los Angelenos may not care about the financial problems of Orange County. Although stations in small markets may have fewer resources, their product may be more relevant to the viewers in their geographic area than the news in the major metropolitan areas.[4]

This finding is no doubt due in large part to the long-term commercial success of NBC prime time programming during the study period (1998–2002). NBC affiliates averaged about 1.7 household rating points and 1.5 demo rating points above all of the competition. Therefore, our statistical analysis takes network affiliation into account.

The amount of competition in a market can influence a station's ability to succeed. The more competitive the market, the greater the difficulty in generating ratings gains. Not surprisingly, we found that the top quarter of markets were the most competitive – the ones with the least amount of variation in ratings among the stations. The stations in the most competitive markets earned an average of 2.2 fewer ratings points than stations in the least competitive quarter of all markets. Because of the impact of market competitiveness on ratings our statistical models take this market characteristic into account.

Lastly, because household ratings declined for local news during the five-year period by almost an entire rating point and the prized demographic ratings declined by four-tenths of a point, we also had to take into account the year of the study. We note all of the noncontent factors that our multiple regressions held statistically constant so that we can make judgments about the kind of content that works regardless of whether a newscast airs early or late in the evening, in Los Angeles or Sioux Falls, on an ABC or NBC affiliate, or where overall news ratings are high or low.

In the charity versus celebrity story choice described above we reached our conclusion by measuring the average commercial success for all of the stories in our sample about civic institutions (including charities) and compared them with the average for celebrity stories – while taking into account the time of each newscast, the market size, its network affiliation, and the year of the study in which these stories originally aired.

– *Todd L. Belt, Marion R. Just*

News Audiences Prefer Hard News to Entertainment

Let's take another example of story choice. If we compare the ratings of an issue-based, policy-relevant story (such as a tax increase on gasoline) versus airing a story about entertainment (such as the premiere of a new movie), we find a similar pattern. Audiences prefer the issue-based story to the entertainment story. Running the issue story will gain an extra one-quarter of a rating point. It will also increase rating and share retention from the lead-in program by nearly 5%. And lastly, it will attract younger audiences, with an increase of about one-fifth of a rating point across the four important groups of young viewers (see Figure 5.2).[5]

What about the critical role the news media play as watchdogs on government? We found that citizens not only need this type of information, they seek it out. Stories that focused on problems in government or the criminal actions of public officials got the highest ratings of all of the story topics we analyzed. In fact, stories about malfeasance in government even outstripped stories founded on scandals involving private citizens. Stories about public malfeasance garnered over one full rating point more than those racier stories. Covering missteps in government also increased lead-in rating and share retention by more than 11%. And public malfeasance stories beat the private-citizen scandal stories by an average of nearly eight-tenths of a rating point among younger audiences.[6] The results speak to the breadth of impact that politics has on viewers. The audience knows what is or is not its business.(See Figure 5.3.)

Finally, these watchdog stories soundly beat out the other "soft news" categories of human interest and celebrities/entertainment. In the end, performing the journalistic watchdog role works – and not just for

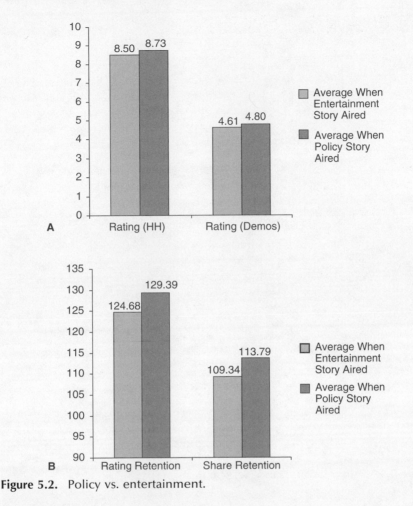

Figure 5.2. Policy vs. entertainment.

democracy but for the bottom line. It builds household audience and share, it improves lead-in retention, and it builds a younger, more desirable audience.

In summary, doing stories that focus on issues, policy, and civic institutions leads to greater station revenues. And fulfilling the democratic mandate of the press to hold government to account is particularly fruitful. Continuing down the path of celebrity, human interest, and superficial sensation is not. Obviously, this finding does not mean that a news diet exclusively of political malfeasance is the answer. We have evidence that even this salutary and engaging topic can be misapplied (see Sidebar 5.3, The WBBM Experiment), but we can say that covering important news builds the audience.

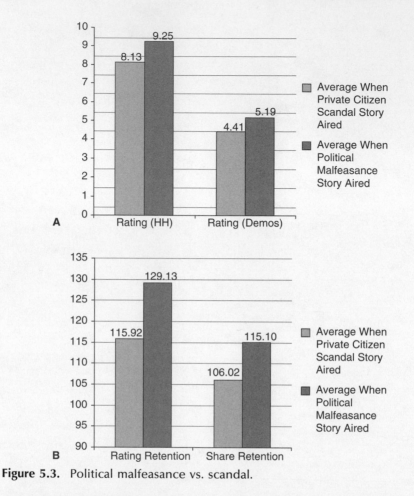

Figure 5.3. Political malfeasance vs. scandal.

SIDEBAR 5.3

THE WBBM EXPERIMENT – WHY IT FAILED

One of the questions some readers will ask on reading this book is, "What about the WBBM experiment? Didn't that station, the CBS affiliate in Chicago, try to go the quality route a few years ago and fail?"

There are lessons to take from WBBM, but those lessons don't contradict anything in this book.

In February 2000, WBBM-TV attempted to reinvent local news in an almost nine-month experiment that became renowned for its aspirations and, ultimately, its failure. The late news on the Viacom-owned-and-operated station had been a ratings disappointment for years. With little to lose, *Channel 2 News at Ten* decided to offer a no-frills presentation of news featuring a single anchor, the highly regarded Carol Marin, who would deliver important stories without hype and happy talk.

Had it succeeded, the WBBM approach would have been copied by other stations looking to break out of the pack. Serious news might have again become a valued brand. And WBBM might have done well (or even better than well) by doing good, or at least that was the thinking. Instead, the station's "noble experiment" became the most closely watched failure on local television, derided as an audience-losing lump of coal that a *Chicago Tribune* editorial likened to "Cod Liver Oil at 10 O'clock." Moreover, the newscast's failure to catch on with viewers appeared to reaffirm broadcast journalists' worst suspicions about the public – that serious news won't sell.

Talk with newsroom leaders about innovation, and it won't be long before someone mentions "the 'BBM experiment." The lesson of its meltdown seems to be, "Don't try anything risky, and if you do, don't use serious news." That's unfortunate because the WBBM experiment is a poor marker on which to calibrate the future course of local broadcast journalism.

What went wrong? In forsaking frightening and fuzzy, the station created a broadcast that was cold, aloof, and exceedingly one-dimensional. It was news about political insiders for political junkies. In the end, ironically, it became what it reviled by airing significantly more of what it might have reduced: crime news.

Our analysis of two weeks of *Channel 2 10 O'clock News with Carol Marin* found a broadcast that was, on balance, unexceptional. Indeed, when we studied newscasts on 40 stations in 12 cities that year, 14 scored higher by our criteria than the WBBM broadcast.

Some critics also maintain that the newscast wasn't on the air long enough to provide much of a measure. As *Chicago Tribune* television critic Steve Johnson said, "When you do something so radical, eight and a half months is not a reasonable test" (Hickey 2001, p. 16).

Still, it's fair to ask whether time was really the problem. The 10 35-minute newscasts we studied were distinguished as much for what they lacked, or chose to ignore, as for what they brought to Chicago's media marketplace. Much of what was unappealing was the result of poor execution – pedestrian writing, unimaginative production, and the aloofness that characterized presentation. But beyond what one might say were mainly production issues, there was the question of

SIDEBAR 5.3 (continued)

content, of the news itself. Though WBBM's reporters excelled in effort and enterprise, the thoroughness of their coverage could not overcome an impression that the same story about the same people was being told over and over again. The result was a sometimes staid, even boring broadcast of limited appeal. "Compared to everything else on television, the show looked very slow, dragging and stagnant," said Northwestern University journalism professor and former NBC News executive Joseph Angotti (Pethokoukis 2000, p. 54).

Chicago has been described as a place where politics is a contact sport. And WBBM provided a nightly play-by-play that featured feuding politicians and corrupt public servants battling special prosecutors, journalists, and, as often as not, each other. Political intrigue became the broadcast's master narrative, the lens through which Channel 2 viewed all of Chicago. Stories about blue-collar crime, a staple of the local market, were replaced with long investigative reports on white-collar corruption. This is not to say the station totally ignored "gunfire erupts" news. On two nights it led with reporter packages about someone firing shots at the publisher of a community newspaper. The story, however, was more about politics than crime. The intended victim, who was not injured, had written articles critical of a well-known politician with whom the suspect was acquainted.

Over 10 weeknights, *Channel 2 News* carried nine stories about politically related crime or corruption, two more stories on this topic than the combined total from 26 other stations in eight different markets that year. There were so many reports on WBBM about wrongdoing by politicians, bureaucrats, and cops, in fact, that crime coverage overall consumed almost one-third (32%) of the average nightly news hole on Channel 2. On other stations studied that year, crime news accounted for about 20% of content.

Not surprisingly, the decision to concentrate on just a few subjects led to a certain imbalance of content. There were a lot of very long stories – 27% were longer than two minutes. But *CBS2* also ran scores of very short items – nearly half its stories were 30 seconds or less – so many short "tells" it actually aired more stories each night than most newscasts. Rather than provide a lot of news in some depth, in other words, WBBM said a great deal about a few things and very little about almost everything else.

Besides concentrating on just a few topics, the newscast was presented in a formal, almost professorial tone. During the first week, anchor Marin sat at a small, waist-high, kidney-shaped table. When not seeing taped reports, viewers usually saw a "head shot" of the veteran anchorwoman with a blue wall in the background. By the second week, she had been moved to stand for part of the broadcast in front of the desk or a large graphics screen. At least one critic claimed the set was better at showcasing Marin than the news. Yet if it was designed to appear intimate, the backdrop instead looked stark, dark, and almost foreboding. The writing and delivery did little to compensate for that impression.

"Mariam Santos is making serious new charges about possible sweetheart deals in the office she wants to re-claim," Marin began the inaugural newscast. "The former city treasurer served time in prison for fraud and extortion and three weeks ago her conviction was tossed out. Now Santos says she needs to go back to work because Mayor Daley's wielding too much clout in her old office." A two-minute report by political editor Mike Flannery on a news conference by Santos, the former city treasurer, followed. When it was over, Santos herself appeared on set and in a three-minute exchange with Marin, repeated many of the claims viewers had just heard. During these exchanges with newsmakers, Marin sometimes came across as lady justice, holder of the scales. She did not shy away from asking a tough question, but she rarely prosecuted with aggressive follow-ups, even when answers were evasive. As a result, Marin sometimes became irrelevant; the politicians said what they wanted to say and otherwise ignored her.

After six and one-half minutes, the city treasurer story was over and Marin turned to the camera. "Another well-known politician, former congressman Mel Reynolds, is still doing time in a North Carolina federal prison," she intoned. "Reynolds says he wants President Clinton to commute his sentence. CBS2 has learned he's gaining support from some surprising places." Reporter Mike Parker's two-minute package followed, after which Parker appeared on the set to answer a couple of questions from Marin. That took another 60 seconds.

Again, Marin turned to the camera and moved down the docket of news about politicians in trouble. "Governor George Ryan, who is facing his own political problems, got a little help from his friends today when fielding a barrage of questions about the truck license scandal." Viewers saw excerpts of a news conference where the governor, joined by a couple of state legislators, attempted to rebut accusations that bribe money collected by state workers to issue truck drivers' licenses had ended up in the governor's campaign coffers.

Next story: "In Highland Park, an investigation is underway tonight into new charges of racial bias by police. It comes as the result of more information uncovered by CBS2 Chicago. Last month, Pam Zekman reported allegations made by some Highland Park officers that their department has a policy of racial profiling. Tonight, Pam takes a look at tactics allegedly used by one of the department's biggest ticket writers." A six-minute, painstakingly documented report showed how some police officers in the Chicago suburb had targeted black and Hispanic motorists for traffic stops.

Not until 17 minutes into the broadcast did CBS2 get to the story its network-owned competitors led with that night – a water main break in the downtown Loop that was expected to cause "system-wide delays" on the elevated train system during next morning's rush hour. Where other stations switched to the scene for live reports, WBBM ran a 24-second anchor tell as pictures of the flooded intersection appeared on the screen.

WBBM's decision to abandon "live, local, and late-breaking" coverage of spot news was a conscious calculation that assumed viewers had grown weary of the steady diet of hype and violence that characterizes local TV news. But by seeking the other extreme, Channel 2 arguably overcompensated and may have become less relevant as a result. On a night competitors carried live reports from a neighborhood that had lost electricity, Channel 2 led with a story on a local chemical manufacturer's agreement with the Environmental Protection Agency to limit the use of a dangerous insecticide (Hickey 2001). Twice during the first week of the new broadcast, WBBM led with reports on computer "denial of service" attacks, which were then much less common.

If WBBM really was "PBS on CBS," as one critic suggested, viewers might have seen more about social issues, health, science, and technology or foreign affairs than other stations. Yet they did not. In only 3 of 12 major topic categories did Channel 2 air more stories than the average of other stations studied that year. It had more items about crime (32% vs. 20%); culture/civilization (17% vs. 8%); and business (11% vs. 6%). On the other hand, it carried fewer stories about (noncriminal) politics (13% vs. 16%); foreign affairs/defense (0.4% vs. 0.7%); health and consumer news (6% vs. 9%); and human interest

(3.4% vs. 8.4%). Perhaps most surprisingly, CBS2 presented significantly less news (8% vs. 13%) about a broad range of social issues, including education, transportation, aging, and poverty, than the average. On the nearly six hours of WBBM newscasts we watched, there were no education stories and one 25-second item about transportation.

And this last statistic, perhaps more than any other, may best illustrate why the "BBM experiment" was doomed to fail. When it came to covering public corruption and political intrigue, Channel 2 was at the top of its game. But news, even in a town as political as Chicago, is not monolithic. City hall may be important, but to the tens of thousands of viewers with children or grandchildren, what happens in the schools is probably more likely to affect their daily lives. Though everyone who gathers around the water cooler may speculate about whether an alderman will be indicted, it's a fair bet the subject of that morning's rush hour commute will also come up.

WBBM didn't fail because it tried to cover important news more thoroughly. It failed because the architects of the *Ten O'clock News* forgot about the audience and about all the many things that touch people's lives. As our analysis reveals, there was too much coverage about too few subjects presented with such solemnity that it's no wonder the broadcast collapsed under its own considerable weight. If one were looking for rich and comprehensive coverage of Chicago, you couldn't get it from WBBM any more than from its rivals.

– Waltes C. Dean, Atiba Pertilla

Step 2.   Invest in Enterprise – Time and Effort Pay Off

One of the biggest challenges in producing local TV news today is budget. To rein in expenses while expanding news programming, reporters are increasingly asked to cover more stories per day. The result is a decrease in the amount of journalistic effort – or enterprise – going into each story. Our study considers the impact that the degradation of enterprise reporting has on local news ratings.

For this analysis, we coded each story for the amount of enterprise reporting that it reflected. A station-initiated investigation was rated at the highest level of journalistic effort, whereas merely airing wire feeds or video news releases (VNRs) would rank as the lowest level of enterprise. We also assigned values to other aspects of journalistic enterprise such as interviews (see Appendix B).

We found that stories that involved greater journalistic enterprise get higher ratings, regardless of the topic, the time at which the newscast

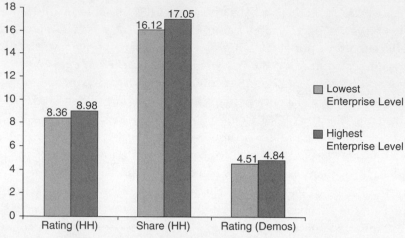

Figure 5.4. Highest vs. lowest enterprise.

airs, the station affiliation, the size or competitiveness of the market, or the year in which the study ran. Audiences are attracted to news stories that involve effort – for example, on-the-spot reporting, as opposed to anchors reading the news.

The appreciation of enterprise is not surprising, considering the news consumption habits of the modern viewer. The average person is exposed to several news outlets before he or she sits down to watch the early or late evening news. If local TV merely provides the same headline service as top-of-the-hour radio or the front page of a tabloid, there is little incentive for the audience to stay tuned. If, on the contrary, a local TV station advances the story, then it can attract the audience's attention.

In our study, stories that involved the highest level of journalistic enterprise earned three-fifths of a household rating point and nine-tenths of a share point more than stories that demonstrated the lowest level of enterprise. The stations that went out of their way to get the story were also preferred by younger audiences by one-third of a rating point.[7] (See Figure 5.4.)

In fact, we found that the amount of journalistic enterprise in a story was at least four times as important as the story's topic in determining audience ratings.[8] Newsrooms that merely focus on topics when determining how to craft the newscast are addressing only a small fraction of what they can control to produce good ratings. Viewers reward stations that put a reporter on the job digging for information and asking tough questions. The audience rewards enterprise. In other words, how a story is done – the treatment – is more important than what the story is about.

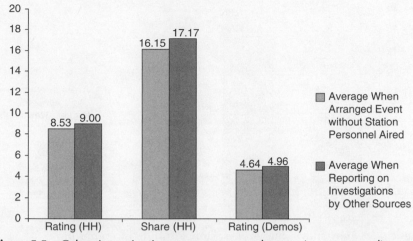

Figure 5.5. Other investigation vs. pre-arranged event (no personnel).

Enterprise encompasses a variety of approaches and strategies, but viewers respond to it even in the broadest sense. One of the chief findings is that audiences stay tuned when a story contributes new information. We found that viewers appreciate news investigations even if the station did not itself initiate the inquiry.

For example, reporting about an investigation launched elsewhere gets a station better ratings than merely sending a cameraperson to a pre-arranged event. Neither approach involves putting a reporter on the scene, but reports of investigations yield higher ratings and share among all audiences, including young people – an extra half of a household rating point, over more than one full share point and one-third of a rating point among the younger demographic groups – compared with simply shooting video of, say, a council meeting or a mayor's announcement.[9] (See Figure 5.5.)

But that doesn't mean it pays to be lazy – quite the contrary.

We compared the ratings when stations aired an investigation initiated by another source versus airing a story comprising only a wire or network feed. Stations that opted for the investigative story over the feed achieved ratings that were half of a rating point higher and more than one full share point higher than those that opted for the feed. Moreover, they also improved their younger demographics by one-third of a rating point compared with stations that chose a feed.[10]

But when it's possible, viewers appreciate when a story goes further than simply reporting on what others have said. We compared some high-level enterprise stories, such as those where reporters interview newsmakers and ask substantive questions, to non-investigative stories that are

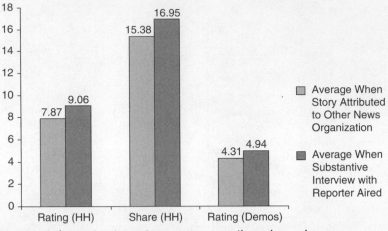

Figure 5.6. Substantive interview vs. story attributed to other news organization.

attributed to other news organizations. The stories with in-person interviews received 1.2 rating points more than stories relying on outside
attribution and yielded a share that was one and one-half points larger.
Additionally, these stories received more than an extra three-fifths of a
rating point among the younger demographic groups.[11] (See Figure 5.6.)

In other words, getting back to the basics of journalism – giving
viewers substance and solid reporting – gets good ratings. Merely
manipulating syndicated material or footage from network feeds or trying to capitalize on what other outlets do may be cheaper in the short
run, but it is costly in terms of the number of "eyeballs." The audience
wants fresh news. It takes time and money to undertake investigations,
and it takes patience, persistence, and contacts to land interviews with
newsmakers. Nonetheless, this kind of journalistic enterprise is important
for building an audience. For news directors and reporters, this means
viewers notice and will reward extra effort.

Step 3.   Make Sourcing Authoritative – Use Data and Consult Experts

Besides putting more journalistic effort into news stories, are there specific
ways of covering stories that also contribute to better audience numbers?
We considered how the use of sources impacts ratings. We analyzed the
sources in each story in our sample. Stories featuring an on-camera
authoritative, credentialed source got the highest score. Those that referenced an expert or provided important facts relevant to the story got a

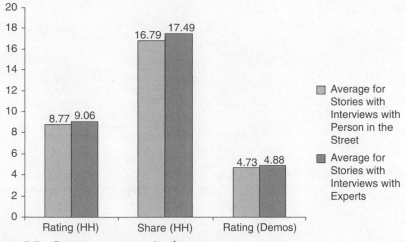

Figure 5.7. Expert vs. person in the street.

slightly lower source score. If the story had one of the major actors, but not experts, that story got an even lower rating. Finally, the lowest scored stories merely made passing reference to an unnamed source.

We found that as stories scored better on our scale of sourcing, they also got better ratings. This was true regardless of the subject. In fact, we found almost no discernible impact of story topic when we compared different levels of authoritativeness in sourcing.[12] The results show that when stations air stories with experts, they are rewarded with higher ratings.

To put this a different way, let's assume that you could cover a story in one of two ways: You could make an effort to interview a credentialed expert on the topic of the story, or you could simply grab someone off of the street and ask her what she thought. Certainly, the "person on the street" is the cheaper, easier way to go about it, but if you did this rather than interview an expert you would lose three-tenths of a household rating point, seven-tenths of a share point, and one-sixth of a rating point among the younger demographic groups.[13] (See Figure 5.7.)

When reporters refer to experts in a story, emphasize the facts, or interview major actors on-screen viewers recognize the added news value. Viewers bring a wide range of experiences and a healthy skepticism to the news. For a story to be believable, it needs hard facts and expert opinion. Local news is perceived as being more credible and less biased than national TV news, but that edge is eroding (Graber 2001). Authoritative sourcing can help news directors keep that edge.

More authoritative stories provide more information. For example, when we compared stories that referenced reliable evidence (such as

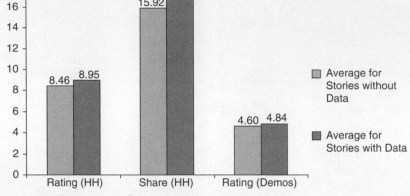

Figure 5.8. Data vs. no data.

published reports) with stories without any experts or data, we found that stories with better evidence saw ratings improve by one-half point, share by 1.4 points, and demographic ratings by one-quarter point compared with stories without the authoritative information.[14] Stories that look good, that are highly visual and emotional, will not on their own build viewership. Our results show that people want reliable information and substance, not just flashy presentation. (See Figure 5.8.)

Step 4. Provide Perspective – Get More Sources and Viewpoints into Stories

Following the suggestion of our news experts, we examined the range of views represented in stories. How well or how poorly were different sides of a story presented? Did obtaining a balance of views improve ratings? To explore the impact of including different points of view on ratings, we measured two characteristics: the number of different sources and the mix of opinions in the story. The *number* of sources speaks to the reporter's effort to get different perspectives, whereas the *mix* of opinions tells us how well the reporter achieved balance in the story.

Our scoring of story sourcing was straightforward. We simply counted the number of sources appearing or cited. The highest score was given to stories that provided three or more sources. The second-highest score was given to stories with two sources. Stories with only one source got a low score, and stories without any sources got the lowest.

We found that using more sources in a story led to higher ratings, regardless of the topic. Just as we found with respect to enterprise and

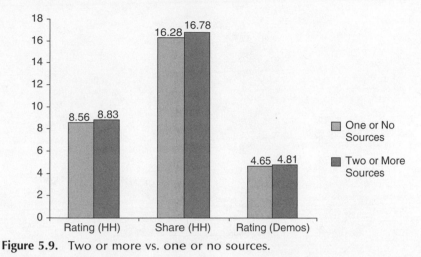

Figure 5.9. Two or more vs. one or no sources.

authoritativeness, the treatment of the story (in this case going after multiple sources), was far more important than what the story was about. In fact, stories with several sources achieved high ratings and shares and better demographics no matter what the topic.[15] The difference between providing one source or no sources compared with two or more sources in a story is measurable in rating points. Getting two or more sources provides an increase of nearly three-tenths of a rating point, one-half of a share point, and one-sixth of a rating point among younger viewers.[16] (See Figure 5.9.)

It is important to note that increasing the number of sources does not automatically translate into a broader range of views. In fact, multiple sources may not offer any opinions at all. To look at the relative balance of the views presented in the story, we had to develop an alternative scoring technique. We scored the stories highest on balance if no single side made up more than 75% of the opinions presented in a given story. We gave a low score to stories that presented only one side of the issue. We gave a mid-range score to stories that presented more than one opinion, but did so in a lopsided way (one side getting more than 75% of the opinions in the story). We then compared the results to ratings.

As in the case of multiple sourcing, a balance of opinions was much more (over three times) important to viewers than topic.[17] Providing a significant mix of opinions instead of just one side of a story gained an extra third of a rating point, nearly two-thirds of a share point, and two-tenths of a rating point among the younger demographic groups in the audience.[18] (See Figure 5.10.)

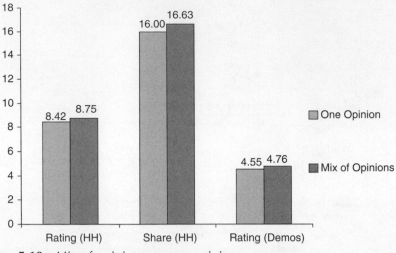

Figure 5.10. Mix of opinions vs. one opinion.

Again, this speaks to the sophistication of the audience. Local TV news viewers want to feel they are getting a complete treatment of the story with all sides represented.[19] This is true whether the differing perspectives are provided through multiple sources or through the presentation of individuals with a mix of opinions on the given issue.

This part of The Magic Formula might seem obvious. But balancing viewpoints would require a bigger change than you might think. The five-year study data show that most stories about controversial issues were not balanced with even two points of view. Indeed, 6 in 10 stories that involved disputes contained only one side of the story or merely a passing reference to a second side. This one-sidedness is a major problem in local TV news, and it is costing stations viewers.

Step 5. Look for Local Relevance – Viewers Watch If They Know How Stories Affect Them

The news directors who helped to design our analysis and the news directors whom we surveyed all agreed that local news needs to be highly local. Our analyses show that viewers agree. They tune in for stories that relate to their community. This finding was particularly apparent when it came to emergencies, such as severe weather, that affected the community. Audiences were especially attracted to stations that devoted significant time and resources to such events.

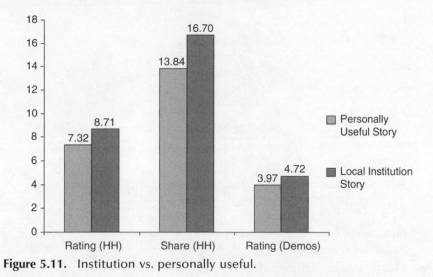

Figure 5.11. Institution vs. personally useful.

Beyond emergency stories, however, we found that less dramatic
stories of community relevance will also appeal to audiences, albeit at a
lower rate. We looked at the ratings for locally significant "hard" news
stories and generic soft news pieces, comparing stories that involved a
major local institution or employer (such as a local plant layoff) to those
centered on personally useful information (such as healthful diets).
These "personally useful" stories have become a hallmark of the
"news you can use" genre popular on local news. We found, though,
that – contrary to what many might expect – viewers preferred stories
with broad civic impact to items of personal interest.

In our study, a story that explained, for example, the impact of layoffs
at a local factory had a 1.4 rating point advantage over a story about
personal health. Stories about community institutions earned 2.9 share
points and three-quarters of an average demo rating point more than
personal interest stories.[20] (See Figure 5.11.)

One could argue that stories involving major civic institutions are
obvious choices both for local newsrooms and for the audience. A
somewhat harder test would be to look at stories that do not affect the
entire community. That kind of story – one that sits on the edge of the
market – often comes up for stations in larger metropolitan areas that
comprise center cities, inner suburbs, outer suburbs, and adjacent rural
areas. Many stories in a diverse market have demographically dis-
tinctive audiences – perhaps the story affects primarily Latinos or
suburbanites.

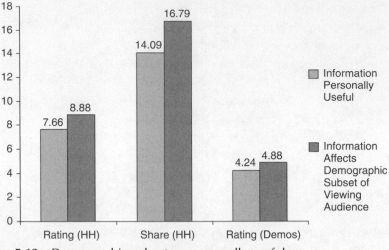

Figure 5.12. Demographic subset vs. personally useful.

We compared the ratings for stories impacting smaller audiences – either geographic or demographic subgroups – with those of "news you can use" stories aimed at the whole audience. We found that civic-minded stories earned one and one-quarter rating points, 2.7 share points, and nearly two-thirds of a rating point more among key demographics than the "news you can use."[21] Again, we found that providing a focus on the community was vastly more important than the topic of the story in generating ratings.[22] (See Figure 5.12.)

These results underscore the conclusion that local news viewers want news that affects their community, not just themselves as individuals. There are numerous competing media where soft news and personal advice abound. These outlets, however, do not cover news that is relevant to the local community. That is where local news fulfills a unique mission, and the audience rewards it when it does.

Step 6.   Make Important Stories Longer – But Don't Pad Shallow Ones

There is a presumption in local news that shorter stories are better for ratings. The idea is that a greater number of stories will help to hold the audience's attention – give a little something of interest to everyone, but above all, not bore anyone. But following all of the practices in The Magic Formula that we have listed so far (getting more sources, doing investigative journalism, explaining the local angle, etc.) would inevitably make stories longer. And that means any newscast following The Formula would necessarily have fewer stories. Because of this, we wondered if story length automatically impacted ratings. To find out, we examined how long stories fared when The Magic Formula was followed and when it was not.

What we found was that longer stories do lose ratings – but only if they are done poorly. Stories that do *not* employ The Magic Formula cost a station more than one-third of a rating point and more than four-tenths of share point when they are extended from 30 to 90 seconds, and they lose one-quarter of a rating point among the younger members of the audience. Long stories that are not about significant topics, that do not have good sourcing or community relevance, lose the lead-in audience by about 3% on rating and share. This is true irrespective of topic. As we have shown, some story topics do better than others, but the choice of topic makes very little difference compared with how the topic is reported.[23] It's much less about what you cover than how you cover it – but fluff and thunder stories don't naturally lend themselves to quality reporting: they don't require much journalistic effort to cover them.

Conversely, longer stories that employ The Magic Formula actually get better ratings the longer they are. The difference between doing a 30-second and 90-second story that employs The Magic Formula is an added two-thirds of a rating point, an entire share point and nearly half of a rating point among the key demographic groups. Additionally, the longer Magic Formula stories help to boost lead-in retention by about 5%. This is dramatic evidence that The Magic Formula has elements that actually "hook and hold" the audience. Time spent on serious reporting, chasing down leads, getting interviews, and making the effort to explain the relevance to the community, is time well spent. Very short stories cannot incorporate these elements, and long stories that do not bother to do so turn the audience off. It makes sense to keep the superficial stories short and the serious stories long; a mix of stories that highlights serious journalism is good for ratings. (See Figure 5.13.)

Recapping The Magic Formula

Each of the techniques of The Magic Formula is at least twice as important in generating audience ratings as the mere selection of the topic. Our study makes it clear that it's not what you cover, it's *how* you cover it that matters. For standard 60-second news stories on all of the

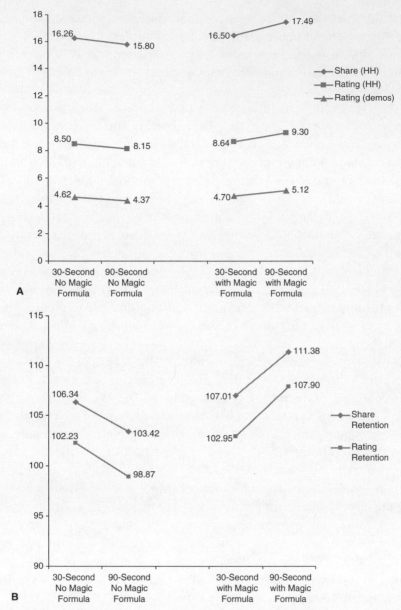

Figure 5.13. Thirty- vs. 90-second Magic/No Magic Formula.

topics we covered, those that included the journalism practices described here outpaced stories that did not by a little more than two-thirds of a rating point, a full share point, and almost one-half a rating point among the demographic groups most sought by advertisers. Moreover, applying

The Magic Formula helps a newscast retain 4% more of the lead-in program's ratings. And as we said at this chapter's start, that adds up to real money in local news. In New York, that would mean an increase in revenue of $3.3 million. In a mid-size market such as Denver, that would mean an increase in revenue of $750,000. These revenue gains could go a long way toward offsetting the increase in staff and training required to implement The Magic Formula. (See Figure 5.14.)

We've touched on a lot of material in this chapter. Here's a quick summary of The Magic Formula.

- Cover Important News – and give it resources and emphasis
  - Aim for a mix of stories that includes coverage of major institutions and issues in the community, including local governance, education, major businesses, and local charities as well as the concerns of large ethnic or geographic groups.
  - Steer away from fluff and fillers that viewers can easily get from entertainment programming.
- Invest in Enterprise – time and effort pay off
  - Give reporters time to investigate important issues in the community. Let them train others.
  - Send reporters out on stories, particularly stories of broad significance that need extra explanation.
- Make Sourcing Authoritative – use data and consult experts
  - Make sure reporters have the time and resources to conduct on-camera interviews.
  - Give reporters time to develop sources on their beats.
  - Press reporters to research the facts around the story and consult experts.
- Provide Perspective – get more sources and viewpoints into stories
  - Encourage reporters to get more than one source.
  - Check the credentials of the sources – are they experts in their fields?
  - Expect a balance of views on controversial issues, especially political questions.
  - Push reporters to get reactions to press releases, not merely to provide a soapbox.
- Look for Local Relevance – viewers watch if they know how stories affect them
  - Even local stories need some explanation about why the audience should pay attention.

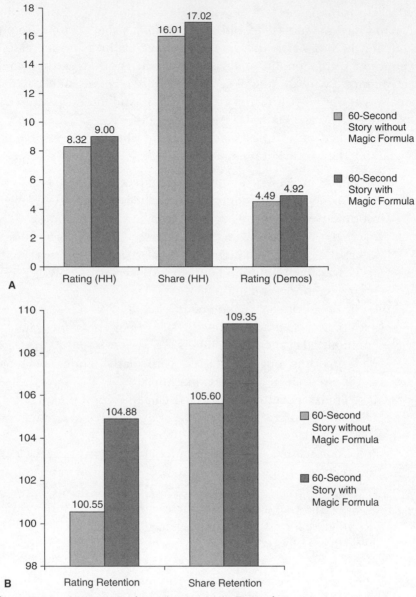

Figure 5.14. Sixty-second Magic/no Magic Formula.

- Provide government and issue stories with enough background so that viewers can tell how the decisions will affect their lives.
- Make Important Stories Longer – but don't pad shallow ones
  - A newscast can contain a mix of story lengths.
  - Don't be afraid to air long stories in each broadcast.

- But make sure the longer stories have real impact on the audience and the key ingredients – interviews, balanced. viewpoints, explanation – that will keep the audience's attention.
- Making empty stories longer – those without sufficient impact or information – will drive viewers away.

CONCLUSION: DOING WELL BY DOING GOOD

We began this chapter by outlining a few assumptions. We said that local TV journalists will voluntarily choose to do the best reporting with the resources at hand, but we also said that commercial considerations combined with the myths of what makes for successful television often thwart journalistic goals. The Magic Formula outlined in this chapter shows that commercial concerns are not necessarily in conflict with the production of a high-quality news product worthy of professional respect. These findings are important for several reasons:

- They contradict the conventional assumption that reporting on the cheap doesn't hurt ratings – it does.
- They reinforce the commercial value of individual reporters going out and getting the story.
- They demonstrate the importance of training for reporters and access to the community because community relevance counts.
- They illustrate the age-old adage that it takes money to make money (investing in good reporting leads to better ratings). Stories that employed The Magic Formula had better ratings than those that did not.
- They demonstrate that even in a difficult market, content will drive audiences rather than glitz.

The results show that local TV news producers are working under faulty assumptions. Instead, if they followed the rules they learned in journalism school, they could actually improve their ratings.

Producers often assume that the general viewing audience prefers soft news and sensationalized stories. Newsroom managers, in turn, may believe that investigative journalism, which costs significantly more than reporting the findings of others, is generally not worth the cost. Not only are these assumptions false, but their reverse is true. Soft news and sensationalism do not build a viewing audience. Getting stories on the cheap to fill the news hole is costly in terms of ratings.

A principal impediment is dependence on short-term ratings results. It is notable that news directors are given only three to four ratings periods ("books") to establish a positive track record at a given station. News directors' résumés are filled with two-year tenures, reflecting the extraordinarily tight leash on which they are held in the highly competitive local news market. The overall decline in ratings has exacerbated the emphasis on immediate results. When ratings go down, news budgets are contracted, often within a budget year. Our results show, however, that journalistic enterprise – which may cost more money in the short term – is one of the factors that leads to larger audiences, and therefore, greater advertising revenue.

In addition to the challenge of defying the long-held business assumptions about what works and what it costs, there are human resource issues involved in improving ratings. Local reporters often do not have the experience and contacts to undertake more enterprise journalism. Reporters have to be well-trained and given time to do their jobs. As one news director told us in our survey: "You can't shortcut the fundamentals."

The emphasis on short-term results and the resources needed for training reporters are formidable barriers. Our findings suggest, however, that meeting those challenges can offer substantial rewards. Our study shows that reporting significant hard news can stimulate viewer interest. Giving reporters the resources to get the story, conduct interviews, do good sourcing, get a balance of opinions, and explain the relevance of the results to the local audience means better local TV ratings. The results indicate that local TV news can and should get back to the basics of good journalism.

Our surveys show that many news directors believe that a return to the basics of good journalism is the best course for winning back viewers. News directors told us that they felt that the way to build audience was through "enterprise reports on issues that matter to the public" and to "provide relevant and compelling stories that affect our community." But news directors feel trapped by commercial interests beyond the simple ratings game.

In our 2001 survey, many of the news directors complained of having to do more with less. They were seeing their budgets and personnel shrink while the demands on the newsroom were growing (see Sidebar 5.3, The WBBM Experiment). This was especially true in the smaller markets (quartiles 3 and 4), where we often found the best journalism. By 2002, many news directors complained that they couldn't retain staff – that the increased workload and lack of support drove away good, experienced newspeople. Worse yet, staff were not being replaced and their jobs were loaded onto other personnel without experience in that particular area. When there was replacement, new inexperienced staff required training – a further strain on already scarce resources. The profit motive, as currently realized in the local TV news business, causes a downward spiral of fewer resources, poorer journalism, and worse ratings.

SIDEBAR 5.4

SAMPLE QUOTES FROM SURVEYS OF NEWS DIRECTORS

Question: What is the biggest change at your station this year?

– Marion Just

2001 Survey	2002 Survey
"Budget cuts; frozen positions, less money and more responsibilities."	"We lost an important management position by attrition due to budget cuts."
"Increasing story count in newscasts without increasing reporting staff."	"Burnout – with more work to do to make up for short staffing and trying to be competitive, folks simply are running on empty a lot."
"The cutbacks have made a lean staff malnourished."	"Having to do more with less. Previously … each person had 1 or 2 specific functions. Now, the corporate mentality is to cross-train everyone and have fewer staff members who can do more things. But that means staff can't focus and do one thing well."
"Downsizing while maintaining full news schedule."	
"For the first time in 10 years as News Director we have downsized staff. We have accomplished it through attrition, but you never like to see staff size shrink. It's a tough mental adjustment."	"Cross-training and multi-tasking – people are being trained to do more than what they may have originally been hired for – for example: producers sub on assignment desk."

SIDEBAR 5.4 (continued)

"Loss of news gathering ability 10–12% due to cuts."

"More newscasts!"

"Adding a 5 P.M. newscast. Don't have staff to make it a local show. [It is] Tough!"

"Cutbacks in staff due to budget restraints."

"90% changeover in staff, including key people: anchors (3), reporters, ND and EP and producers."

"6 of 9 contracts renewed and we had to hire 6 new people and train them!"

"Anchor turnover – need rebuilding reporting staff. Also great turnover among photographers."

"Lost a majority of experienced reporters."

"3 news directors in one year."

"The tightening of our budget last year bled into this year, hurting our ability to hire and retain quality people."

"Departure of long-time anchor and managing editor."

"Losing several veteran reporters to the private and public sector and replacing them with reporters who have considerably less experience."

But the facts, based on research beyond the capacity of most stations or even most consultants, reveals a different approach to help local TV news get back on track. What is required is giving staff more time to cover fewer stories better. By investing in good reporting, stations can do better stories, get better ratings, and afford more staff. They can raise the bottom line and boost morale at the same time.

In the next chapter we will explain how to apply The Magic Formula to four of the most important and common topics newsrooms cover every day.

6   Steps to Better Coverage

Many local television news stations could do a better job in their coverage by taking the path already traveled by successful stations. How can reports about serious issues such as politics, health, education, and crime draw viewers? In this chapter we explain by looking at how the "typical" story is crafted in each topic area and then offering ways that stations can improve on those stories. Most importantly, we show that this kind of coverage will not lose viewers and can actually increase audience and ultimately revenues.

COVERAGE OF CRIME

If there is one area where a station might want to alter its coverage it is crime. Crime stories make up nearly one-quarter (24%) of all stories broadcast. Moreover, crime stories are most likely to be first in a newscast. Whether this kind of attention is warranted is a valid question. In terms of audience appeal, crime stories get nearly identical ratings as noncrime stories. And this is true whether or not the story is local or national. But because of local TV's focus on crime, learning to cover the topic successfully may help stations to better build and hold their audiences.

The Typical Crime News Story

The typical crime story is highly local. Of all the topics we studied, crime is the second most likely to be local in nature (social issue topics are first). This may not be surprising given the fact that audiences are more concerned with crime in their immediate communities rather than crimes elsewhere. Crime coverage is also more likely to be sensational than

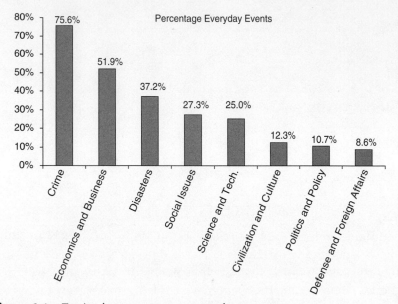

Figure 6.1. Topics by percentage, everyday events.

other story topics, with the lone exception of disasters. Yet, despite the fact that they are most likely to come at the beginning of the newscast and are highly sensationalized, crime stories also tend to be about relatively common incidents. In our sample, we found that 76% of crime stories covered things that happen every day. In other words, there's not much "new" in crime news, nor in the way stations try to cover it. (See Figure 6.1.)

There's generally little thought or planning behind crime stories. Indeed, crime stories are much more likely than others to be aired as a response to a breaking event (second, again, only to disaster coverage). And crime stories tend to be less enterprising – leaving the viewer only with details of what happened, but not why. Is this the type of crime coverage audiences want, or can more in-depth coverage sustain, or even build, the TV audience? (See Figure 6.2.)

Making Crime Pay

Although crime stories get similar ratings to other types of stories, our research found that covering certain kinds of crime and using a broader variety of approaches to crime coverage can result in better ratings. That would begin with skipping some of the everyday, "garden variety" crime that dominates coverage. We found that stories focusing on ordinary

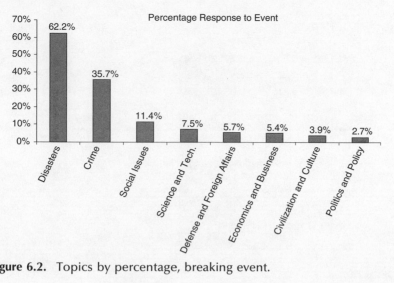

Figure 6.2. Topics by percentage, breaking event.

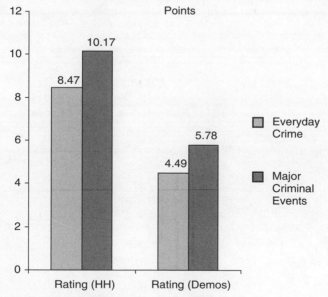

Figure 6.3. Everyday crime vs. major criminal events.

crimes outnumbered those involving major criminal events by a ratio of more than 3 to 1. Stories that focused on commonplace crimes, however, lost 1.7 household rating points and 1.3 demo rating points compared with major crime stories.[1] (See Figure 6.3.)

Moreover, the notion that crime must "bleed to succeed" is not supported by the facts. Everyday crime stories, the kind normally focused on

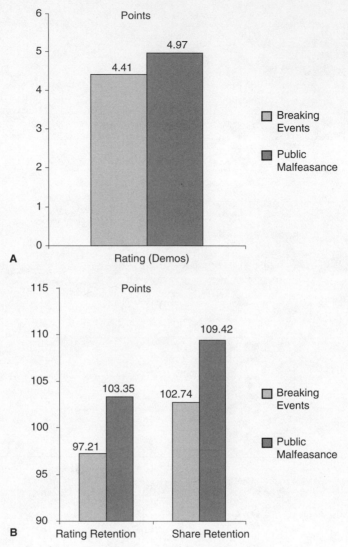

Figure 6.4. Breaking crime news vs. public malfeasance.

shootings and stabbings, are likely to *lose* viewers – about three-fifths of a rating point among the most desired demographics (men and women in the 18–49 and 25–54 age range) – when compared with stories about unusual or wide-reaching crime, such as malfeasance by public officials. Crime stories that focus on breaking events lose ratings from and barely retain the market share of the lead-in program, whereas the stories that focus on public malfeasance build the audience in both categories.[2] (See Figure 6.4.)

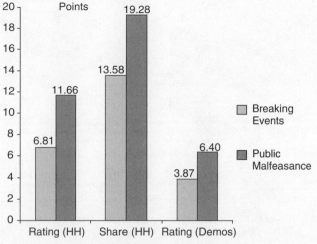

Figure 6.5. Major crime beats celebrity crime with viewers.

When it came to the subgenre of celebrity crime, we saw even less viewer interest. Counter to the conventional wisdom, viewers liked celebrity crime stories least of all the crime stories we studied. When celebrity crime was compared with substantive, major criminal events, the celebrity stories fared exceptionally poorly. Major crime stories gained 4.8 rating points, 5.7 share points, and two and one-half prime demographic points more than celebrity crime stories. And while celebrity crime stories lost ratings from the lead-in program, major crime stories significantly built on the lead-in audience (major crime stories improved on the lead-in rating by 12%, whereas celebrity stories lost 15% of the lead-in program's ratings).[3] (See Figure 6.5.)

Enterprising Crime

Viewers appreciate enterprise journalism. When stations take the time to go out and investigate stories, get interviews, and put the newsmakers on the air, audiences tune in and stay tuned. The same is true when these methods are applied to crime stories.

Given the choice between quickly reacting to a crime event – "spraying" the scene and passing on a few facts – or airing an investigative report that offers background, develops characters, and addresses a larger theme, the more complete story is likely to get better ratings. When we compare longer stories (60 seconds or more) that report the details of a criminal investigation with short stories (30 seconds or less) that are merely snapshots of an incident, the longer, more thoughtful

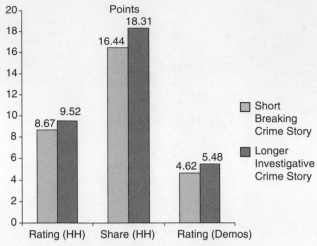

Figure 6.6. Long and thoughtful beats short and breaking.

reports get .85 of a rating point, 1.85 share points, and .85 of a demographic rating point more than a short story devoted to "spot news" coverage of an unanticipated crime or incident.[4] (See Figure 6.6.)

Crime in the Balance: Sources, Opinions, and Experts

As with other topics, viewers appreciate a balance of sources and views in crime stories and like to hear from "expert" sources. Audiences tune in when reporters take the time to get multiple sources to provide a mix of opinions. When sourcing is more extensive, stories gain one-third of a rating point, six-tenths of a share point, and one-quarter of a rating point among the young demographic groups over crime stories that provide no sourcing at all.[5] (See Figure 6.7.)

And source expertise is a plus. When reporters sought out multiple sources and multiple viewpoints from experts, their crime stories scored more than one-half of a rating point, more than one full share point, and four-tenths of a demographic rating point more than when the story featured uncredentialed sources and presented an unbalanced set of opinions.[6] (See Figure 6.8.)

Don't Sensationalize Crime

If sensationalized visuals really did "hook" an audience, we would expect them to work in crime stories. However, when we analyzed sensationalized visuals – visuals that are repeated beyond the point at which they add

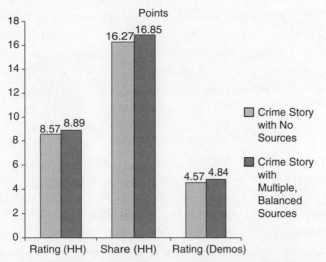

Figure 6.7. Multiple and balanced sources help crime stories.

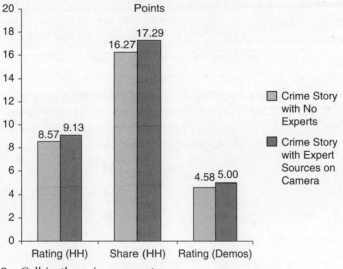

Figure 6.8. Call in the crime experts.

information – we found no significant difference between those that used the visuals and those that did not. Sensationalized crime stories showed a tendency to get slightly (though not significantly) lower ratings than stories without them. When stations repeatedly air images such as flashing lights and yellow police tape when covering crime to excite people rather than inform, they are not helping themselves. Our data suggest they might even be hurting themselves – and scaring the community as well. Stories

employing these visuals have been shown to make audiences disproportionately fearful about becoming victims of violent crime in their
communities (Bryant, Carveth, and Brown 1981). Thus by avoiding
overuse of eye candy video, stations would help their relationship with
viewers, do better journalism, and perform a public service.

Community Relevance

Audiences want crime coverage that deals with important institutions in
their area, not random, common street crime. A crime story that focuses
on an important community institution gets three-quarters of a rating
and share point, and nearly one-half of a rating point more among
younger demographic groups than the merely "interesting" crime story.[7]

But stories don't have to be about major community institutions to be
successful with viewers. Stories can also explain how seemingly random
incidents impact the community. It's unlikely, for example, that a station
would assign a reporter to do a story on a "smash and grab" automobile
break-in. But if that occurrence is used to illustrate a larger problem, with
the reporter providing the facts and figures of where break-ins occur and
how they affect local auto insurance rates, the incident becomes relevant
to a much larger segment of the viewing audience. (See Figure 6.9.)

In addition to allowing the reporting process to work its magic, stations
will be rewarded if they apply to crime stories the editorial standards and
routines that govern other kinds of news. For example, when reporters

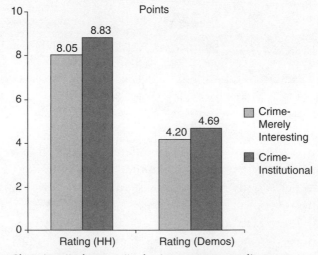

Figure 6.9. Showing "relevance" of crime attracts audience.

pitch stories about *nonviolent* crime (crimes against property make up about three-quarters of all crime in the United States, according to the Bureau of Justice Statistics[8]), they often will have to demonstrate why the subject is relevant to viewers. This isn't a bad practice. It makes reporters think harder about how to frame the story and what evidence they will need to support the story as they tell it.

In the case of spot news, however, the relevance standard is often waived – just getting some pictures and a few details is usually considered sufficient, especially if it's "late breaking." Yet the fact that something bad happened and the station has the video does not build viewership. Without context or explained relevance, most of the audience will not think the event is important.

Demonstrating relevance may require no more than a few lines of copy. But it often means the reporter will have to put some time into research – although this is increasingly easy given all the information available online. Most important, the audience notices. Stories with data are associated with higher ratings more than stories without hard information.

COVERAGE OF GOVERNMENT AND POLITICS

Coverage of government and politics is often considered a ratings loser on local TV. It is "institutional" news – inherently dull and visually challenged – and too complicated to do in the time constraints local stations face.

Yet there is no doubt that the decisions of local, state, and national government officials can have a much greater and more lasting influence on viewers' lives than stories about yesterday's movie premiere or last night's drive-by shooting. In fact, government and politics stories are more likely than other stories to include an important ingredient of "The Magic Formula" – a focus on ideas, issues, or policies. Government and politics stories are far more likely than nongovernment and politics stories to focus on ideas and issues (25% compared with 11%).

One reason government and politics news has a reputation for boring audiences, and worse, driving them away. It is faulty advice from consultants that prevents newsrooms from considering new ways of covering this kind of news (see Sidebar 6.1, How Faulty Research Leads TV to Misplay Politics). The consequence is that government and politics get disproportionately little coverage compared with their vital importance to viewer's lives. Why do government and politics stories have such a bad reputation, and how can stations report these stories in ways that will improve both the quality of the stories and their audience appeal?

SIDEBAR 6.1

HOW FAULTY RESEARCH LEADS TV TO
MISPLAY POLITICS

A 2002 study by the Project for Excellence in Journalism and Best Practices in Journalism, with the aid of the Pew Research Center for the People and the Press, found that the way market research questions are asked can make all the difference in how viewer interest in local political news is perceived by the newsroom.

A standard survey from one of the nation's major television consulting firms – typical of those used industry-wide – had plenty of targeted questions on whether audiences want specific types of consumer news, including everything from where to shop to how to avoid getting ripped off. There were also questions to gauge interest in subjects from parenting tips to pet care. But the question about politics was put as follows: "How interested are you in news reports about issues and activities in government and politics?" The less specific the question is, the less useful the answer, according to polling professionals. In this case, question's wording about interest in politics was so general that respondents' answers were meaningless, and preditcably, interest was low.

What would happen if the questions about politics were framed as specifically as those about pet care? The Pew Research Center conducted a nationwide poll that included the standard consultant question on politics.[9] Only 29% said they would be very interested in "reports about issues and activities in government and politics." Yet when people were asked whether they'd be interested in "news reports about what government can do to improve the performance of local schools," the percentage of "very interested" jumped to 59%. Similarly, when participants were asked whether they'd be interested in reports on what government could do to ensure that public places were safe from terrorism, the percentage of "very interested" rose to 67%. Similar interest-level percentages were tallied for stories about reducing health-care costs. All of these topics, from schools to health care to public safety, have everything to do with politics and government.[10]

This experiment in research methods suggests at least two lessons:

First, the research that has dominated TV consulting about covering public life is faulty. The vague and ambiguous standard questions on politics are inadequate measures of what the public wants – they will inevitably generate low levels of interest due to their lack of specificity. They are less social science than self-fulfilling prophecy.

Second, the reframed questions offer a guide for TV journalists about how to make stories about public life more relevant and more popular. Journalists should frame stories about government and politics in a way that is relevant to people's lives – how government controversies affect their schools, their health, and their safety. Reporters should connect the dots between the problems that people face with what government is doing or could be doing about these problems. Journalists ought to focus on people and their problems, not politicians and theirs. As ratings for local TV news decline, setting aside old-style consulting and doubtful research can help stations to navigate an increasingly difficult future.

– Tom Rosenstiel

Making News about Government and Politics More Successful

Let's begin by examining the conventional wisdom that government and politics stories do not build audience. To test that assumption, we compared the ratings for government and politics stories with all other kinds of stories. In the five years of our study, we analyzed the content of 3,239 government/politics stories, accounting for 9.7% of the 33,911 local TV news stories in our sample. What did we learn?

First, we discovered that stories about government and politics are not poison. They got about the same ratings as other stories among all households and the important young demographic groups. It made no difference whether government/politics stories aired early or late or in a large or small market. We also found that the government/politics stories actually had a slight edge in holding the lead-in share and rating over other kinds of stories – about 1.7% more of their lead-in rating and share. So, the premise that government and politics coverage drives audiences away is not supported by the evidence.

In spite of the generally low esteem newsrooms give government/politics stories, they aired twice as many in the presidential election year of 2000 as they did in any other year of our five-year study. So newsrooms apparently believe that sometimes government/politics stories attract audiences. (See Figure 6.10.)[11]

The Typical Story about Government and Politics

To try to understand how government and politics stories should be played, we identified five main story types: what is going on in the mayor

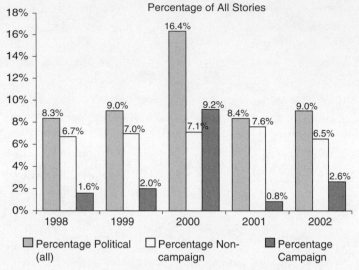

Figure 6.10.   Political stories by year: campaign vs. noncampaign.

or governor's office (administrative action); in the legislature or city council (legislative action); in various agencies of government, such as the Food and Drug Administration or the state Environmental Protection Agency (agency action); government and politics in general; and finally, stories about election campaigns.

Viewing those types more broadly, the two most common categories of stories were about governance (44%) and electoral politics (27%). Governance stories were made up of stories that addressed government or politics in general, as well as stories about legislative, administrative agency, or executive action (17%, 15%, and 12%, respectively).[12]

Most governance and campaign stories are about pre-arranged events (governance stories 75.6% and campaign stories 63.2%). Instead of going out and getting a governance story, newsrooms respond to the offerings of government or campaign public relations operations for coverage. And 41% of the time when stations respond to one of these pre-arranged events, no reporter is seen on the screen. Why are government/politics stories presented this way?

First, newsrooms find it easier to allocate resources if they can plan the newscast as much as possible in advance, so pre-arranged events have an advantage. In addition, pre-arranged events are usually easier to cover than other kinds of stories because the events' organizers do a lot of the work. Knowing that interesting visuals are keys to getting a story aired, organizers turn press conferences into "media events" where the

Table 6.1. Journalistic enterprise: political stories vs. nonpolitical stories

Level of Enterprise	Political Stories		Nonpolitical Stories	
	Stories	Percentage	Stories	Percentage
Station-initiated investigation	20	0.62	337	1.10
Report of investigation by others	26	0.80	437	1.42
Interview with reporter's questions	109	3.37	1,094	3.57
News series (non-investigative)	37	1.14	1,101	3.59
Response to a spontaneous event	87	2.69	7,007	22.84
Response to pre-arranged event	2,337	72.15	13,729	44.76
Wire or feed from other source	557	17.20	6,294	20.52
Attributed to other news organization	31	0.96	415	1.35
Other	35	1.08	258	0.84
TOTAL	3,239	100.00	30,672	100.00

pictures dominate – making the surrounding area and props both camera-friendly and interesting. At the national level, presidents are successful in gaining media attention to bill signings by moving the events into the White House Rose Garden, or even National Parks or other backdrops. Local media stunts used to stimulate coverage have included turkey awards to politicians on Thanksgiving and parents pouring soda down a drain to protest soft drink sales at an elementary school. People who want news coverage have learned that images or conflict drive coverage. Airing contrived visuals and focusing on conflicts, however, have the potential for turning viewers off government and politics altogether (Patterson 1994; Cappella and Jamieson 1997). Our analysis shows that political stories do not need to be spiced up by staged visuals to sell.

As we noted in Chapter 5, viewers tend to watch newscasts that feature reporters going out and getting the story (journalistic enterprise) instead of reporting pre-packaged events. We found, however, that very few stories on any topic in our sample involved a high level of journalistic enterprise. The lack of enterprise particularly characterized government and politics stories. For example, station-initiated investigations accounted for a mere 1.1% of all stories but only half that amount (.62%) of government and politics stories. (See Table 6.1.)

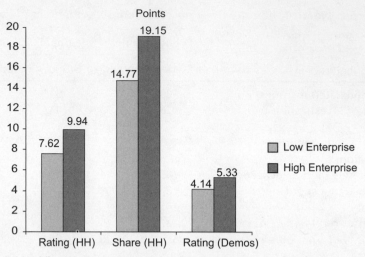

Figure 6.11. Viewers want enterprise in government and politics coverage.

The bulk of government/politics stories are about pre-arranged ("day-book") events – a whopping 72%. Reporters generally let government and politics stories come to them instead of going out and investigating them. Failing to fulfill the press's watchdog role is detrimental to citizens, but it also decreases the size of the local news audience.

In Chapter 5, we described how we coded "enterprise," an assessment of the level of journalistic effort in each story. Stories with higher levels of journalistic enterprise (such as investigations) were given higher scores and lower levels of enterprise (such as running feeds from other sources) were given lower scores (see Appendix B for value coding).

We found that as enterprise scores increased among government and politics stories, so did ratings. The ratings differences between doing a low-enterprise and a high-enterprise political story were dramatic. Stories that reflected the highest levels of enterprise generated household ratings two and one-third points higher than stories reflecting the lowest level of enterprise. Stories with the highest enterprise scores also generated a share that was 4.4 points above stories with the lowest scores. And demo ratings that were 1.2 rating points higher than the lowest enterprise quality stories.[13] (See Figure 6.11.)

Viewers want to see investigations into government and politics and high-quality reporting when it comes to important political issues. They reward stations that put the effort into stories about local government. Let's look at the type of journalistic enterprise that worked best in getting higher ratings – interviews.

Interviews in which the reporter asks substantive questions of the newsmaking politician or government official were the most popular government and politics stories with viewers. To demonstrate this effect, Figure 6.12 shows the differences between a high effort story – an interview with a newsmaker in which there is substantive questioning by the reporter – and easier, low enterprise ways of covering the story, such as taking a wire feed or covering a pre-arranged event. In every case, the interview outperformed the other "easier" methods by at least two household rating points, four household share points, and at least one full rating point more among the younger viewers for whom advertisers are willing to pay a premium.[14] So the first step to making political coverage more successful with viewers is moving beyond reacting to the daybook and putting more effort, or enterprise, into the reporting.

Balanced Coverage

Our analysis of The Magic Formula suggests that doing longer stories that include multiple sources with various viewpoints also can enhance ratings. That may not be surprising considering that news about government and politics is especially sensitive to balance. But in-depth reporting not only costs more, it takes time away from other potentially audience-building stories. Is it worth the effort to do this type of reporting?

We isolated all of the government and politics stories that provided multiple sources and a mix of opinions in coverage. There were 721 such items, amounting to 22.3% of government and politics stories. That number was more than twice as high as the 9.3% of nongovernment or politics stories that managed to combine a mix of sources and opinions. The greater balance of government and politics stories suggests that local news staffs are already aware of the need for a range of views in covering this topic.

We compared multiply sourced to one-sided government and politics stories to see which type of story garnered more viewership. The result? Balanced government and politics stories received better ratings than the same category of stories with only one point of view. The balanced stories with multiple views recorded household ratings nine-tenths of a point higher, 1.8 share points higher, and one-half of a demographic rating point higher than the single view, poorly sourced stories.[15] (See Figure 6.13.)

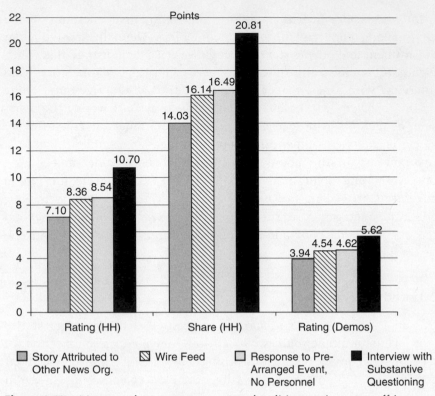

Figure 6.12. More work on government and politics stories pays off in more viewers.

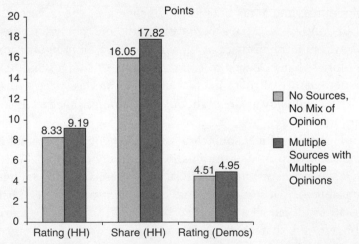

Figure 6.13. In covering government and politics, a mix of opinion really matters to viewers.

The conclusion is that to get better ratings, reporters should seek multiple sources in their coverage of political stories. Viewers need a mix of opinions and sources to understand the meaning and significance of the story. This approach translates into better ratings.

Adding Credibility

Because government/politics stories often involve controversy, it is important for reporters to assure their audiences that these stories are credible. There are other ways to do this besides multiple sourcing.

We ranked the level of credibility of each government and politics story, giving the highest credibility scores to stories where experts were interviewed on camera, lower credibility scores to stories in which there was merely a reference to such experts, even lower credibility scores for interviews with major actors in the story but no experts, still lower credibility scores to interviews with the "person on the street" (except for polling stories where the person on the street *was* the expert), and the lowest credibility scores for stories in which there was an unnamed source or no source at all.

What we found was that government and politics stories with the highest credibility scores – on-camera interviews with credentialed experts – outperformed the lowest credibility stories – no source at all – by 1.8 household rating points, more than four share points, and nine-tenths of a rating point among younger viewers.[16] (See Figure 6.14.)

Thus, credible political stories, that is, stories that include experts or refer to what they have to say, actually attract viewers. Multiple sources and expert interviews make government and politics stories more – not less – interesting to viewers.

Governance

We found that in terms of commercial success, governance – stories that addressed government or politics in general, as well as stories about legislative, administrative agency, or executive action – is a winning topic. Compared with other kinds of government and politics stories, coverage about what the government was actually doing earned over three-quarters of a rating point more, one and two-thirds of a share points more, and .44 of a rating point more among the important demographic groups. Governance stories also retained over 5% more of their lead-in audience compared with other kinds of government and

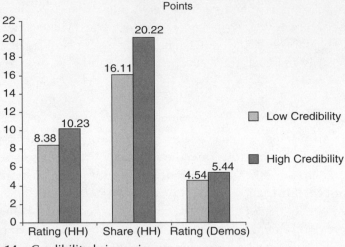

Figure 6.14. Credibility brings viewers.

politics stories.[17] As with all of our findings, this proved to be true irrespective of the time slot, the network affiliation of the station, the size of the market, or the year the story was aired. Viewers want to know how the actions of local government affect their lives. They tune in when this is explained, they tune out when it is not. (See Figure 6.15.)

Stories about governance were almost evenly split between those focused on policy and those focused on strategy.

In fact, surprisingly, strategy edged out policy as a focus of government stories (37.5% vs. 33.3%, respectively). It should be noted that the strategy focus, or what some call "horse-race coverage," plays a large role in all government/politics story types. It is an even bigger part of the election stories, as detailed in the next section. But when we look at the use of the strategy frame in noncampaign stories, we find no evidence that its use either helps or hurts viewership. (See Figure 6.16.) In other words, when covering what the government is doing – after the election – the tactics and strategy will not attract more audience.

Campaigns and Elections

When it comes to strategy, however, campaign stories are very different from governance stories. The content of campaign stories on local news is typical of what scholars have described for many years: Most of the coverage of campaigns and elections is about "the game"– what strategies the campaigns are using and who is ahead or behind in the polls. In our sample we found that 9 out of 10 campaign stories (90%) were about

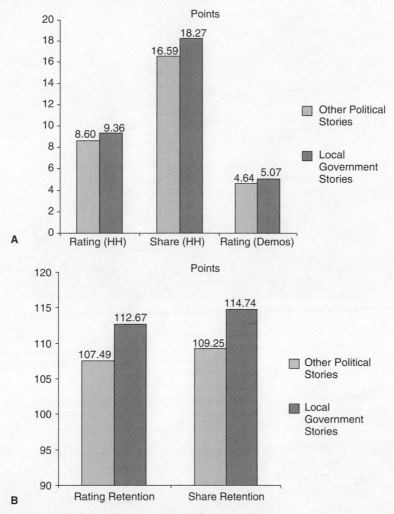

Figure 6.15. Local government pieces bring audience ... and keep it.

strategy. By contrast, only 4% focused on the candidates' policies and ideas, or their stances on the issues. Of course, this horse-race coverage doesn't help citizens choose a candidate unless they want to pick a winner.

Journalists have reason to cover campaigns like a game. An election, after all, is a contest. There are winners and losers. Many journalists presume that using sports as a metaphor for political conflict makes the story more interesting. But this approach leads journalists to report campaigns as if they were "only a game" and not about choices that substantially affect viewers' lives. The "game frame" trivializes politics

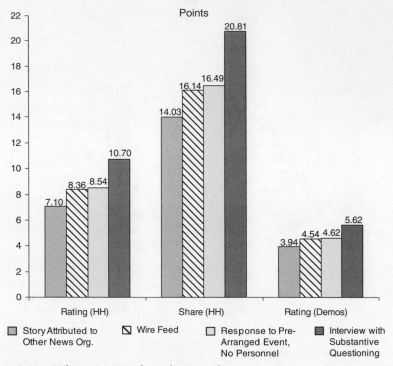

Figure 6.16. Where issues play a larger role.

and distances campaigns from voters' real concerns. Furthermore, the game frame encourages reporters to second-guess the strategic choices and political motivations of candidates, which gives campaign coverage a cynical cast (Patterson 1994).

Focusing on the horse race also offers cover for reporters. Sidestepping the substance of policy proposals and positions helps reporters avoid charges of bias. Reporters cannot be seen as taking ideological sides if all they talk about is the venal motivations of all candidates and the respective styles of their campaigns. Moreover, it is easier and quicker to cover polls and strategies than to cover issues, which often requires background research into specific problems and policies.

Stories about campaigns and elections in our sample represented both national elections (46%) and local elections (54%). We found that national campaign stories were slightly more likely than local campaign stories to be about political strategy (94.5% vs. 88.0%). Almost all of the national strategy-oriented stories, 83.9%, came from network wire feeds. Local campaign stories generally exhibited a different level of enterprise than national stories. They were predominantly covered by having a reporter show up at a pre-arranged campaign event (51.6% of local election stories). Local stories were less likely than national stories to have experts on camera for an interview to explain the relevance of the story (54.3% national vs. 29.7% local). Perhaps this is because reporters believe that local campaign stories do not need to be explained as much as national stories. Or perhaps this is because the national stories come from network feeds, and the networks have better resources for tracking down experts for interviews. Because they contained fewer interviews, local stories included fewer sources and fewer points of view than national ones. Among the national stories, 38.6% had three or more sources, whereas only 15.9% of the local stories had three or more sources. Also, 33.5% of national stories contained a mix of opinions, whereas 29.5% of local campaign stories did so. How did these trends in coverage of campaigns and elections affect ratings?

The most significant finding in our analysis of campaign and election stories was that focusing on strategy actually *loses* audience compared with another focus, such as candidate qualities or debates about issues. Campaign stories that focused on strategy got one and one-third fewer rating points, nearly three fewer share points, and three-quarters of young demographic rating points fewer than campaign stories that focused on aspects of the campaign other than the horse race. Similarly, stories that focused on strategy were less able to retain the rating and share of their lead-in programs by 10%.[18] (See Figure 6.17.)

If the game frame is not a winner in campaign stories, what does the audience want? We found that the way to boost ratings when covering campaigns is by focusing on the relevant ideas, issues, and policies that are at the heart of elections. Choosing to focus on the substance of the campaign yields an extra one and one-third rating points, 2.9 share points, and .85 rating points among the young demos.[19] (See Figure 6.18.)

The lesson here is that stations should not be afraid to educate viewers about the impact of the election. Normally a "show and tell" story is considered of lesser value as news because it does not add new information. Our analysis suggests that a story does not always have to contain new information, so long as the information in the story is new to the viewer – as it often is in the context of an ongoing campaign with complicated issues in play. Rather than focusing on gamesmanship, reporters on the campaign trail should focus on what the candidates will do once in office, and who they are, the things that can affect viewers' lives.

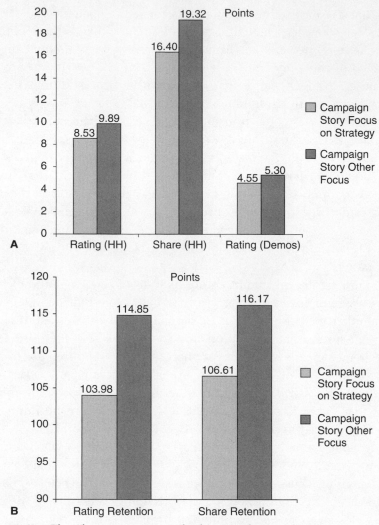

A

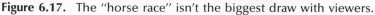

B

Figure 6.17. The "horse race" isn't the biggest draw with viewers.

Conclusion on News about Government and Politics

Stations generally do a better job of sourcing political stories than other stories. But they could do even more and air political stories more often to good effect. When it comes to politics, there is no need to make the viewers "eat their spinach." Newsrooms do not have to force-feed their audiences for a station to fulfill its democratic mandate. People are interested in government and politics when the relevance of a story is explained to them, when news is balanced, and when evidence and

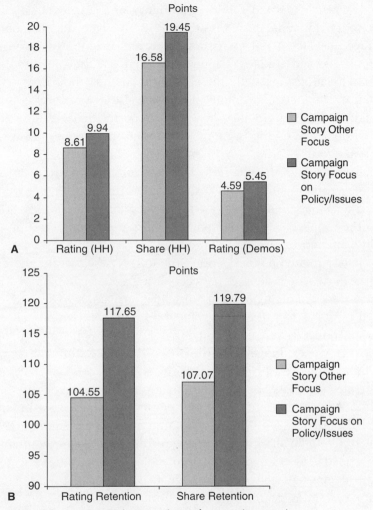

Figure 6.18. Viewers want issue-oriented campaign stories.

experts are used to support the story. Better political reporting means better ratings for the station.

Nor are people merely interested in who is ahead or behind in an election campaign. They want to know how the results of the election will affect their lives. Without information about the stakes of elections and what the conflicts are about, citizens can be turned off by political conflict. Stations that choose to cover the horse race instead of the issues may be turning voters off to politics and their newscast. If politics is turning people off, it may be the coverage, not the topic, that is at fault.

To do government and politics news right – and get viewers – a station needs to provide some extra resources to give viewers detailed, balanced coverage that focuses on the issues. Reporters assigned to government/ politics beats need time to track down the experts. They have to develop personal relationships with these experts so that they can get their assistance when facing deadlines. Reporters also need access to the facts to make their stories credible. And lastly, reporters have to have time to do their own investigations. All of these things require training as well as time and effort.

Considering all of the criteria we isolated for crafting successful stories about government and politics, it should not be surprising that we found that stations that aired longer political stories got better ratings, but only when they applied our keys to political story treatment (most of which, notably, are part of our Magic Formula).

For poorly treated political stories, the longer they are, the more audience they lose. The difference between airing a 30-second, poorly treated political story (following none of our guidelines) and a 90-second, poorly treated story is a loss of eight-tenths of a rating point among all households, and one full share point and one-half a rating point among younger viewers. However, longer government and politics stories, when done well, build audience. The difference between a 30-second and a 90-second well-treated story is a boost in household rating by two and one-quarter points, a share increase of nearly four points, and an increase in younger viewers by one and one-third demo rating points. (See Figure 6.19.)

Obviously, to do all of the things we recommend, a station might have to expand the amount of time devoted to politics. But long political stories that are reported well can have a significant and positive impact on ratings and are clearly worth the effort.

COVERAGE OF HEALTH

There can be no doubt regarding the importance of news about health and medicine in viewers' daily lives. As a result, health stories are often heavily promoted. Still, we found sparse health coverage, only half the amount of coverage of government and politics. Furthermore, health stories are generally positioned toward the end of the newscast. As we found with government and politics, health stories overall do no better or worse than other stories in terms of viewership. So how are health stories generally covered, and how could they be improved so that they will help build audience?

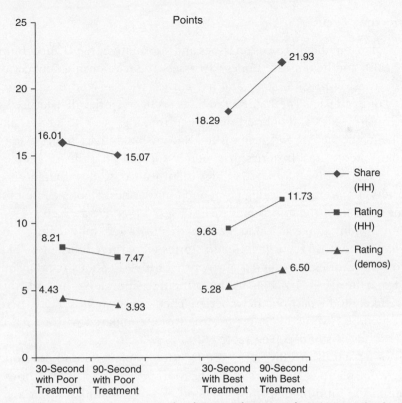

Figure 6.19. With government and politics, it takes more than time to win viewers.

The Typical Health News Story

Health stories make up a small proportion of local TV news despite their obvious importance to viewers. In our sample, we found 1,367 health stories, making up 4% of all stories in newscasts. Health stories were slightly more likely to be local than national: 801 (58.6%) local items compared with 566 (41.4%) national items. Health stories, by their very nature, are often not time sensitive and almost never are "late-breaking." Therefore, they get slotted late in the program so they can be heavily promoted throughout the newscast.

In spite of their lack of immediacy, health stories, for the most part, can be classified as important news. In our sample, health stories were five times more likely than other stories to focus on ideas, issues, and policy (56.5% vs. 10.9%, respectively). Health pieces were also three times as likely as others to focus on substantive trends (6.2% vs. 1.9%, respectively). An example of a "substantive trend" health story is a decline in deaths from a particular disease as a result of a new treatment.

Hard News Focus

To what extent did this focus on issues and substantive trends affect ratings for health and health-care stories? To assess the relationship between the seriousness of a health story and its ratings, we classified each story in terms of its impact. The highest rankings went to stories that focused on health-care issues and policies, mid-range rankings went to stories about trends in the health and medical fields, and low-impact scores went to human-interest health stories that merely focused on ordinary people or celebrities. We found that the high-significance stories gained three-quarters of a household rating point and almost one-half of a demo rating point more than the low-significance stories.[20] (See Figure 6.20.)

Our examination also found that health stories generally featured high levels of enterprise reporting. Health stories were three times more likely than other stories to be based on reports of investigations (station-initiated or otherwise), twice as likely to include interviews, and six times more likely to be part of a news series. They also were less likely merely to respond to events (39% for health stories compared with 69.5% for other kinds of stories). (See Table 6.2.)

In other words, health stories are frequently planned and developed. When not planned, health stories are more likely than other stories to come in the form of feeds from the station's ownership group or a syndicated content supplier.

In terms of credibility, more than half of all heath stories (53.2%) included interviews with experts, such as doctors. Only 36.7% of nonhealth stories included expert interviews. Health pieces were also more than twice as likely to reference authoritative data – such as disease statistics – than other stories (13.9% vs. 5.5%). And health reports more often provided multiple sources of information. More than 20% of them offered three or more sources compared with just under 14% for other stories. So if health stories have many of the hallmarks of The Magic Formula – significantly more so than other stories – why are their ratings so similar to other stories?

One of the possible reasons for the unimpressive ratings may be lack of balance. Nearly half (49.4%) of all health stories presented only one view of the story. That was true of only 23.1% of all other stories. This suggests that many health stories simply announce a new treatment or medicine, with little critical analysis. These health stories may amount to medical advertisements. They may even be produced or based on feeds from drug companies or hospital companies.

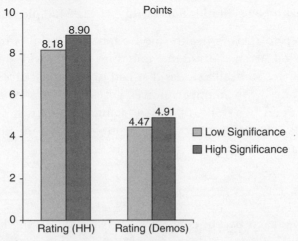

Figure 6.20. Health story significance and ratings.

Table 6.2. Journalistic enterprise: health stories vs. nonhealth stories

	Health Stories		Nonhealth Stories	
Level of Enterprise	Stories	Percentage	Stories	Percentage
Station-initiated investigation	33	2.41	324	1.00
Report of investigation by others	49	3.58	414	1.27
Interview with reporter's questions	92	6.73	1,111	3.41
News series (non-investigative)	236	17.26	902	2.77
Response to a spontaneous event	97	7.10	6,997	21.50
Response to pre-arranged event	437	31.97	15,629	48.02
Wire or feed from other source	393	28.75	6,458	19.84
Attributed to other news organization	17	1.24	429	1.32
Other	13	0.95	280	0.86
TOTAL	1,367	100.00	32,544	100.00

Health stories are also often geared to one specific subgroup of the population, such as the elderly or middle-aged women. We found that 23.4% of all health stories were targeted at a demographic subgroup, whereas only 2.3% of other stories had such targeted appeal. So how can health coverage be improved?

Making Health News Stories Successful – Using Multiple Sources

The first step to making health stories more successful is making them more balanced. We compared the ratings for health stories that had two or more sources to health stories that had one or no sources. We found that the stories with multiple sources got four-tenths of a household rating point and two-thirds of a share point more than stories that had one or no sources. When it comes to health stories on the news, viewers like to get a second opinion.[21] (See Figure 6.21.)

Relevance

Another important part of doing a health story is making it relevant to the viewing audience. We found that audiences preferred medical breakthrough stories that explain and detail impacts on people's lives as opposed to simple lifestyle health tips. National stories about health and medicine that made their relevance clear scored well – gaining two more household rating points, four more share points, and 1.6 more rating points among younger demographic groups than health stories that were merely personally useful.[22] Apparently the audience has a high threshold for "news they can use"– perhaps because such health tips are numerous and easily ignored. (See Figure 6.22.)

Provide Data

Stories about health and medicine can sometimes be difficult to understand. Moreover, the stories need to be very credible because they may involve life or death decisions. We compared audience ratings of the health/medicine stories that provided facts and statistics with those that did not. We found that stories that provided facts got three-quarters of a household rating point, 1.7 share points, and .42 demo rating points more than stories without data.[23] Viewers are savvy – they want to have information to back up claims made in medical stories. (See Figure 6.23.)

Take Time to Explain the Story

Because stories about health and medicine are often beyond the knowledge of the casual viewer, newsrooms need to take time to educate

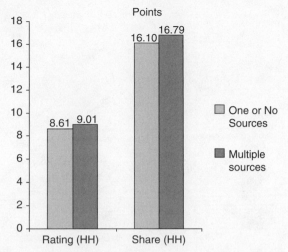

Figure 6.21. A second opinion helps health report ratings.

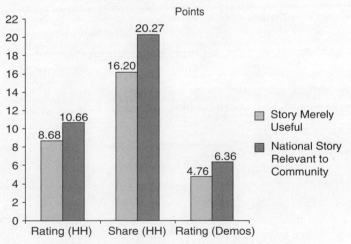

Figure 6.22. Viewers want real news they can use in health stories.

the audience by explaining the story clearly. We found that taking time to do health stories more completely also can help ratings.

There was a large variation in the length of the health stories we looked at. Some stories were as short as 11 seconds, whereas one story was 6 minutes and 42 seconds long. We divided the health stories in our sample into three equal groups based on length. The first group, the shortest, ranged from 11 to 29 seconds. The middle group ranged from 30

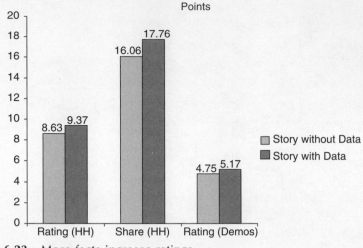

Figure 6.23. More facts increase ratings.

to 99 seconds. And the longest group was 100 seconds or longer. The difference in ratings between the shortest (11–29 seconds) and longest (100+ seconds) groups was more than half a rating point, .84 share points, and three-tenths of a rating point among the younger demographics. This is not to say that stations should simply run longer stories.[24] Our other suggestions are critical to improving audience. (See Figure 6.24.) But following them may also require making stories longer.

Conclusion on Health News

Our findings challenge the notion that stories about health and medicine are only interesting to older viewers or demographic subgroups. Health and medicine news has mass appeal, even among younger viewers. Focusing on the hard news aspects of stories, getting multiple sources, finding the community relevance of nationally important stories, providing facts and statistics, and taking time to explain the story helps to increase the audience when airing health news. (See Figure 6.25.)

As in other areas, we found that length seemed to help ratings for health stories. This was because, in many cases, stations covered health the right way: doing enterprise, getting data, tracking down sources, and the like. When we take a closer look at the relationship of length to the hallmarks of good coverage, we find that story length only works in building audience when health stories are covered well (i.e., employ The Magic Formula). Figure 6.25 demonstrates that health stories covered

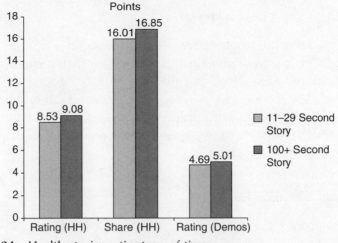

Figure 6.24. Health stories – tincture of time.

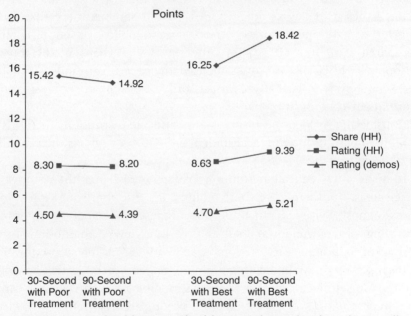

Figure 6.25. Longer health stories build ratings but only when done well.

poorly lose audience as they get longer. By contrast, a health story covered well gains three-quarters of a household rating point, more than two share points, and one-half of a demo rating point when expanded from 30 to 90 seconds.

COVERAGE OF EDUCATION

News that affects the schools in our local communities is tremendously important. The stories personally affect everyone with a child in school and the children themselves. But the influence of education reporting goes beyond students and parents. One-third of all public sector employment is in education. Education affects local quality of life and, on a larger scale, economic competitiveness. So how does local TV news treat this important topic?

The Typical Education News Story

In our sample, we found 884 stories about education (2.6% of all stories) – about half the coverage of health news. Education coverage is highly localized; only 22 education stories dealt with national issues. Like health news, education news is more than twice as likely to be about issues or policy as other stories. In our sample, more than one-quarter of education stories (27.6%) were policy or issue related, compared with only 12.3% of other stories. Perhaps predictably, a whopping 31.8% of the stories focused on civic institutions – notably the school system itself. By contrast, only 7.5% of other news stories were about civic institutions.

Considering its focus on ideas, policy, and the institutions themselves combined with its intense localism, education coverage has the potential to be exemplary.

In some ways education stories were reported better than stories in other areas, but there were shortcomings. It's true that education stories show almost twice as much of the highest hallmarks of enterprise reporting – investigations and substantive interviews – than other stories (7.1% of education stories compared with 3.7% of non-education stories). However, we found an inordinate tendency in education coverage for reporters to be reactive – to be responding to events such as press conferences (71.2% of education stories, compared with 46.7% of other stories). We will explore what this means for ratings in the next section.

In terms of story credibility, education stories were largely similar to other stories. Expert sources appeared in 19.9% of education stories, compared with 16.5% of other stories. And stories about education were just slightly more likely than other stories to have hard facts (7.6% vs. 6.0%). Education stories featured more sources of information than other stories. They were more likely to feature two or more sources as other stories (42.2% of education stories, compared with 29.5% of other stories). And they were also more likely than other stories to present a mix of opinions, with 27.7% of education stories having a mix of opinions compared with 15.8% of other stories.

Considering the extra effort reporters put into providing more sources and points of view in education coverage, it is not surprising that education stories were longer than other stories. In our sample, the average education story was 70 seconds, compared with 61 seconds for all other stories. Obviously, education stories already employ many of the features we recommend for building audiences.

Making Education News Stories Successful

As a group, education stories get nearly identical ratings as other types of stories. This was true for all our different commercial success indicators: Household Rating and Share, Demographic Ratings, and Rating and Share Retention. What can be done to make education stories more attractive to viewers? One thing that stood out was enterprise.

Education Success: Getting Interviews

When it comes to education news, viewers particularly like to see reporters going out and getting interviews. They want to hear the story from the newsmaker – they want to be taught by an authoritative figure. We found that when a station sends a reporter out to get an interview as part of an education story, it generates better ratings than if the station had simply sent a photographer out to shoot a pre-arranged event. Stories with interviews got ratings that were two and one-quarter household rating points, 4.6 share points, and 1.2 demographic points more than stories that were covered merely as footage of a pre-arranged event.[25] The advantage of putting real people into an education story is that it brings home and enlivens what can otherwise be a dull and distant report. (See Figure 6.26.)

Education stories are an important source of news just waiting to be covered. But to cover education right, reporters need to spend more time in class. They need to better understand the complex issues surrounding public and private schools and to do that they should consult the experts. They should have little trouble finding them because every parent, teacher, and student knows something about the schools.

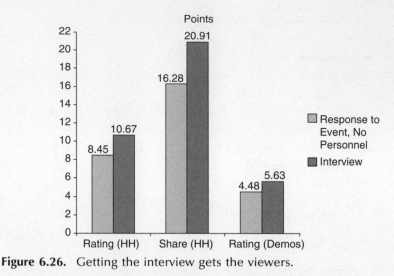

Figure 6.26. Getting the interview gets the viewers.

SIDEBAR 6.2

EDUCATION COVERAGE

Of the more than 250 small groups that have completed our newscast "stacking exercise" (described in Chapter 4) only a handful chose the education story (about plans to cut the school budget in the following academic year) as the lead. There were, however, some participants who bucked the trend and viewed education as a priority: "We need to look for stories that affect the most people and education is a hot topic – lots of people care," a TV journalist in one city told us. A newswoman from a station in the Southeast put it this way: "Children are our future. This is the kind of story that defines who we are. The state's reputation rests on this issue. And kids evoke a lot of emotion." But more often stories about schools were put in the middle of the newscast, and usually news staffers decided to give them quick voice-over treatment – exactly the opposite of what viewers want from education stories, according to our research.

At a station in Oklahoma, however, one group moved education to the head of the class. The group comprised four photographers. "Go find some teachers, students, or parents," their spokesman told us. "The desk could have made some calls and lined somebody up. We could explain where the funds that have been cut are going to go and focus on one central character [such as a parent, student, or teacher].

We could show a teacher at home correcting papers or a student at a football game or doing homework to get them in a personal setting. It would be especially good to find a teacher who is on the bubble. And ask them what the announcement means to them. It's really a water cooler story."

It was striking how little time it took four visual thinkers to come up with ways to turn what most saw as an institutional topic with no pictures into a potentially compelling tale. And they did it by employing a fundamental storytelling technique: Choose a strong central character, tell his or her story, and weave the larger story around that individual's experience. To the photojournalists this was no big deal. "We have to do this all the time," said one of them.

– Walter C. Dean

SUMMARY

In the end, there is no single "silver-bullet" for improving coverage and ratings. Different practices work better with different kinds of stories. But ultimately, quality journalism is what sells – even on topics that might appear dry or distant.

To report about government and politics successfully:

- Focus on government – the community problems government is trying to solve and what government is doing about those issues – when covering local politics.
- Do solid enterprise reporting.
- Provide multiple sources that reflect a balance of opinions.
- Use hard information and interview experts on-screen for credibility.
- Focus on issues and ideas in campaigns stories that affect voters instead of the horse race/strategy.

To cover crime successfully:

- Employ enterprise: Explain the story behind the incident – provide background and develop central characters.
- Establish relevance: Place an incident in context – show how it relates to a larger theme, problem, or community institution.
- Broaden sourcing: Seek more points of view and obtain expert testimony or opinion.

To cover health successfully:

- Focus on important issues and substantive trends.
- Use multiple sources.
- Explain relevance: Don't just report a medical breakthrough, show how it affects someone.
- Use data to place information in perspective.
- Take time to explain the story: Go beyond the headline – educate the audience.

To cover education successfully:

- Cover more than announcements: Get ideas from students, parents, teachers, and taxpayers.
- Find the newsmakers, and interview them.
- Shoot stories where education occurs: Go to class; know what's really happening there.

7 Putting It All into Action: Techniques for Changing Newsroom Cultures

At this point you might be thinking: This all sounds good in theory, but how realistic is it? Statistics and quantitative analysis are fine for books or classrooms, but local TV newsrooms are in the real world. In TV, you get results or you get lost. That, after all, is why the average tenure of news directors is something less than two years. The successful get promoted to spread whatever "magic" they have somewhere else. The less successful are sent packing (see Sidebar 7.1, The View from the Hot Seat).

SIDEBAR 7.1

THE VIEW FROM THE HOT SEAT

By Scott Libin

Every news director, general manager, media-company executive, and owner I know encourages, appreciates, and supports quality journalism. As long as it works. "Television news is a product, just like any other," my former boss Rob Hubbard said, according to the Minneapolis *Star Tribune*. "If Target puts something in the store that isn't selling, no matter how good it is, you have to adjust it."

The adjustment Hubbard was referring to began with my 2003 departure as news director from KSTP-TV, the Twin Cities ABC affiliate. Rob and I agreed I wasn't the guy to take the station in the new direction he had chosen: a style a lot like the industry's "live, local and late-breaking" approach.

SIDEBAR 7.1 (continued)

In fairness, my five years at KSTP constitute a pretty good run for a television news director – especially for one whose station stayed in third place for virtually that entire time.

So, what went wrong? If I knew, I'd probably still be running KSTP's newsroom. But in the 20-plus years I've spent reporting, managing, and teaching television news, I have developed some ideas about what's ailing the industry.

Immediacy Trumps All

In newsroom after newsroom where I have spoken with journalists as part of the Committee of Concerned Journalists' "Traveling Curriculum," they say they care most about enterprise, educating the public, and helping viewers make more-informed decisions. Then, when forced by a decision-making exercise to choose a lead story for a fictitious newscast, those same staffers with very few exceptions choose based on what's "new since 6," "happening now," or – above all – "breaking."

Already, the definition of "breaking news" has been stretched dramatically, with some stations even packaging planned events under the rubric. I know of at least one that promises to deliver it every morning. When there isn't true breaking news the station simply picks a routine story and treats it as if it were breaking. Throbbing graphics, alarming sound effects, and stricken-looking reporters add to the effect.

The unfortunate result is diminished viewer response and, eventually, diminished credibility for news operations that use the label too liberally.

There Are Few Truly New Ideas

Or so you'd think watching TV news, anyway. The cutting-edge quickly becomes cliché. Even the expression "out of the box," which once sounded so innovative and iconoclastic, has turned truly trite through over-use. The fact is today's television news products have far more in common than what distinguishes them from one another.

When a station's big, bold initiatives don't generate results quickly enough, it tends to retreat to what it knows how to do: high story count, sensory-bombardment graphics, and a breathless sense of artificial urgency. It's a familiar formula, and we trust viewers won't remember that they didn't like it much last time around.

We Like Our Choices Stark

Color came to television half a century ago, but we in the newsroom are much more at home in a world of black and white. Consultants urge reporters and writers to "find the conflict" in stories, and too often the outcome is a simplistic interpretation of complex issues: heroes and villains, right and wrong, supporters and opponents. Stations make sanctimonious claims to provide "both sides of the story," as if there were only two sides to any story worth telling.

Our biggest bias is not what our critics claim – some supposed liberal agenda or an obsession with negative news. Our biggest bias is that we are most comfortable with the least-complicated situations, issues, and decisions. To paraphrase the old axiom, we tend not to let the facts get in the way of a good story. This is especially true for untidy facts that just confuse what would otherwise be such a straightforward story. We fall for a false dichotomy every time – true or false, always or never, good or bad – focusing almost all of our attention on the far ends of the spectrum. Our reporting too seldom ventures between the poles, where most of life takes place.

Demographics Drive Decisions

Television's dark secret is that it really doesn't value older viewers as much as younger ones. Blame the advertisers who pay the bills: They don't consider anybody over 55 adequately susceptible to the marketing messages TV delivers best. Our target demo, which was once 25 to 54, keeps getting younger. Viewers 18 to 34 are now the most sought-after and the most elusive when it comes to news programming.

For a while, we hoped young singles who saw nothing of relevance in reporting on local communities or public policy would change their ways when they got married, bought homes, started paying property taxes, and began sending their kids off to public schools. So far, not so good. Demographers tell us the habits younger consumers develop between the ages of about 17 and 25 tend to stay with those consumers as they mature. They seem more than happy getting more and more of their news from cable, late-night comedy, and the Internet.

Meanwhile, we in local TV privately, if not publicly, are quite willing to alienate older audiences to attract younger ones. And we've been more effective at the former than the latter.

Before we alienate all of those older viewers, however, we might want to take another look at the buying power of slightly older

SIDEBAR 7.1 (continued)

demographics. I'm not suggesting we give up on finding ways to be more relevant to young viewers. I am suggesting we not abandon the best customers we have in the process.

The pessimistic prognosticators may be right: There may come a day when most markets can't support three or four television stations doing news. There have been some casualties already. There has been a great deal of expansion, too, over the last decade – despite the dire predictions not so many years ago that terrestrial broadcasting itself was on the verge of extinction. We aren't dead yet.

Scott Libin is a member of the leadership and management faculty at the Poynter Institute. He is a former television reporter, anchor, and news director.

So how do you put into action what we used social science tools to discover? Can a station practically apply what we've discovered to improve ratings and profits? Yes, and in this chapter we tell you how.

Our answers don't come from a book or a management consultant, but from TV newsrooms themselves – our discussions with more than 2,000 broadcast journalists in more than 40 stations around the country. In the years we've been conducting trainings in TV newsrooms, we've had the opportunity to observe various station cultures, scrutinize different newsroom systems, and hear firsthand about what does and does not work. What follows are road-tested ideas about putting theory into practice.

LET GO OF THE MYTHS

To produce better content that will really attract viewers, journalists have to first let go of deeply ingrained assumptions about the audience, the medium, and their own abilities. Putting the ideas in this book into action requires an open mind. Because resources are limited, TV news is about making choices. You cannot do "more of everything," much less do it well.

The right choices begin with really letting go of the notion that of all the kinds of news viewers *could* watch, they would choose to tune in night after night to be "shocked and amazed." We recognize that some down-market stations will find a comfortable niche airing "flash and trash." But the evidence of declining ratings over several years demonstrates that this is not a good long-term strategy. In other words, respect the audience. And don't view the ideas in this book as things you can try only when you have the time. If newsrooms continue to heap precious resources on "hook-and-hold" stories, they won't be able to "add" other ideas from this book. In the same way that one reprograms muscle memory when trying to improve a tennis serve, a swimming stroke, or a golf swing, the first step is to stop relying on the habits you are trying to change.

DEFINE YOUR MISSION THEN BUILD YOUR JOURNALISM AROUND IT

Next, if you do want to veer from the status quo – and doing so involves risk – you must have something to which to grab hold. A news organization must have a clear sense of purpose. To make money or win ratings isn't enough – every station wants to be Number 1. But wanting to win doesn't help the 23-year-old producer trying to figure out how to "stack" a newscast at 4 A.M. Nor is purpose always a brand.

Some stations choose a brand and then attempt to mold the news product around it. This approach is backward. Instead, a station should identify what for it are the most important values and build *both* its journalism and its brand around those values.

A news organization has many purposes, not the least of which is to make money. But there is a long list of others: to educate, inspire, entertain, get people to think, help viewers make informed choices, connect people, document the daily history of a community, be a "watchdog" of government, give voice to the voiceless, promote a greater good, protect life and property, help set the public agenda, take people where they cannot go themselves, be a filter for information, and tell the truth.

These aims are all laudable, but sometimes they conflict. Watchdog reporting, for example, takes more time, resources, and a different set of skills than covering a traffic accident or house fire. Judgments have to be made about every story, from whether it should be covered to how much time it will get on the air. That decision making improves when there is a consensus about priorities that reflects the values of the organization and the people who work there. Here are some questions to help you think about priorities:

- How do you define "news"?
- What does your definition of news assume about the community?

- Does your definition meet the community's diverse needs?
- What does it assume about viewers?
- What does it assume about you and your news organization?
- How does your definition of news affect what is covered, the allocation of airtime and newsroom resources, and the promotion and the placement of stories in newscasts?

Asking these questions raises what may be the key issue in the apparent disconnect between broadcast news organizations and their viewers: Do fundamental differences exist in how the newsroom and the community defines "news," and if so, what are the implications for the news organization, its mission, and the station's business model? Without some agreement about the organization's hierarchy of news, individual employees will understandably apply their own definition of what is and is not important.

UNDERSTAND THE ROLE OF JOURNALISTIC REFLEXES

Without clear priorities, decision making reverts to habit and, over time, these habits become reflexive: "It's now a chase, drop everything, we've got to roll." The myths that govern local TV are often unconscious. They are a set of attitudes that become automatic responses. So a major step in change is examining whether these routines are *always* the best way to achieve the organization's journalistic and commercial goals.

DISCRIMINATE BETWEEN "SPOT" NEWS AND "BREAKING" NEWS

Never is the chasm separating the potential and the reality of local TV wider than when they meet, as they often do, at the intersection of breaking news and enterprise.

"There is a tension between providing depth and being first," someone at a Midwest station told us. "We can't chase everything and also do quality." Certainly, stations need to "win breaking news." Yet there's confusion about what "breaking" really means. One assignment editor told us she defines breaking news by referring to what she calls "The News Director Pacing Scale": "The more, faster, pacing in front of the news desk equals a bigger, breaking story." This definition, however, simply reflects what excites newspeople.

Confusion over how to respond to unanticipated events only increases as stations must do more with the same resources. As one broadcast journalist put it, "We lack the staff to compete – we cannot win breaking news AND do all the rest." Said someone else, "Innovative approaches and ideas from the daybook are the *best* stories, but breaking news is *fast*."

Winning breaking news, however, doesn't have to be either-or. One way to make better choices is to distinguish between *spot* news and *breaking* news. Breaking news means "big deal, right now, drop everything and go." Spot news means an event will remain an *incident* and will be treated accordingly until there is evidence that it is other than commonplace. Here's a checklist for drawing that distinction:

- In the hierarchy of unplanned news, what kinds of events must you cover and cover first?
- What is your purpose in running this spot news story? What are you trying to accomplish by placing it in the newscast where you have it? What have you done to tie this event to other events or to the bigger picture? Why will the viewer care?
- Would you air this story if you did not have pictures?
- Would you air this story if you had a better enterprise story?
- If covering an unplanned event requires pulling a reporter and photographer from another story, what criteria do you use to make this decision?
- What kinds of unplanned events are unlikely to make air even if you have tape of the incident or event?
- Of the unplanned events you do *not* care about, should you consider whether they are part of a larger trend that *may* be newsworthy and should eventually be reported?

If a newsroom chooses to be more selective about what it covers, it *will* miss stories. When that happens, consider these questions:

- Who's keeping score? Do you care about this story because the competition had it or because the viewers needed it?
- Would you have called someone in on overtime to cover this story?
- Did not covering an unplanned event allow the newsroom to do something else? What did that other story bring to the newscast?
- Should the newsroom recap or follow up? If the story is not worth pursuing after you chose not to cover it, why was it so important in the first place?

- What have you learned? Were there ways you could have worked smarter? Should you revise your rules of engagement? If so, how do you let everybody know the lessons learned or the new reality?

In the same way a station must differentiate between breaking news and spot news, it should also strive to define what it considers "hard" and "soft" news. Is hard news primarily about immediacy, or is it about a story's long-term impact? Is soft news simply an evergreen or feature that can be aired anytime, or can an interesting, but less-immediate story be considered for the A block of a newscast? The answers to these questions will affect everything from the stories you choose to how they are covered to where they are placed in the rundown. They are critical to your relationship with the audience and, ultimately, the success of your broadcast.

OTHER TOOLS FOR ASSESSING YOUR WORK

Such checklists as described in the previous section can be powerful tools for helping individuals and newsrooms (as well as teachers and students), make coverage choices more conscious. Here are several other tools to assess what you're putting on the air.

Inventory Newscast Content

If local newspeople had a better idea of the amount of spot news they aired or of the overall impression created by the emphasis on crime and violence, we believe they'd be surprised. There is a certain irony in this considering the industry's passion for ratings and audience research. Yet we have found that newsrooms usually have more data about their product's appeal than they do about its substance. With the exception of quarterly or semi-annual consultant reports, few newsrooms systematically review, much less analyze, the content of broadcasts. That's unfortunate because it needn't be expensive or cumbersome.

- *Regularly audit newscasts* by reviewing one or two weeks of line-ups. What were the lead stories, who appeared in the stories, what did the pictures show, what topics were given what kinds of story treatment, what patterns appeared, and what impressions were left? Importantly, what wasn't on the air?
- *Audit the geography of coverage.* Get a map of your coverage area and some colored push pins. Over a period of three or four weeks, stick a

pin at the address of every location at which you've shot tape.
Eventually, you'll have a clear display of the geography of your
news coverage. Pay particular attention to the places you *haven't*
been.

- *Audit individual stories.* Dan O'Donnell, the news director of WGAL-
  TV in Lancaster/Harrisburg, Pennsylvania, likes to review stories by
  diagramming them as one would a sentence. Themes are identified,
  as well as assertions and the evidence on which those assertions are
  based. How many facts are in the story? What has the viewer really
  learned from watching it? A hollow story does not do well in this
  exercise.

Broaden the Source Base

As we have seen, viewers appreciate stories that are well sourced and
contain a variety of viewpoints and information. The challenge is how to
mine this knowledge quickly and efficiently. Here are some strategies:

- *Conduct a source audit.* How many names in the Rolodex belong to
  middle-aged white guys who wear ties and have an office in a
  government building? One kind of source means one perspective
  and viewers want more than one point of view. Make a list of all the
  people who have appeared in stories over the course of a week or a
  month. Do any patterns stand out? After identifying who's been on
  the air, think about who's missing.
- *Identify the places where "real people" hang out.* One way to find people
  other than the "usual suspects" is to look for places where they
  gather. In the case of working parents, it could be a day-care facility
  or a bowling alley on league night. Ethnic churches or restaurants
  are great places to tap into communities of color. Then visit these
  places, meet people, hand out business cards, and collect names and
  numbers of folks who can be called the next time a story needs
  someone with special knowledge or life experiences.
- *Build an e-mail Rolodex.* The TV set is a newsroom's entry point into
  thousands, perhaps tens of thousands, of households. With most
  homes and offices now having Internet access, stations can build
  viewer source lists and then efficiently query groups of people likely
  to have specialized information. For example, if a medical reporter is
  working on a story about hip replacement surgery, he might send an
  e-mail to ask if anyone has undergone or knows of anyone who's
  undergone that procedure.

- *Make all your contacts sources.* All it takes is a question such as: "What are you concerned about, what bugs you?" Keep track of the answers, perhaps on a shared page in the newsroom computer system. Review the responses and look for patterns. Find a pattern and you've got a story or even a series of stories. And by keeping track of the names and numbers of the people you've talked to, you've even got somewhere to start.
- *Recruit viewers to help choose the news.* Several local stations, and even one network evening news broadcast, have experimented with a feature called "You Choose the News." Editors pick several topics that *could* be covered and then ask viewers to vote by phone or e-mail for the story they would most like to see. A reporter is assigned to cover the winning topic, and the story is presented later in the week.
- *Mine viewers for story ideas.* Many news organizations have phone numbers or places on their Web sites where viewers can submit story proposals. Often, these don't work well because the queries are usually answered by voice mail or with a computerized response. One station, however, occasionally takes a camera into the newsroom during newscasts and invites viewers to call reporters and producers. It's surprising how quickly the phones start ringing.

Getting viewers to talk back is only a first step. To mine these conversations effectively, newspeople must become more conscious about how they listen to nonjournalists and about their ability to understand what they hear. Instead of asking for a story, ask what's on people's minds, what they're concerned about, and what they've noticed about their community and their lives. Instead of listening for a 10-second sound bite, listen for patterns. Then search for a quote that symbolizes the pattern. "My commute is taking longer," "I worry about keeping my job," "Young people are disrespectful," "The city is sure doing a lot of digging around here." These are all statements but implicit in each is a question. If other viewers are asking the same question – and often it's simply "Why is this happening?" – a reporter can find the answer and, in doing so, a story.

IMPROVE NEWSROOM ORGANIZATION, COMMUNICATION, AND PLANNING

Spend just a few minutes in a television newsroom and you are likely to hear a conversation that goes something like this: Question: "What's Jim working on?" Answer: "A minute-thirty package with a live open and donut that goes at the top of the second block." Question: "What did he come up with?" Answer: "Some good shots, a couple of [sound] bites and a stand-up close." This exchange is notable for what isn't discussed. Yet it's indicative of the degree to which the production of the news increasingly overshadows the content of broadcasts.

The logistics of just getting all the promos, "teases," "supers," graphics, "bumpers," "stingers," "whip-arounds," and various live shots produced is so complicated that precious little time is left for editorial reflection or collaboration. It is why someone in every newsroom we visit observes that, "We are communicators but we have problems communicating among ourselves." Newsroom conversations, we have found, usually reflect the priorities of the news organization. Talk mostly about logistics, and logistics become the most important value of the newscast.

TALK ABOUT CONTENT

In busy newsrooms, it is unrealistic to expect that systematic discussions of content will just bubble up on their own. Rather, collaboration must be wedged, even forced, into the daily agenda. Here is how some newsrooms do it:

- *Reality checks*. Schedule a time during the day when people in the field call in to update the newsroom on the progress of stories. When they do, don't converse just about logistics. Talk about content. What's the story about? What does it need to be better? Don't forget sports and weather.
- *A bridge line or speakerphone*. Stations often use a bridge line or conference call for special occasions, such as election night or a major sports event. Consider using the bridge every day. When people call in for the reality check, transfer them to the bridge or a good-quality speakerphone so that several people in different parts of the newsroom can participate in the call.
- *A newsroom start page* is one way to literally get everybody on the same page. Creating a "home" page that will appear when staffers log in to the newsroom computer system allows the sharing of information (memos, schedule changes, etc.), the solicitation of story ideas and comments, and the sharing of links, tips, sources, and research.[1]
- *Reporter notes*. Some stations have a section in the newsroom computer called "Reporter Notes." Each day, broadcast producers discuss stories with the reporter-photographer teams in the field and

then fill in the answers for questions such as: "What is the focus of the story?" "People interviewed?" "Best video?" This forces the producers and crews to communicate and provides some guidance to those who must create supporting material for a story that is still being shot.

- *Hand-off notes.* At many stations, there's a gap of several hours between the time the late-news shift leaves for the day and the early morning staff comes in. Much the same thing happens on weekends. How do you brief the next-up broadcast when you don't see people face-to-face? Leave a "hand-off note" that describes what's been done, what must still be completed, and where everything is located. As important, let the next shift know what is unclear but brewing. In addition, that is, to the coffee.

IMPROVE ENTERPRISE AND FOCUS

At a respected station in the upper Midwest, we asked newsroom staffers to identify the elements that together make a good lead story. Here is their list. We then asked how many of the stories on *their* newscasts rose to this level. The answer was notably consistent: between 10 and 20% of the

- Emotion
- Relevancy
- Character-driven
- Consequence/impact
- Compelling
- Good pictures/visuals
- Dramatic
- Offers new information
- Longer (2 minutes or more)
- Emotional attachment
- Smart – values viewer's intelligence
- Shows a side you might not see
- Empowers – answers "What can I do?" question
- Quality of life
- Advances the story
- Offers something viewers didn't know
- Audience relates to characters in story
- Conflict or tensions
- Contains a plot, twists
- Engaging, character-involved
- Happening now
- New – sense of discovery
- Timeliness
- Valuable information
- Perspective
- What others offer "Only on" – distinct from
- Goes beyond the surface
- Frames a central/larger issue
- Intellectual engagement between audience and reporter

stories were lead "worthy." What steps, we asked, could a newsroom take to improve the ratio, even by as little as 10%? Here's what they told us:

Start sooner to get more time to work on the story.

Examine what makes a good lead story.

Instill a culture of expectation.

Encourage risk-taking.

Improve editorial oversight with two levels of review – in addition to producers reading scripts, ask (a respected anchor) to look at them, too.

Is the 1:00 P.M. check-in about control or help? We need help for our stories while we still have time to fix them.

Day-after script reviews

More input from photographers – have both the reporter and photographer on conference calls.

The roadblocks noted here are typical of what newspeople say gets in the way of quality – not enough time, low expectations, too little collaboration, and the wrong kind of oversight. Yet these are all things any station can change, and they can do it without spending a lot of money. The answer is to modify newsroom practices and procedures.

RETHINK THE MORNING MEETING: SOME NEW APPROACHES

For most newsrooms, the editorial process begins at a morning meeting that usually starts between 8:30 and 9:30 A.M. and sometimes runs as long as an hour. These used to be called editorial meetings but they've really become much more than that. Not only are stories chosen and assigned to reporters and photographers, they are often doled out to the various late afternoon and early evening broadcasts. Producers, in fact, have a pretty good idea by the time they walk out the door what will be in their broadcasts and even where they will slot a particular story. All this occurs, of course, before much of the day's news is even committed, much less reported.

In one of the sessions we conducted a news staffer observed that, "On days that we know big stuff is going on, meetings are fast. Other days they go on and on." Why? "We can't decide. We hear everybody out. We spend a lot of time trying to pick leads." So begins what one person sarcastically referred to as "the grand process" of choosing, framing, guiding, and eventually approving stories.

At other stations, however, meetings are faster because they have an agenda and spend only a few minutes on any one item. If they can't choose a lead they settle with identifying some *potential* lead stories and agree to make the final decision later.

Each approach involves trade-offs. Long meetings allow for more breathing room and, in theory, encourage discussion and reflection. Shorter meetings require that attendees be more organized and focused on decision making.

Regardless of which style a manager prefers, here are several strategies that will improve every meeting:

- Use the first few minutes to teach. Show a story or read a lead or tag that worked especially well. This teaching does not always have to be done by managers. Let the producers take turns spotlighting "best practices." Do this every day and do it first.
- Don't spend more than a couple of minutes on any one item.
- Start on time and keep the meeting short for reporters and photographers who have assignments that day.
- If the boss is late, don't wait.
- Recap and review at the end of each major decision and at the end of the meeting.
- Some part of every major editorial meeting should be devoted to reviewing yesterday and thinking about tomorrow.
- Managers should serve more as facilitators and teachers than as judge and jury.

DESIGNATE A "BLACK HAT"

One way to strengthen reporting is to generate internal criticism of the news product. Get a black hat (a baseball cap works nicely) and assign it to a different person in the meeting each week. Their job is to be the "nudge," and they have a free pass, in fact a duty, to question assumptions, challenge reflexes, and press for excellence. This person is to act as a devil's advocate to strengthen the quality of the stories. Too often, this task is left only to managers, which is not only unfair but ineffective.

HOLD A LOOK-AHEAD MEETING

A staffer at a station in Idaho had this description of the way local broadcast journalists work: "Most newsrooms are not very civilized. We are hunter-gatherer societies. We know in the morning that we'll eventually be hungry so we start foraging. We are totally focused during the day in pursuit of food for hungry producers. But because we're not well organized, we bring home a rat instead of a gazelle."

Nobody has enough time to think or plan. But newsrooms can add 16 hours to the clock by starting a day ahead. At some stations, people meet for a few minutes in the afternoon to consider next-day possibilities, especially enterprise offers. This is when story ideas can be helped, rather than just accepted or vetoed, which is what often happens if they are introduced for the first time in the morning meeting. The manager in charge of this day-before meeting should have the authority to launch one or two enterprise offers, so reporters and photographers can begin lining up shooting and interviews. The manager, who understands the story and its nuances, can present it at the morning meeting, thereby giving the reporter a head start.

This arrangement, of course, places significant responsibility on the person who commissions these next-day stories. But it's preferable to a system where a bunch of largely untested ideas are thrown out to a committee, which then attempts to quickly construct a vision that the reporter is sent scrambling out the door to try to match over the next few hours.

MAKE THE EDITORIAL PROCESS MORE "STORY FRIENDLY"

TV newsrooms invest untold energy "testing" stories to see if they meet the bars of brand, relevancy, target audience, and so forth. Usually this occurs only twice in the editorial life cycle of a story: when the story idea is offered at the morning meeting and at the end of the day when the script is submitted for approval. Stories, and the people who report them, need more than tests; they need help. And the earlier they can get that help, the greater the chance they'll be able to take advantage of it. Some strategies:

- *Have a place – a holding pen – for good story ideas and follow-ups.* Some stations do this on a dry-erase board, others on computer. The more people who see it the better because they might have an idea to move a story along.
- *Assign advocates to holding-pen stories.* Assign someone to shepherd a holding-pen idea – to research it, to flesh it out, and to keep bringing it up until the story either gets commissioned or is put out of its

misery. This person does not always have to be a reporter, producer, or the assignment editor. Spread out the work by assigning advocate jobs to everyone, including photographers.

- *Target stories for extra help.* Spend the last five minutes of the meeting helping to choreograph a story by brainstorming possible approaches, sources, picture opportunities, and the like. Use the creativity in the room to consider how the story might be made special.

- *Brainstorm.* The collective wisdom of several people is greater than any one individual. And if there isn't time to brainstorm ideas at the morning or afternoon meetings, get a few people together some other time. Don't forget to include the photographers. They think visually and can add creative energy to the product.

- *Take chances on people and ideas.* The late Marty Haag often said that in the almost two decades he ran the newsroom at WFAA-TV in Dallas, he often had to force himself to just say "yes" to ideas he wasn't sure would fly. Why? Because he wanted people to develop confidence in their own judgment and abilities. More often than not, Haag said, the stories turned out OK. Sometimes, in fact, they were "real home runs." Haag was also known to occasionally leave the office early so he could get home to watch the news in his living room just like other viewers.

- *Create "Journalists' Choice" days.* Circumvent the jury process by giving reporters and photographers one or two days a month to do any story they want. This sort of freedom stimulates creativity as well as a sense of pride in one's work.

SIDEBAR 7.2

FIND THE FOCUS: A CHECKLIST

Working with Deborah Potter of the research and training organization NewsLab, we developed a series of story-specific questions that any broadcast journalist, but especially assignment and planning editors, should ask to organize themselves and their newsrooms throughout the reporting and editing process.

- What's this story really about?
  - What is the central point of this story?
  - Why does the community need to know about this?
  - If it's a "big" topic, how can we break it down so it's easier to tell?

- If it's a "small" topic, is there a story behind the story? Does this development reflect a larger trend or theme?
- Who will care about this story?

- What information do viewers need?
  - What question or questions *must* this story answer to be worth watching?
  - Will viewers know something after seeing this story that they didn't know before it aired?
  - If viewers can put this new knowledge to use, have we told them how?

- Who has the information?
  - Where or from whom can we learn the facts?
  - Who can put the facts in perspective?
  - Where is the central place of this story? Is that where we're shooting?
  - Who and what will *not* be covered in this story?

- What's the best way to tell this story?
  - What drives this story – plot, character, picture, detail, fact, sound?
  - What is the best technique to give the viewer *the most important information* in this story? Anchor copy, voice-over/sound on tape, package, live?
  - What techniques can we use to tell the rest of the story?

MAKE QUALITY CENTRAL TO THE NEWSROOM CULTURE

Some news stories are easy to cover. But these "easy gets" don't draw the audience that a more complete journalism attracts. As the data show, viewers are interested in seeing well-told stories about the important or interesting. But this is hard work – harder, frankly, than relying on fires, accidents, and crime to create a false sense of urgency. To build newscasts around storytelling and significance rather than visual stimulation, newspeople have to become smarter. They must improve their knowledge about the subjects they cover and the storytelling skills they employ to impart that information. Moreover, this learning must take into account the realities of the marketplace; the size, experience, and capabilities of the staff; the resources of the station; and the expectations of management. Finally, the learning process must be able to unfold within the hectic, stressful environment that is today's local TV newsroom. Here are some steps to making quality central to the newsroom culture.

Instill a Coaching Culture

Local TV newsrooms are usually populated by a mix of experienced veterans and energetic up-and-comers. This is an ideal environment in which to instill a teaching and coaching culture. It's rewarding for the veterans, valuable for the younger staffers, and a necessity for stations that must attract employees to replace those who move on. Journalists want to work in a place of which they can be proud and where they can improve their professional skills.[2]

Yet there remains little investment by ownership in mid-career journalism training. Certainly consultants provide some, and so do a few non-profits. A few of the larger broadcast groups conduct "boot camps" for reporters and producers. But these are typically held only once or twice a year and only one or two people from each station can attend. In fact, the overwhelming majority of training in the local TV newsroom takes place in the front seat of a crew car as reporters and photographers drive to and from assignments, in edit booths as they put their stories together, or at producer's desks as they read over scripts. All in all, it is strikingly haphazard.

A first step is to recognize the importance of training and to make it a part of the newsroom mission. Put somebody in charge, identify areas of need, develop a plan, and then assess the impact and improve the methods. Coaching is not just the responsibility of managers. The expectation is that everyone should be *both* a *teacher* and a *student*.

At WEEK-TV in Peoria, staffers felt they needed help with writing, so five of the best writers conducted several two-hour seminars. They shared tips, and then reporters, producers, and anchors agreed on new writing rules. The group followed up by conducting weekly script reviews and handed out awards for the best work.

"Automatics"

WTSP-TV in Tampa–St. Petersburg has used "automatics" as a way to get everybody on the same page and then to progressively raise the performance bar. Groups of staffers, say photographers, brainstorm a list of minimum standards based on the specific work they do and the circumstances in which they perform it. These automatics might range from "I will always have gas in my car and tape in my camera" to "I will have fun at my job and learn and teach something every day."

Management doesn't impose the rules, but managers do use them in conducting employee evaluations. Importantly, the automatics are not considered eternal, though some of them may be. Employees meet at least a couple of times a year to review the goals and reaffirm the choices they've made. As skills improve, they raise the bar.

Systematically Recognize Achievement beyond Ratings

Another strategy is to recognize daily "wins." If this is done at the beginning of the morning meeting, it can be used to "tee off" an example of a best practice. For example:

- It's a win to take a "dull and boring" topic and turn it into an engaging and interesting story.
- It's a win when at least one primary newscast leads with an enterprise story versus spot news or a planned event.
- It's a win when every crime story has explicit relevance to the viewers.

Teach Not Just the How but Also the Why

When it comes to the tools and techniques of television, local news-people certainly know how things work. But they are less likely to understand why. If they were more conscious of what happens on the receiving end of television, they'd be more likely to pick up the right tool.

Deborah Potter, a former network news correspondent who has done extensive local newsroom research and training, scoured academic studies to develop a summary of viewer responses to some common TV production and storytelling techniques.

- Stacking a newscast by putting similar stories together for purposes of "flow" may impede the recall of stories. Elements of stories merge or become confused with elements of another causing confusion and mental "meltdown."
- Viewers are likely to forget what they saw and heard before a negative image was shown. They will remember best what they see during and after negative images.
- A combination of fast-paced editing (changing from scene to scene) and emotional content can overload viewers. They pay attention and remember they saw something, but they can't recall the details.
- Viewers say they find stories produced using highly emotional techniques (music, sound effects, slow motion, flash frames, and

obtrusive voice) less enjoyable, less believable, and less informative than stories with identical content produced without them.

- Graphics in stories can decrease memory for audio information at the time of the graphic, particularly if the content is difficult or unfamiliar. This was true even when the audio matched the graphic.
- A study that compared a typical inverted pyramid–style newspaper story – most important news on top and less important information as the story goes on – to a story containing the same information arranged chronologically found that people remembered the chronological story 15% better.
- When programming that leads into a newscast is arousing, viewers tend to not remember much that happens during the first two minutes of the newscast.
- In general, viewers tend to remember best the last stories they see in a newscast, the first stories less well, and the middle stories the least. Emotional stories and stories with good video can overcome this effect (Lang and Potter 2000).[3]

Detailed summaries can be found at NewsLab.org.

CONCLUSION

At first glance, most local TV is visually attractive. Yet when one looks at the content and editorial structure of the news, the result is less impressive. That is why before they clip on a microphone or light up a live truck, broadcast journalists should reflect about the definition of news, think about how stories are covered and presented, and be more conscious of the role journalistic reflexes play in this process. They must also understand why the medium works the way that it does.

The message here is two-fold. First, the way a newsroom operates – the morning meeting, the assignment desk, the script review, the newscast stacking, the language people use – reflects the collective values that become culture. Moreover, it is through process that these values are propagated. The second point is that process, both individual and organizational, can be changed at little or no financial cost. It's more a matter of working smarter than it is of hiring more staff or buying more equipment.

The broadcasting industry has already invested untold fortunes in technology, sets, audience research, consultants, and talent contracts. To improve content, the most important factor in viewing, its time to focus on the people who produce content.

8   The Road Ahead: The Future of Local TV News

Outside of all the findings in this book – all the data, all the suggestions – there is the question of the future of the medium itself. Where is local TV news heading?

The business, along with journalism itself, is already changing. With an explosion of new outlets presenting news, audiences are fragmenting across more places and technologies. Consumers no longer rely primarily on one medium, but increasingly they graze across a range of different media each day, getting their news in pieces.

The audience for most journalism also is aging. This includes local TV. Young people are not acquiring the habit of reading newspapers, watching network news, listening to news on radio, or, indeed, watching local TV news. But the young are not apathetic. They do, it turns out, consume news. They also read. But they are getting their news from Internet sources, podcasts, and even cable news/comedy shows such as *The Daily Show with Jon Stewart*. These trends have major implications for local TV journalism. There is no reason, based on what we know about the history of news consumption habits, to believe that with age they will migrate to the older media in significant numbers.

There is a major financial implication to the new technology and the explosion in outlets it has spawned. Generally it has meant that most local TV stations are losing audience, which in turn is putting pressure on revenues.

All of this is ceding more power away from journalists and toward the viewers, all of whom can pick and choose what they want to know, in what style of presentation, when, and from what media. The young, in particular, increasingly want their news on demand, giving them maximum control of what they get and how, a phenomenon reflected in the fact that the Internet is the one medium in which they consume news in greater numbers than their elders.

Some consumers are also becoming active producers themselves – if not of news then of discussion about news – through blogging, podcasting, their own Web sites, and more. What in 2005 were being called video blogs, or vlogs, are still in their infancy, but they are growing. Advocates of the new culture of news/talk use phrases such as "We Media" and "citizen journalists," and they speak of consumers becoming "pro-sumers," a hybrid of consumers and producers.

Whatever one thinks of these changes, they are happening undeniably. Ignoring them isn't a viable option for any media outlet looking to thrive in the new environment. The critical issue for local TV news professionals is coming to accept them and to understand their implications. The most fundamental of these changes is that as consumers gain more independence and power, news consumption is becoming less of a prepared lecture and more of an open dialogue, with all the advantages and disadvantages that implies.

In turn, journalists are less and less gatekeepers with exclusive control over what facts the public will and will not have access to. Instead, their new roles increasingly are those of authenticators, contextualizers. They will need to help citizens to better sort through the avalanche of information and to identify what they can trust and believe – the authenticator role. And this likely means they will have to do more of the deeper reporting that will help people make sense of what this information means, to make connections so people can put information to use – the contextualizer role. In short, they will have to put the pieces together and tell the audience the story. They also must put more emphasis on being originators, uncovering what otherwise would be kept secret.

For local TV news, the changes have already meant that the arenas over which they once had particular advantages, such as sports and weather, are now available from other sources on demand.

Some elements of local TV news are showing no signs of change. One is the expectation of big profits. Another is the reliance on newsrooms as cash generators for their owners. A third is the stretched resources on which most newsrooms rely, which profoundly influence the kind of news they can produce. This translates into more pressure on local TV newspeople as they make decisions about how to deploy resources, what news to cover, how to cover it, and what not to cover.

Many broadcast journalists may be inclined to say that much of this is beyond their control: "We're not in the driver's seat any more, so we had better just go along to get along." But this suggestion of powerlessness, we believe, is mistaken for two reasons. First, if TV newspeople allow the business side to dictate and design what the newsroom produces, that product will not be as good. Business people are in the business of selling, not producing the news.

The second risk is that local TV journalists will give up. This attitude as a prescription for change is backward. It is a reaction to the symptoms rather than a treatment for the current challenges and changes facing TV journalism. The way to regain audience and influence is to create a product that people want. As those wants are now changing, local TV needs not just the freedom to adapt but encouragement to do so as well. This process will be more a transition than a leap. But for it to happen successfully, there must be a willingness to experiment and even to risk failure.

If the business side remains so focused on the next quarter's profit and loss statement or in servicing the massive debt left over after purchasing more stations, there will be little money or energy to innovate. And if that happens, local TV will find itself stuck even more in the past. So how do local TV newspeople need to rethink what they do to stay up with or ahead of it all? We see four major changes that local TV people should think about as they look ahead.

THE DECLINE OF APPOINTMENT NEWS CONSUMPTION

The first change is that local TV newspeople will have to change the way they think of attracting people to the news. For the last half century, local TV news has been built around appointment viewing. People would gather at specific times – the dinner hour, or after prime time, or early morning – to get their news. This will have to change. Local TV newspeople are going to have to begin thinking of producing news in a way that accommodates the growing expectation that the latest news will be available whenever the consumer might want it, not just when a program is airing.[1]

LOCAL TV NEWSROOMS WILL NO LONGER BE JUST ABOUT TV

The second change is that local TV newspeople will have to think of themselves as more than just "TV" people. Local TV newsrooms have to become multi-platform information centers, available on TV, online, on

Palm Pilots or PDAs, on audio and video iPods, on phones, and on products that do not yet exist.

In effect, the newsroom will have to become the soul of the operation. Not the newscast. The newscast will often not even be the medium. This means more than "repurposing" old material. It means understanding the next technology and how that technology must and will change journalism, without changing its purpose.

THE PRODUCT WILL DIFFER SOMEWHAT IN EACH NEW PLATFORM

How local TV newspeople approach each of these platforms is less certain.

Online, the news could look something like a newscast, only one that the consumer navigates, rather than watching in a linear fashion. Or local TV newsrooms may decide to make their Web site something less tied to the legacy of local TV and adopt a more truly multimedia personality, perhaps with a look and feel that is distinct to the Web. Some stations may experiment with allowing consumers to "create" their own newscasts, "stacking" the stories for themselves, and then letting the users watch a continuous Webcast. Others are already using their Web sites more as marketing organs than as news outlets, turning them into virtual infomercials. There are various options, and likely different stations will experiment in different ways. But whatever look or approach stations take, one change is coming unambiguously. Stations cannot look to the Web mainly as a place to drive people to their newscast. The Web will become its own destination. It already has, and given that younger audiences are not developing the local news consumption habit in the same way previous generations did, that will only continue. Those stations that do not come to understand this new reality – and accept it – will lose.

The product of local TV news designed for PDAs, iPods, or mobile phones will likely have to look different, be designed for a smaller screen, be easier to load, and be easier to navigate.

Then there are the newscasts – the legacy media.

Stations have already begun to experiment with how these might change. Some stations have moved in the direction of mimicking 24-hour cable news. In an 18-hour day, as much as one-third of the programming carried by some stations is devoted to news. Yet, our belief is that imitating the CNN or any other cable news model is not the answer. For one thing, the demands of continuous newscasting have meant that most cable news is conducted through live stand-ups and live interviews, leaving little time for research, fact checking, and reporting. It is prone to what we call the "Journalism of Assertion," versus the strengths of the traditional "Journalism of Verification" and storytelling, where facts are double-checked, scripts are refined, and pictures are matched to words.

In a faster broadband environment, where video is searchable and more easily downloaded, the cable model will also increasingly not adapt as well as traditional storytelling packages. Packaged "containers" of information are more easily searchable and give more power to consumers to find what they want over having to sit through a continuous stream of whatever the newscaster or commentator happens to be talking about at a given moment.

Stations could have their newscasts begin to mimic the feel of the Web. In 2005, News One in New York had audiences go online in the afternoon and vote for how the station should build or stack the nine o'clock newscast that night. Stations might even reverse their current balance of thinking and begin to use their newscasts to drive audiences to their deeper platform – online – where consumers could navigate longer stories, peruse original documents, see full interviews rather than just the sound bites, and more.

Local TV news producers need to recognize that telling a good story still remains an important constant. In a medium such as the Web where newsrooms have less control over what viewers see and hear, a compelling story becomes even more vital. Our "Magic Formula" provides the elements of putting together just such a story. This leads us to our next point.

THE PACKAGES, OR STORIES, WILL HAVE TO GET BETTER

Whatever path stations take, one change seems unavoidable. The stories that are the backbone of a newsroom will have become better than they are now. And the range of what stories get the kind of deep treatment that make them compelling will have to widen. Local TV newsrooms will have to grow beyond being specialists in "spot news" and weather. There are several reasons why we think that the storytelling in local TV newsrooms will have to deepen in quality and widen in scope.

First, the story – rather than the newscast – will be the essential unit consumers are seeking in the new technology environments, whether online or via phones and other platforms. Those stories have to be worth searching for, and worth returning for. The anchors may become less central in a newscast that, in effect, consumers are building through their searches.

Second, some of the most basic concepts of flow, of stacking a newscast, and of "hooking and holding" the audience by trying to manipulate them into continuing to watch, all will increasingly falter. Accustomed to making their own choices in navigating the Web – rather than just clicking channels – people will be more likely to leave a source because they have so many other choices.

Third, stations chasing each other for "live, local, and late breaking" will likely have diminishing returns. The technology of airing live significant events will still have appeal in newscasts, and possibly also online. Early experiments suggest that posting live video as it is happening can draw significant traffic. But stations cannot create brands around these occasional episodes. In the twenty-first century, scoops may only last a few seconds.

The growing importance placed on storytelling has a series of other implications.

ANCHOR TALENT WILL NOT BECOME IRRELEVANT, BUT IT MAY BECOME LESS DOMINANT

If more of the brand of the station is built online and in other delivery systems, the reliance on anchor chemistry, on byplay, on the look of the set, and on so many other "atmospheric" aspects of local TV news obviously become de-emphasized. Stations will still deliver the newscasts. But the newscasts themselves will become a smaller part of the puzzle.

NEWS ORGANIZATIONS WILL NEED TO BUILD EXPERTISE

As stations inevitably build themselves somewhat less around the likeability of the anchors, they will depend more on the news staff's skills and the knowledge of the storytellers – which may indeed include the anchors doing more reporting. The crux of this storytelling strength will be the knowledge of the reporter-storytellers about their subject matter. This can develop more than one way. Magazine programs such as *60 Minutes* continued to use skilled generalists as their correspondents, while they developed deeper expertise in their producers. Local TV newscasts could use this approach, but it would mean hiring more people who would not be on the air.

The need for reporter expertise will mean developing specialties, or beats. The beat system in this new environment will have to emphasize topics rather than buildings. To a degree, local stations will have to move somewhat from covering communities as geography to also covering communities of interest. There will be no avoiding the inevitable need: Local stations will have to allow or demand that their reporters (and producers) develop beat expertise locally. Relying on generalists who can make pretty stories but who barely scratch the surface of the substance of those stories will no longer suffice.

BROADEN THE RANGE OF TOPICS THAT GET TOP COVERAGE

More reporting effort, time, and devotion will need to go into subjects that currently are malnourished. The culture of live, local, and late breaking and the myths of local TV thinking have led to the predicament of devoting most of the time and reporting energy to three topics: crime, accidents, and disasters. In the new environment, audiences will require local TV newsrooms to deliver more than that, especially on new platforms online and elsewhere. This means newsrooms will have to make choices that are difficult, as we noted in the last chapter. But if local TV stations seriously devote themselves only to the subjects and approaches that work in the old environment of the appointment broadcast, those things will not be enough and may not work at all in the new environment, where the local TV station is head-to-head against the newspaper Web site and other rivals perhaps unknown.

USE THE WEATHER EXPERIENCE AS A MODEL

We believe there is a model, and a lesson, for the future of local TV news in the medium's past – weather. In the earlier days of local TV news, weather was something of an afterthought – a place for pretty girls and schtick. In the case of one San Francisco station, a critical qualification for the position of weatherperson was the ability to write temperatures backward with a grease pen on a sliding Plexiglas panel.

In time, some stations hired stand-up comedians to handle the topic. David Letterman once delivered the weather in a bunny suit in Indianapolis.

As research began to indicate that weather was becoming a central reason why people tuned in, and a competitive advantage for stations, that changed. Weather presenters became experts. Many were sent back to school to become certified by the American Meteorological Society, and stations brandished their expertise in their promos. (When was the last time a station promoted a reporter's advanced degree in something other than law, medicine, or weather?) Stations also began to upgrade technology to improve forecasting, investing heavily in Doppler radar, which is essentially a news gathering tool for weather. This, too, became something to promote.

Today, weather is still the Number 1 reason people watch local TV news in many markets. Weather is a primary attraction for viewers because local TV has invested in expertise and equipment to produce highly sophisticated weather journalism. In fact, the quality and sophistication of the weather reporting on most stations far exceeds that of the reporting on any other subject. Local TV owns that topic. It covers it better than newspapers and, locally, often better than the Weather Channel or other sources. The depth of information, and the respect with which local stations approach viewers on this topic, has made it a strength as well as an enormously profitable franchise.

To succeed in the age of the new media, local TV can follow its own example. Consider weather as a model. It has proved that depth works. Weather reporting has proved you can own a subject and make it a brand.

THE CASE FOR EXPERTISE

In sports, some stations have followed this lead. In some markets, coverage of high school sports, especially football, is a major part of station branding, and a reason for the station helicopter. In other places, stations have failed to get beyond the highlight stage of sports coverage. In those stations, sports has been cut back and the audience ceded to ESPN.

There are other examples where stations have invested and created brand. Some do it in consumer reporting. At WRC-TV in Washington, D.C., the "Does It Really Do That" series by reporter Liz Crenshaw tackles products people have seen heavily advertised on TV and checks whether the claims are for real. She uses viewers (fellow citizens and consumers) to test the products, and they become her independent authorities. It is a nice example of the new authenticator role. At KMEX-TV in Los Angeles, a Spanish-language station, the newsroom hired an attorney to cover immigration. Various stations have hired doctors to cover health.

Beyond the occasional examples, however, most TV is done with general assignment reporters, particularly in late and early morning news. And on average they are doing roughly two stories a day. Stations will need to think differently about this. With the rise of the Web individual stories will matter more. And just passing on a few sketchy details or some cover footage won't be enough. They will have to be worth keeping on the Web for hours, or even days. It will be multimedia, not just visual. And if people are to make time for it, it must be more valuable than what they are getting now. It must have more value than immediacy.

News organizations will also have to place less emphasis on a coverage of efficiency and put more importance on reporting routines that allow for depth. They will have to beef up their reporting staffs, and the staff's expertise. Stations will have to rediscover the role of the researcher and create more "one-person brands" – reporters whom viewers recognize for their work. This may also mean creating some "one-person bands," in which reporters take their own pictures, and edit their own stories, perhaps from a laptop in the field.

Various possibilities will need to be tested. Some folks will succeed at these experiments, whereas others will not. But old ways will have to be jettisoned. In time, stations should reconsider such things as the need for dual anchors on every newscast, a practice that is probably the most economically inefficient in local TV. With the salary paid one anchor, most stations could hire two reporters and in some cases three or four.

AND THEN . . .   •

Perhaps most important, stations will need to abandon some of the faulty assumptions that have governed the thinking of local TV newsrooms for more than a generation. This will be difficult. It means letting go. But that is the only way in the end that they will be able to do the most vital thing, broaden the base of stories that they really own, broadening, in effect, their definition of what news they give real commitment to. In short, stations will have to stake their identities on news content, not on a more abstract or cosmetic notion of brand.

In the end, the changes facing local TV news are immense, as they are for all of journalism. But they represent an opportunity, not simply a threat. The winners will be those who are willing to abandon old thinking while embracing the enduring qualities that make journalism important in the first place.

APPENDIX A

Design Team Members

The following members of the Design Team participated in the 1997 meeting. They are listed with their positions at that time followed by their affiliation as of 2005.

John Corporon, retired Tribune company news executive; board of governors, Overseas Press Club.

Randy Covington, news director, WIS, Columbia, South Carolina; instructor, University of South Carolina School of Journalism and Mass Communications.

Alice Main, executive producer, WLS, Chicago; author.

Paula Pendarvis, director of news and local programming, WGNO TV, New Orleans.

Gordon Peterson, principal anchor, WUSA TV, Washington, D.C.

Jose Rios, vice president of news, KTTV, Los Angeles.

Jim Snyder, retired Post-Newsweek news executive; deceased.

Gary Wordlaw, vice president of news, WJLA TV, Washington, D.C.; vice president and general manager, KSTW TV, Seattle.

Other members of the Design Team who were not present at the New Orleans meeting:

John Cardenas, news director, KPHO TV, Phoenix; news director, WBNS, Columbus, Ohio.

Marty Haag, senior vice president of broadcast news, Belo Corp.; executive in residence, Division of Journalism, Southern Methodist University.

Natalie Jacobson, principal anchor, WCVB TV, Boston.

Dan Rosenheim, news director, KRON TV, San Francisco; news director, KPIX TV, San Francisco.

Kathy Williams, news director, WKYC TV, Cleveland; news director, KRIV, Houston.

Participation in the Design Team does not imply agreement or endorsement of the conclusions in this book. Design Team members help develop the criteria; they did not participate in the analysis of the data for the book.

APPENDIX B

Quality Grading Criteria and Value Codes*

Significance

Designates the extent to which the story focuses on in-depth issues.

MEANING	VALUE
Focus on ideas, issues, or policy	10
Focus on public malfeasance ("watchdoggery"; criminal potential)	10
Focus on monumental events	9
Focus on public/private/civic institutions/actors	8
Focus on substantive trends	7
Focus on unusual events	6
Focus on politics (strategy and gamesmanship stories)	6
Focus on breaking events	5
Focus on everyday incidents	4
Focus on everyday crime	4
Focus on people/popular behavior/human interest	3
Focus on celebrities/entertainment	2
Focus on scandal/sensation	1
Station personnel or network promotion	0
Cross-talk	0
Focus on sports (everyday segment)	0
Focus on weather (everyday segment)	0

Journalistic Enterprise

Designates the method used in gathering the news story.

MEANING	VALUE
Station-initiated investigation	8
Report of investigation initiated by others	7

*Prior to compression to 0–1 range for use in statistical models.

(Journalistic Enterprise *cont.*)

Interview – substantive questioning by reporter	7
Interview – nonsubstantive questioning by reporter	6
News series (non-investigative)	6
Response to spontaneous event (crime, accident, weather, disaster)	6
Response to pre-arranged event (press conference, trial, Wall Street)	4
Response to pre-arranged event/tape/no on-scene station personnel	3
Wire or feed from network/other source (inferred/nonlocal anthologies)	3
Story attributed to other news organization	1
Corporate/Video news release (inferred)	1
Story attributed to supermarket tabloid news organization	0
Story attributed to rumor or gossip	0
No attribution/explanation	0

Balanced Sourcing

Designates number of sources provided in story.

MEANING	VALUE
Three or more sources	5
Two sources	3
One source	2
Passing references/Unnamed sources only	0
No source	0

Balanced Viewpoints

Designates number of viewpoints provided in story.

MEANING	VALUE
Mix of opinions (no one opinion more than 75%)	5
Mostly one opinion, passing reference to other	3
All of one opinion	1
Undisputed event reporting	NA

Authoritativeness

Designates the credibility of each story via inclusion of relevant and expert sources.

MEANING	VALUE
Expert, credentialed source, on-camera interview	3
Reference to expert/serious data, no on-camera presence	2
Major actor in story (if not expert, credential source)	1
Person on the street (when citizens not major actor)	1

Passing reference/Unnamed source   0
Undisputed event reporting   0
No sources   0

Community Relevance

Designates the effort of the news organization to present story as relevant to the audience.

MEANING	VALUE
Emergency info – affects viewing area	8
National info – affects viewing area	7
Information – affects presidential election - no local linkage	6
Information – affects major community institution/event or employer	6
Information – affects dominant geographic area of viewing audience	5
Information – affects Carib/Latin American/Spanish-language nation	4
Information – affects other geographic subset of viewing audience	3
Information – affects demographic subset of viewing audience	3
Information – generally useful/interesting to viewing audience	2
National story – no connection to viewing area	2
International story – no connection to viewing area	2
Information – personally useful to viewers	1
Information – unrelated to community	0

Sensationalism

Designates type of use of video or still visuals in the story. Note: Higher values indicate less sensationalism.

MEANING	VALUE
Still graphic/photo/title, neutral	3
Taped action, neutral	3
Live action, neutral	3
Still graphic/photo/title, somewhat sensational	2
Taped action, somewhat sensational	2
Live action, somewhat sensational	2
No graphics/photos/titles/action	1
Still graphic/photo/title, mostly sensational	0
Taped action, mostly sensational	0
Live action, mostly sensational	0

APPENDIX C

Content Analysis Intercoder Reliability Analyses

1998. One coder was designated as the control coder and worked off-site for the duration of the project. At the completion of the general coding process, the three on-site coders, working alone and without access to the control coder's work, recoded one-sixth of the broadcasts completed by the control coder. Daily scores were found to be reliable within ±0.79 points per day, as per the comparative daily broadcast scores.

1999. For this project, the principal coding team comprised six people, who were trained as a group. One coder was designated as the control coder and worked off-site for the duration of the project. At the completion of the general coding process, the on-site coders, working alone and without access to the control coder's work, recoded 40% of the broadcasts completed by the control coder. Daily scores were found to be reliable within ±0.59 points per day, as per the comparative daily broadcast scores of general coders versus the control coder.

2000. For this project, the principal coding team comprised four individuals, who were trained as a group. One coder was designated as the control coder and worked off-site for the duration of the project. At the completion of the general coding process, the on-site coders, working alone and without access to the control coder's work, recoded 40% of the broadcasts completed by the control coder. Daily scores were found to be reliable within ±0.78 points per day, as per the comparative daily broadcast scores of general coders versus the control coder.

2001. For this project, the principal coding team comprised five individuals, who were trained as a group, augmented by two precoders. One coder was designated as the control coder and worked off-site for the duration of the project. At the completion of the general coding process, the on-site coders, working alone and without access to the control coder's work, recoded 33% of the broadcasts completed by the control coder. Daily scores were found to be reliable within ±0.74 points per day, as per the comparative daily broadcast scores of general coders versus the control coder.

2002. Testing performed similar to prior years to measure uniform coding showed that daily scores were reliable within ±0.49 points per day for all broadcasts.

APPENDIX D

Sample of Local TV News Stations

STATION	MARKET	YEAR
KOAT	Albuquerque	1998
KRQE	Albuquerque	1998
KOB	Albuquerque	1998
WSB	Atlanta	1998
WGNX	Atlanta	1998
WXIA	Atlanta	1998
WCVB	Boston	1998
WBZ	Boston	1998
WHDH	Boston	1998
WKBW	Buffalo	1998
WIVB	Buffalo	1998
WGRZ	Buffalo	1998
WVNY	Burlington	1998
WPTZ	Burlington	1998
WLS	Chicago	1998
WBBM	Chicago	1998
WMAQ	Chicago	1998
WEHT	Evansville	1998
WEVV	Evansville	1998
WFIE	Evansville	1998
WJXX	Jacksonville	1998
WJXT	Jacksonville	1998
WTLV	Jacksonville	1998
WLAJ	Lansing	1998
WLNS	Lansing	1998
WILX	Lansing	1998
KABC	Los Angeles	1998
KCBS	Los Angeles	1998
KNBC	Los Angeles	1998

WHAS	Louisville	1998
WLKY	Louisville	1998
WAVE	Louisville	1998
KSTP	Minneapolis	1998
WCCO	Minneapolis	1998
KARE	Minneapolis	1998
KMSP	Minneapolis	1998
WABC	New York	1998
WCBS	New York	1998
WNBC	New York	1998
WTAE	Pittsburgh	1998
KDKA	Pittsburgh	1998
WPXI	Pittsburgh	1998
KMOV	St. Louis	1998
KTVI	St. Louis	1998
KSDK	St. Louis	1998
KOMO	Seattle	1998
KIRO	Seattle	1998
KING	Seattle	1998
WTXL	Tallahassee	1998
WCTV	Tallahassee	1998
WTWC	Tallahassee	1998
KGUN	Tucson	1998
KOLD	Tucson	1998
KVOA	Tucson	1998
WJLA	Washington	1998
WUSA	Washington	1998
WRC	Washington	1998
KAKE	Wichita	1998
KWCH	Wichita	1998
KSNW	Wichita	1998
KTVA	Anchorage	1999
KTUU	Anchorage	1999
WCVB	Boston	1999
WBZ	Boston	1999
WHDH	Boston	1999
KGWN	Cheyenne	1999
KKTU	Cheyenne	1999
WLS	Chicago	1999
WBBM	Chicago	1999
WMAQ	Chicago	1999
WEWS	Cleveland	1999
WOIO	Cleveland	1999

WKYC	Cleveland	1999
WFAA	Dallas	1999
KTVT	Dallas	1999
KDFW	Dallas	1999
KXAS	Dallas	1999
WEHT	Evansville	1999
WTVW	Evansville	1999
WFIE	Evansville	1999
WAPT	Jackson	1999
WJTV	Jackson	1999
WLBT	Jackson	1999
WATE	Knoxville	1999
WVLT	Knoxville	1999
WBIR	Knoxville	1999
KATV	Little Rock	1999
KTHV	Little Rock	1999
KARK	Little Rock	1999
WHAS	Louisville	1999
WLKY	Louisville	1999
WAVE	Louisville	1999
WPLG	Miami	1999
WFOR	Miami	1999
WSVN	Miami	1999
WTVJ	Miami	1999
KSTP	Minneapolis	1999
WCCO	Minneapolis	1999
KARE	Minneapolis	1999
KMSP	Minneapolis	1999
WGNO	New Orleans	1999
WWL	New Orleans	1999
WVUE	New Orleans	1999
WDSU	New Orleans	1999
WABC	New York	1999
WCBS	New York	1999
WNBC	New York	1999
WPVI	Philadelphia	1999
KYW	Philadelphia	1999
WCAU	Philadelphia	1999
KGO	San Francisco	1999
KPIX	San Francisco	1999
KRON	San Francisco	1999
KOMO	Seattle	1999
KIRO	Seattle	1999

KING	Seattle	1999
KAKE	Wichita	1999
KWCH	Wichita	1999
KSNW	Wichita	1999
WCVB	Boston	2000
WBZ	Boston	2000
WHDH	Boston	2000
KMGH	Denver	2000
KCNC	Denver	2000
KUSA	Denver	2000
KSTP	Minneapolis	2000
WCCO	Minneapolis	2000
KARE	Minneapolis	2000
KMSP	Minneapolis	2000
WABC	New York	2000
WCBS	New York	2000
WNBC	New York	2000
KNXV	Phoenix	2000
KPHO	Phoenix	2000
KPNX	Phoenix	2000
KTVK	Phoenix	2000
KSFY	Sioux Falls	2000
KELO	Sioux Falls	2000
KDLT	Sioux Falls	2000
KGUN	Tucson	2000
KOLD	Tucson	2000
KVOA	Tucson	2000
KAKE	Wichita	2000
KWCH	Wichita	2000
KSNW	Wichita	2000
KTVQ	Billings	2001
KULR	Billings	2001
WSOC	Charlotte	2001
WBTV	Charlotte	2001
WCNC	Charlotte	2001
WFAA	Dallas	2001
KTVT	Dallas	2001
KDFW	Dallas	2001
KXAS	Dallas	2001
WXYZ	Detroit	2001
WDIV	Detroit	2001
KITV	Honolulu	2001
KGMB	Honolulu	2001

KHON	Honolulu	2001
KHNL	Honolulu	2001
KTNV	Las Vegas	2001
KLAS	Las Vegas	2001
KVBC	Las Vegas	2001
KABC	Los Angeles	2001
KCBS	Los Angeles	2001
KNBC	Los Angeles	2001
WABC	New York	2001
WCBS	New York	2001
WNBC	New York	2001
KOCO	Oklahoma City	2001
KWTV	Oklahoma City	2001
KFOR	Oklahoma City	2001
WPVI	Philadelphia	2001
KYW	Philadelphia	2001
WCAU	Philadelphia	2001
KATU	Portland	2001
KOIN	Portland	2001
KGW	Portland	2001
KTVX	Salt Lake City	2001
KUTV	Salt Lake City	2001
KSL	Salt Lake City	2001
WFTS	Tampa	2001
WTSP	Tampa	2001
WTVT	Tampa	2001
WFLA	Tampa	2001
WJLA	Washington	2001
WUSA	Washington	2001
WRC	Washington	2001
KOAT	Albuquerque	2002
KRQE	Albuquerque	2002
KOB	Albuquerque	2002
WBRZ	Baton Rouge	2002
WAFB	Baton Rouge	2002
WCVB	Boston	2002
WBZ	Boston	2002
WHDH	Boston	2002
WLS	Chicago	2002
WBBM	Chicago	2002
WMAQ	Chicago	2002
WOLO	Columbia	2002
WLTX	Columbia	2002

WIS	Columbia	2002
KMGH	Denver	2002
KCNC	Denver	2002
KUSA	Denver	2002
WZZM	Grand Rapids	2002
WWMT	Grand Rapids	2002
WOOD	Grand Rapids	2002
KITV	Honolulu	2002
KGMB	Honolulu	2002
KHON	Honolulu	2002
KHNL	Honolulu	2002
KTRK	Houston	2002
KHOU	Houston	2002
KPRC	Houston	2002
KMBC	Kansas City	2002
KCTV	Kansas City	2002
WDAF	Kansas City	2002
KSHB	Kansas City	2002
KTNV	Las Vegas	2002
KLAS	Las Vegas	2002
KVBC	Las Vegas	2002
KABC	Los Angeles	2002
KCBS	Los Angeles	2002
KNBC	Los Angeles	2002
WPLG	Miami	2002
WFOR	Miami	2002
WSVN	Miami	2002
WTVJ	Miami	2002
WKRN	Nashville	2002
WTVF	Nashville	2002
WSMV	Nashville	2002
WABC	New York	2002
WCBS	New York	2002
WNBC	New York	2002
KXTV	Sacramento	2002
KOVR	Sacramento	2002
KCRA	Sacramento	2002
KSFY	Sioux Falls	2002
KELO	Sioux Falls	2002
KDLT	Sioux Falls	2002

APPENDIX E

2005 Follow-up Study

In 2005 the Project for Excellence in Journalism decided to conduct a small follow-up study of local TV news to determine whether the basic findings about local news content gained over the course of the five-year study still held true.

Methodology

The 2005 follow-up study used newscast rundowns from Video Monitoring Services (VMS) (available from Lexis-Nexis) to gather data about newscast content. The rundowns included: start and end times of each story (used to determine story length), descriptions of the story topic matter, and indication of the names and/or identities of additional sources used in reporting the story.

The basis of the study was a sample of 50 newscasts from 10 different markets. Markets were randomly chosen from a list of the 40 largest TV markets (i.e., markets for which VMS rundowns were available). This produced the following list of markets: Los Angeles, Philadelphia, Washington, Houston, Phoenix, St. Louis, San Diego, Cincinnati, Salt Lake City, and Grand Rapids. Network affiliations were then assigned at random to determine a specific station to study in each market, which resulted in the inclusion of three ABC stations, three CBS stations, and four NBC stations. Newscast dates were selected at random to produce a full work-week of newscasts (i.e., Monday through Friday) scattered over the period January to May 2005. The exact dates were: January 14 (Friday), February 10 (Thursday), March 21 (Monday), April 27 (Wednesday), and May 17 (Tuesday). Rundowns were then pulled from Lexis-Nexis for the corresponding dates. Because of gaps in the VMS database it was not possible to randomly select the early or late newscast for study in each market, but the sample was balanced to include five programs of each type.

Substitutions were made when no newscast could be found for the newscast from the desired station for the desired time period. These substitutions were (a) a newscast from the same day of the week made by the same station in different weeks (i.e., different sample day used, such as one week earlier or one week later); (b) a newscast from the sample day made by the same station but in a different time period (i.e., different time slot); (c) a newscast from the sample day made in the same time period but aired by a competing channel in the market (i.e., different station). The substitutions tended to balance each other out: For example, if in one market two early newscasts had to be substituted for a late newscast, in a different market the reverse was true. Because the goal of the study was to measure local TV news in the aggregate, rather than comparing the performance of individual stations, these substitutions did not upset the follow-up study's purpose.

Findings

The final database used for the study contained 1,184 stories (as compared with 6,000 to 8,000 stories in each year of the fuller local TV news study). The study found that crime was still the most prevalent topic on local TV news, accounting for 32% of all stories. Stories about disasters and catastrophes accounted for 10%, whereas health and consumer stories were 8%. Coverage of human interest, politics, and social issues were all below the levels found in the full five-year study.

TOPIC	PCT. OF STORIES
Crime	32%
Disasters/Catastrophes	10%
Health/Consumer	8%
Accidents/Bizarre events	8%
Culture/Civ.	8%
Human interest	7%
Politics	6%
Social issues	6%
Business	6%
Foreign affairs/Defense	6%
Sci/Tech	3%
Miscellaneous	1%
GRAND TOTAL (does not equal 100 due to rounding)	100%

The follow-up study found that the pacing of newscasts in 2005 was very similar to the findings of the five-year study: The longest stories tend to appear at the beginning of newscasts, with story length quickly dropping over the remainder of the program. In 2005, the average story length was 65 seconds, as opposed to an average story length of 61.3 seconds in the full study.

STORY NUMBER	AVG. LENGTH IN SECONDS
First story	159
2	88
3	63
4	59
5	60
6	67
7	72
8	49
9	51
10	72
11	55
12	57
13	48
14th story	34

Finally, the study examined whether or not the "hook and hold" approach – placing dramatic stories about public safety at the head of the newscast and "soft" lifestyle news at the end – still predominates in the local TV news. The 2005 findings show that the hook-and-hold pattern is all but ubiquitous.

As the first row of the table indicates, "public safety" news accounts for 54% of all stories, civic news for 24% of all stories, and "soft" news for 22% of all stories. However, in 78% of all newscasts, the first story is about public safety, and public safety news remains the most likely topic of newscast stories through the 7th story in the newscast. Soft news stories barely appear in the first set of newscast, but from the 10th story onward they account for a plurality.

Although the 2005 study was not as comprehensive as the full study, the follow-up study confirms that many of the trends observed in the original study still apply: Public safety news is most prevalent, and story pacing places easily hyped public safety news at the beginning of the newscast and "teasable" soft news at its conclusion. The even higher amount of crime news found in the 2005 study suggests that newsrooms are more committed than before to the hook-and-hold approach.

	CIVIC NEWS	MISCELLANEOUS	PUBLIC SAFETY	SOFT NEWS
All stories	23.6%	0.7%	54.3%	21.5%
First story	12.2%	0.0%	77.6%	10.2%
2	18.0%	0.0%	68.0%	14.0%
3	16.0%	2.0%	78.0%	4.0%
4	12.0%	0.0%	74.0%	14.0%
5	22.0%	0.0%	70.0%	8.0%
6	16.0%	0.0%	68.0%	16.0%
7	32.7%	0.0%	49.0%	18.4%
8	40.8%	2.0%	36.7%	20.4%
9	36.2%	0.0%	38.3%	25.5%
10	29.5%	4.5%	27.3%	38.6%
11	25.0%	0.0%	32.5%	42.5%
12	32.4%	0.0%	38.2%	29.4%
13	21.4%	0.0%	39.3%	39.3%
14th story	16.0%	0.0%	32.0%	52.0%

Notes

CHAPTER 1. A PROLOGUE: WHAT THIS BOOK IS FOR

1   The second installment of the two-part "Walls" story ran the next night, and the audience was up slightly to a 7 rating, one point higher than the four-week Tuesday night average of 6.
2   The segments that aired before "Too Old to Drive?" ranged in topic from a live report about the New Mexico legislature to a report on a wildfire to a report on a casino in someone's home.
3   A Pew Research Center for the People and the Press survey found 59% of respondents said they regularly turned to local TV news compared with 38% for cable news channels and 34% for national evening news, ("News Audiences Increasingly Politicized," June 8, 2004).

CHAPTER 2. THE KNOWLEDGE BASE

1   There is a small amount of academic research exploring what local audiences want and specifically whether the content of news matters. Some researchers have studied the programming in one market or a few markets. See for example, Phyllis Kaniss, 1991, *Making Local News*, Chicago: University of Chicago Press; John H. McManus, 1994, *Market-driven Journalism: Let the Citizen Beware?* Thousand Oaks, CA: Sage Publications; James T. Hamilton, 2004, *All the News That's Fit to Sell: How the Market Transforms Information into News*, Princeton, NJ : Princeton University Press.
2   All of the quotes regarding news quality come from the members of the Design Team.
3   The first group comprised the very largest markets in the country where 25% of the urban population of the country live. The second group was drawn from a larger number of markets, consisting of those that served the next quarter of the population in urban areas, and so on, down to the quarter of the population living in the smallest media markets. These market quartiles paralleled the Nielsen market-size index drawn from DMAs (Nielsen Media Research Local Universe Estimates, 2006). Random samples were taken from each market-size quartile.

Because the number of markets in the top quartile is only seven, a few of the largest markets were studied more than once over the five-year time frame.

4   See Nielsen Media Research, "Definition of Terms." To account for sweeps-to-sweeps fluctuation in ratings, an average figure for each of the eight aspects of commercial success was calculated for an entire year. This meant that ratings from four sweeps periods were averaged together for each station analyzed. The window of this analysis was from November of the year prior to the study, which is the first sweeps period of the TV season, to July of the content study year, which is the last sweeps period of the season. All eight measures became our dependent variables for the statistical models. To make our findings clearer, we report them separately in terms of their impact on ratings, share, and improved retention over lead-in audience.

CHAPTER 3. "I-TEAMS" AND "EYE CANDY": THE REALITY OF LOCAL TV NEWS

1   WBBM captured attention in February 2000 when the station experimented with a supposedly serious-minded newscast (see Sidebar 5.3.3, Chapter 5). The newscast didn't succeed and after nine months the station returned to a more traditional program in October 2000 that has remained on the air ever since, including 2002 when we conducted a full study of the Chicago market.

2   The Project for Excellence in Journalism conducted a study of 50 local newscasts drawn at random from 10 TV markets between January and June 2005. In contrast to the five-year study, which was based on review of videotapes, this smaller study is based on newscast rundowns that provide basic information on subject matter, story length, and the use of outside sources. For more details see Appendix E.

3   In fact, the very sameness of local news that we've observed from one part of the country to another is why we feel so strongly that our results from the 50 markets we studied can be applied to the country as a whole.

4   Honolulu, the submarine's homeport, was one of the markets studied in 2001.

5   Depending on which criterion one uses, it can be argued that this universe of higher-quality reporting is really much larger. For example, if one includes stories about issues or trends or those with multiple sources that offer a mix of opinions, the amount of high-quality work grows to one-quarter (25%) of news items. This larger statistical universe could arguably be seen as a core of more substantive content that has remained consistent over the five years of the study. Stories with the highest degree of enterprise, station-initiated investigations, composed just 1.1% of stories, falling each year from a high of 1.6% of stories in the first year of the study to 0.7% in the fifth year.

CHAPTER 4. THE MYTHS THAT DOMINATE LOCAL TV NEWS: THE X-STRUCTURE AND THE FALLACY OF THE HOOK-AND-HOLD METHOD OF TV NEWS

1   See Project for Excellence in Journalism, "Local TV: Audience," in *The State of the News Media 2004*. Available online at: http://www.stateofthemedia.com/2004/narrative_localtv_audience.asp?cat = 3&media = 6.

2   Craig M. Allen, 2001, *News Is People*, Ames, Iowa: Iowa State University Press, p. 205.

3   In the three years of training, more than 250 small groups completed the newscast stacking exercise. Each group was made up of a cross-section of newsroom employees such as anchors, reporters, producers, photographers, videotape editors, and, occasionally, someone from another department such as production, promotion, or engineering. Depending on the size of the news staff, an average two-day station visit resulted in newscast lineups from between 8 and 14 small groups. As each small group reported out the results of its deliberations, the lineup was noted, along with an explanation for the decision about each story. Newscast lineups and comments from participants in the stacking exercise were recorded by facilitators on flip chàrts that were later transcribed by Committee of Concerned Journalists staffers. Unless otherwise noted, the quotations in this chapter were taken from postsession reports that were later given to each station.

4   The exact figure was 45.5%. Radio and Television News Directors Foundation, 2003, *Local Television News Survey of News Directors and the American Public*, "Questionnaire," question 53, p. 81 (http:www.rtnel.org/ethics/2003 suryey.pdf)

5   Allen, News Is People, p. 205.

6   According to the FBI's Uniform Crime Report for 1999, the metropolitan areas of Minneapolis-St. Paul and Philadelphia had roughly equivalent crime rates in that year, whereas the crime rate in Miami was twice as high as the rate in those two areas (data for Wichita are not available).

7   Lead stories about health or political malfeasance got ratings that averaged six-tenths of a rating point more than stories about everyday crime. This finding was true irrespective of market size, station affiliation, competitiveness of the market, newscast time slot, or the year in which we studied the newscast. The statistical analysis used to generate this finding and all subsequent ratings findings is multiple regression analysis. Eight ratings measures of interest are analyzed as dependent variables: household rating and share, ratings among men and women ages 18 to 49 and 25 to 54, and rating and share retention as compared with the final quarter hour of the lead-in program. Independent variables include the market size (quartile), station affiliation, the competitiveness of the market (inverted standard deviation of household ratings of newscasts in the market during the time slot of interest such that larger values = less deviation, thus more competitive), time slot (early/late), study year, and the predictor variable of interest. All independent variables have been compressed to a range of 0 to 1 for ease of interpretation. Unless otherwise specified, the variable of interest is a variable that reflects one of two dichotomies. First, one story type or one mode of story treatment (= 1) versus all other stories or modes of treatment (= 0). Second, one story type or one mode of story treatment (= 1) versus another type of story or mode of treatment (= 0). The analysis noted here is an example of the second type of dichotomized variable. For lead stories, the data set is unweighted (equal number of lead stories per station); for all stories, the data are weighted by the number of stories aired per station. For brevity, reported regression estimates will omit control variables. For this estimate, the coefficient for the variable in question yields the following estimates: for Women 18–49: $b = .736$, $SE = .244$, $p < .01$,

$R^2 = .220$; for Women 25–54: $b = .857$, $SE = .289$, $p < .01$, $R^2 = .184$; for Men 18–49: $b = .628$, $SE = .200$, $p < .01$, $R^2 = .221$; for Men 25–54: $b = .681$, $SE = .234$, $p < .01$, $R^2 = .208$; $n = 717$ for all estimates (lead stories only).

8   For Rating Retention: $b = 8.151$, $SE = 3.337$, $p < .05$, $R^2 = .243$; for Share Retention: $b = 3.381$, $SE = 3.073$, $p < .05$, $R^2 = .080$; $n = 2418$ for both estimates (lead stories only).

9   For Women 18–49: $b = .185$, $SE = .080$, $p < .05$, $R^2 = .175$; for Women 25–54: $b = .197$, $SE = .094$, $p < .05$, $R^2 = .145$; for Men 18–49: $b = .156$, $SE = .065$, $p < .05$, $R^2 = .178$; for Men 25–54: $b = .202$, $SE = .076$, $p < .01$, $R^2 = .165$; for Rating Retention: $b = 4.710$, $SE = 1.240$, $p < .001$, $R^2 = .241$; for Share Retention: $b = 4.444$, $SE = 1.145$, $p < .001$, $R^2 = .072$; $n = 5420$ for all estimates (all stories).

10 For Women 18–49: $b = .396$, $SE = .178$, $p < .05$, $R^2 = .178$; for Women 25–54: $b = .387$, $SE = .210$, $p = .066$, $R^2 = .148$; for Men 18–49: $b = .368$, $SE = .146$, $p < .05$, $R^2 = .183$; for Men 25–54: $b = .444$, $SE = .170$, $p < .01$, $R^2 = .171$; $n = 907$ for all estimates (all stories).

11 Difference among Women 18–49 is .073 rating points ($F[1, 33909] = 5.429$, $p < .05$); Difference among Women 25–54 is .071 rating points ($F[1, 33909] = 5.429$, $p = .05$); Difference among Men 18–49 is .081 rating points ($F[1, 33909] = 9.817$, $p < .01$); Difference among Men 25–54 is .083 rating points ($F[1, 33909] = 7.647$, $p = .01$).

12 Difference among Women 18–49 is .106 rating points ($F[1, 33909] = 6.880$, $p < .05$); Difference among Women 25–54 is .113 rating points ($F[1, 33909] = 5.801$, $p = .01$); Difference among Men 18–49 is .082 rating points ($F[1, 33909] = 6.045$, $p < .05$); Difference among Men 25–54 is .007 rating points ($F[1, 33909] = 7.221$, $p = .01$).

13 P. J. Bednarski, "The Shape of Things to Come" *Broadcasting & Cable*, January 5, 2004, pg. 33).

14 Household Share: $b = .437$, $SE = .199$, $p < .05$, $R^2 = .068$, $n = 5,130$.

15 Longer stories that feature enterprise reporting, authoritative sources, and a mix of views are significantly better at retaining or building viewership in all time periods. See discussion in Chapter 5.

16 For Women 18–49: $b = .307$, $SE = .156$, $p < .05$, $R^2 = .165$; for Women 25–54: $b = .401$, $SE = .181$, $p < .05$, $R^2 = .133$; $n = 6,322$ for both estimates.

17 For Household Rating: $b = .339$, $SE = .072$, $p < .001$, $R^2 = .065$; for Household Share: $b = .574$, $SE = .137$, $p < .001$, $R^2 = .080$; for Women 18–49: $b = .214$, $SE = .044$, $p < .001$, $R^2 = .096$; for Women 25–54: $b = .277$, $SE = .052$, $p < .001$, $R^2 = .084$; for Men 18–49: $b = .165$, $SE = .036$, $p < .001$, $R^2 = .096$; for Men 25–54: $b = .218$, $SE = .042$, $p < .001$, $R^2 = .093$; $n = 33,911$ for all estimates (all stories).

18 Our definition of "live" reporting strictly included only stories in which the events being reported in the story were happening live, on-camera while the reporter or cameraperson was at the scene. It did not include pieces such as a reporter standing on the front steps of a local courthouse after dark to report on a decision handed down that morning, or a reporter standing next to a highway to report on traffic conditions. Stories that met our criteria for live reporting made up just 1.2% of the stories we studied.

19   Charlie Tuggle, Dana Rosengard, and Suzanne Huffman, "Going Live, as Viewers See It." Newslab, 2004, available online at: newslab.org.

20   Andrea Miller, "Me News: What Draws Attention to Breaking News?" Newslab, 2004, available online at: http://www.newslab.org/research/breakingnews.htm.

21   For Household Rating: $b = .340$, $SE = .173$, $p < .05$, $R^2 = .087$; for Women 18–49: $b = .220$, $SE = .105$, $p < .05$, $R^2 = .104$; for Women 25–54: $b = .259$, $SE = .123$, $p < .05$, $R^2 = .095$; for Men 18–49: $b = .200$, $SE = .084$, $p < .05$, $R^2 = .105$; for Men 25–54: $b = .241$, $SE = .099$, $p < .05$, $R^2 = .106$; $n = 4,340$ for all estimates.

22   Pew Research Center for the People and the Press, "News Audiences Increasingly Politicized," June 8, 2004.

23   For Rating Retention: $b = 6.521$, $SE = 2.953$, $p < .05$, $R^2 = .243$; for Share Retention: $b = 6.370$, $SE = 2.718$, $p < .05$, $R^2 = .080$; $n = 2,418$ for all estimates (lead stories).

24   Comparison for full Enterprise scale (see Appendix B for variable coding); for Household Rating: $b = 1.310$, $SE = .508$, $p < .01$, $R^2 = .082$; for Women 18–49: $b = .899$, $SE = .295$, $p < .01$, $R^2 = .213$; for Women 25–54: $b = 1.073$, $SE = .350$, $p < .01$, $R^2 = .177$; for Men 18–49: $b = .662$, $SE = .242$, $p < .01$, $R^2 = .212$; For Men 25–54: $b = .764$, $SE = .283$, $p < .01$, $R^2 = .201$; $n = 2,418$ for all estimates (lead stories).

25   Newslab, "The Savvy Audience for Local TV News: Are Stations Turning Viewers Off?" 2002. Available online at: http://www.newslab.org/research/savvyaudience.htm.

26   For Household Rating: $b = -.264$, $SE = .120$, $p < .05$, $R^2 = .071$; For Women 18–49: $b = -.170$, $SE = .071$, $p < .05$, $R^2 = .174$; For Women 25–54: $b = -.186$, $SE = .084$, $p < .05$, $R^2 = .145$; For Men 18–49: $b = -.158$, $SE = .059$, $p < .01$, $R^2 = .177$; For Men 25–54: $b = -.193$, $SE = .068$, $p < .01$, $R^2 = .164$; For Rating Retention: $b = -4.432$, $SE = 1.112$, $p < .001$, $R^2 = .239$; For Share Retention: $b = -4.032$, $SE = 1.027$, $p < .001$, $R^2 = .070$; $n = 33,911$ for all estimates.

27   Length variable measured in seconds. For Household Rating: $b = .00146$, $SE = .00036$, $p < .001$, $R^2 = .071$; for Household Share: $b = .00256$, $SE = .00069$, $p < .001$, $R^2 = .080$; for Women 18–49: $b = .00089$, $SE = .00021$, $p < .001$, $R^2 = .174$; for Women 25–54: $b = .00114$, $SE = .00025$, $p < .001$, $R^2 = .145$; for Men 18–49: $b = .00069$, $SE = .00018$, $p < .001$, $R^2 = .177$; for Men 25–54: $b = .00082$, $SE = .00020$, $p < .001$, $R^2 = .165$; $n = 33,911$ for all estimates.

28   In May 2005, the top-rated shows on TV, *Desperate Housewives* and *American Idol*, each averaged 25 million viewers each.

29   Allen describes "news for the masses that the masses embrace" as

a news broadcast that mixed news, sports and weather; was headlined by a two-person usually male-female anchor team and had weather and sports anchors in dominant supporting roles. Exhaustive visualization was another defining feature, as were reporters who went to the scene and used pictures to communicate stories. Short interview clips called "soundbites" were in. The paradigm of words, known in TV as the "talking head," was out. Action, too, was a goal, as were eye-catching studio sets, mood-changing music and soft-sell promotion. Blotter news like meetings and news conferences was limited so that investigative exposes, medical reports, consumer affairs, personal money matters and lifestyle news could be seen. All the anchors and reporters conversed with one another in a way that made the viewer their friend. Put all together, the people's newscast was an electronic extension of a viewer's family; in binding symbol, the smile. (Allen 2001, p. 69)

30   A separate RTNDFA survey of news directors from the fourth quarter of 2000 found that the median amount of time that they had held their current job was two years and the mean amount of time in their current job was 3.4 years. See http:www.rtnda.org/research/money.shtml.

31   See Allen, *News Is People*, p. 215. Though the consultants claimed they did not dictate news content, Allen concluded they didn't have to. "Local newsrooms had become so conditioned to what was in the research that they responded by rote." Nor was there any lack of data. From research centers such as the Magid campus in Marion, Iowa, scores of analysts used high-speed computers to poke and prod the collective mind of "Joe six pack." During just a five-day period in 1995, for example, Audience Research & Development completed 28 500-person surveys for local TV markets ranging in size from Washington, D.C., to Twin Falls, Idaho. And these 14,000 interviews were among 240,000 telephone contacts the company made with local TV news viewers that year (Allen 2001, p. 247).

32   Nielsen Media Research, "About Nielsen Media Research," available online at: http://www.nielsenmedia.com/about_us.html.

33   See Project for Excellence in Journalism, "Local TV: Audience," in *The State of the News Media 2004*, available online at: http://www.stateofthemedia.com/2004/narrative_localtv_audience.asp?cat = 3&media = 6.

CHAPTER 5. THE MAGIC FORMULA: HOW TO MAKE TV
THAT VIEWERS WILL WATCH

1   We average together all four of the demographic (Men and Women 18–49 and 25–54) estimates for discussion and graphical presentation. Estimates for Household Rating: $b = .322$, $SE = .143$, $p < .05$, $R^2 = .072$; for Women 18–49: $b = .165$, $SE = .085$, $p = .052$, $R^2 = .175$; for Women 25–54: $b = .201$, $SE = .100$, $p < .05$, $R^2 = .146$; for Men 18–49: $b = .172$, $SE = .063$, $p < .05$, $R^2 = .178$; for Men 25–54: $b = .217$, $SE = .081$, $p < .01$, $R^2 = .166$; for Rating Retention: $b = 3.929$, $SE = 1.319$, $p < .01$, $R^2 = .241$; for Share Retention: $b = 3.949$, $SE = 1.217$, $p < .01$, $R^2 = .072$; $n = 3853$ for all estimates.

2   Our multiple regression models are weighted least squares estimates weighted by the number of stories a station aired in our sample.

3   For similar reasons we had to account for the size of the market where a local news story was taped because the smallest market quartile generally receives 1.5 rating points more than the largest market quartile in terms of household and a full rating point more in terms of desirable demographics.

4   In our multiple regression analysis we also held constant the network affiliation because we discovered that the NBC network affiliates were getting better ratings than other affiliates during the period of our study.

5 For Household Rating: b = .231, SE = .134, p = .086, R^2 = .070; for Women 18–49: b = .185, SE = .080, p < .05, R^2 = .175; for Women 25–54: b = .197, SE = .094, p < .05, R^2 = .145; for Men 18–49: b = .156, SE = .065, p < .05, R^2 = .178; for Men 25–54: b = .202, SE = .076, p < .01, R^2 = .165; for Rating Retention: b = 4.710, SE = 1.240, p < .001, R^2 = .241; for Share Retention: b = 4.444, SE = 1.145, p < .001, R^2 = .072; n = 5,420 for all estimates.

6 For Household Rating: b = 1.119, SE = .355, p < .001, R^2 = .084; for Women 18–49: b = .740, SE = .210, p < .001, R^2 = .188; for Women 25–54: b = .891, SE = .248, p < .001, R^2 = .145; for Men 18–49: b = .697, SE = .172, p < .001, R^2 = .196; for Men 25–54: b = .783, SE = .201, p < .001, R^2 = .182; for Rating Retention: b = 13.207, SE = 3.261, p < .001, R^2 = .265; for Share Retention: b = 9.084, SE = 3.027, p < .01, R^2 = .081; n = 706 for all estimates.

7 For Household Rating: b = .621, SE = .120, p < .001, R^2 = .071; for Household Share: b = .929, SE = .231, p < .001, R^2 = .080; for Women 18–49: b = .323, SE = .071, p < .001, R^2 = .174; for Women 25–54: b = .427, SE = .084, p < .001, R^2 = .145; for Men 18–49: b = .261, SE = .058, p < .001, R^2 = .178; for Men 25–54: b = .307, SE = .068, p < .001, R^2 = .165; n = 33,911 for all estimates.

8 Average betas for rating and share, Enterprise = .024 vs. Topic = .001; Average betas for demo ratings, Enterprise = .024 vs. Topic = .006.

9 For Household Rating: b = .476, SE = .202, p < .05, R^2 = .071; for Household Share: b = 1.025, SE = .387, p < .01, R^2 = .080; for Women 18–49: b = .337, SE = .119, p < .01, R^2 = .175; for Women 25–54: b = .374, SE = .141, p < .01, R^2 = .146; for Men 18–49: b = .232, SE = .098, p < .05, R^2 = .178; for Men 25–54: b = .330, SE = .114, p < .01, R^2 = .165; n = 7847 for all estimates.

10 For Household Rating: b = .500, SE = .197, p < .05, R^2 = .071; for Household Share: b = 1.206, SE = .379, p < .001, R^2 = .080; for Women 18–49: b = .326, SE = .117, p < .01, R^2 = .175; for Women 25–54: b = .392, SE = .138, p < .01, R^2 = .146; for Men 18–49: b = .213, SE = .096, p < .05, R^2 = .178; for Men 25–54: b = .311, SE = .112, p < .01, R^2 = .165; n = 7313 for all estimates.

11 For Household Rating: b = 1.184, SE = .299, p < .001, R^2 = .086; for Household Share: b = 1.575, SE = .577, p < .01, R^2 = .087; for Women 18–49: b = .709, SE = .177, p < .001, R^2 = .188; for Women 25–54: b = .874, SE = .209, p < .001, R^2 = .161; for Men 18–49: b = .373, SE = .146, p < .05, R^2 = .183; for Men 25–54: b = .558, SE = .171, p < .01, R^2 = .174; n = 922 for all estimates.

12 Average betas for rating and share, Authoritative Sourcing = .025 vs. Topic = −.005; average betas for demo ratings, Authoritative Sourcing = .019 vs. Topic = .002.

13 For Household Rating: b = .445, SE = .108, p < .001, R^2 = .071; for Household Share: b = 1.039, SE = .207, p < .001, R^2 = .080; for Women 18–49: b = .221, SE = .064, p < .001, R^2 = .174; for Women 25–54: b = .289, SE = .075, p < .001, R^2 = .145; for Men 18–49: b = .197, SE = .052, p < .001, R^2 = .178; for Men 25–54: b = .165, SE = .061, p < .001, R^2 = .165; n = 33,911 for all estimates. Note: values plugged-in for discussion and graphing are .333 for "person on the street" and 1.000 for "expert" (see Appendix B for "authoritativeness" variable coding prior to compression to 0–1 range).

14   For Household Rating: b = .488, SE = .120, $p < .001$, R^2 = .074; for Household
Share: b = 1.380, SE = .230, $p < .001$, R^2 = .086; for Women 18–49: b = .242,
SE = .071, $p < .001$, R^2 = .176; for Women 25–54: b = .319, SE = .084, $p < .001$,
R^2 = .147; for Men 18–49: b = .174, SE = .058, $p < .01$, R^2 = .179; for Men 25–54:
b = .215, SE = .068, $p < .01$, R^2 = .166; n = 5,217 for all estimates.

15   Average betas for rating and share, Number of Sources = .029 vs. Topic =
−.003; average betas for demo ratings, Number of Sources = .027 vs.
Topic = .003.

16   For Household Rating: b = .279, SE = .051, $p < .001$, R^2 = .072; for Household
Share: b = .498, SE = .099, $p < .001$, R^2 = .080; for Women 18–49: b = .157,
SE = .030, $p < .001$, R^2 = .175; for Women 25–54: b = .192, SE = .036, $p < .001$,
R^2 = .146; for Men 18–49: b = .125, SE = .025, $p < .01$, R^2 = .178; for Men 25–54:
b = .143, SE = .029, $p < .01$, R^2 = .165; n = 27,663 for all estimates.

17   Average betas for rating and share, Balance of Views = .036 vs. Topic = .009;
average betas for demo ratings, Balance of Views = .037 vs. Topic = .011.

18   For Household Rating: b = .334, SE = .072, $p < .001$, R^2 = .072; for Household
Share: b = .626, SE = .138, $p < .001$, R^2 = .081; for Women 18–49: b = .219,
SE = .043, $p < .001$, R^2 = .176; for Women 25–54: b = .254, SE = .050, $p < .001$,
R^2 = .147; for Men 18–49: b = .161, SE = .035, $p < .01$, R^2 = .179; for Men 25–54:
b = .200, SE = .041, $p < .001$, R^2 = .166; n = 11,931 for all estimates.

19   The widely held perception is that educated people prefer newspapers and largely
ignore TV news. Actually, people from all education levels and income groups
watch local TV news in similar proportions.

20   For Household Rating: b = 1.395, SE = .348, $p < .001$, R^2 = .076; for Household
Share: b = 2.864, SE = .668, $p < .001$, R^2 = .085; for Women 18–49: b = .742,
SE = .206, $p < .001$, R^2 = .178; for Women 25–54: b = .880, SE = .244, $p < .001$,
R^2 = .149; for Men 18–49: b = .603, SE = .169, $p < .001$, R^2 = .181; for Men
25–54: b = .763, SE = .198, $p < .001$, R^2 = .169; n = 2,901 for all estimates.

21   Slight variations between the "news you can use" results in Figures 5.11
and 5.12 are due to different numbers of stories in the multiple regression
equation estimates. The estimates for Figure 5.12 and the discussion here
are as follows: for Household Rating: b = 1.225, SE = .402, $p < .01$, R^2 = .096;
for Household Share: b = 2.706, SE = .758, $p < .001$, R^2 = .095; for Women
18–49: b = .593, SE = .235, $p < .05$, R^2 = .246; for Women 25–54: b = .792,
SE = .279, $p < .01$, R^2 = .216; for Men 18–49: b = .511, SE = .195, $p < .01$,
R^2 = .257; for Men 25–54: b = .660, SE = .227, $p < .01$, R^2 = .243; n = 1,208 for
all estimates.

22   Average betas for rating and share, Focus on Demographic Subset = .100 vs.
Topic = −.019; average betas for demo ratings, Focus on Demographic Subset
= .149 vs. Topic = .023.

23   Regression equations used to generate the length-related figures include
terms that reflect interaction of focus coverage by length. Average betas for
rating and share, Journalistic Treatment = .102 vs. Topic = −.003; average
betas for demo ratings, Journalistic Treatment = .122 vs. Topic = .007; average
betas for lead-in rating share retention, Journalistic Treatment = .089 vs.
Topic = .002.

CHAPTER 6. STEPS TO BETTER COVERAGE

1 For Household Rating: b=1.696, SE=.761, $p<.05$, R^2=.069; for Women 18–49: b=1.256, SE=.431, $p<.01$, R^2=.189; for Women 25–54: b=1.492, SE=.514, $p<.01$, R^2=.159; for Men 18–49: b=1.065, SE=.356, $p<.01$, R^2=.178; for Men 25–54: b=1.347, SE=.423, $p<.01$, R^2=.175; n=554 for all estimates.

2 For Women 18–49: b=.550, SE=.247, $p<.05$, R^2=.315; for Women 25–54: b=.574, SE=.291, $p<.05$, R^2=.283; for Men 18–49: b=.538, SE=.203, $p<.01$, R^2=.290; for Men 25–54: b=.597, SE=.234, $p<.05$, R^2=.289; for Rating Retention: b=6.142, SE=2.944, $p<.05$, R^2=.386; for Share Retention: b=6.688, SE=2.927, $p<.05$, R^2=.148; n=334 for all estimates.

3 For Household Rating: b=4.848, SE=1.365, $p<.001$, R^2=.225; for Household Share: b=5.709, SE=2.750, $p<.05$, R^2=.154; for Women 18–49: b=2.550, SE=.824, $p<.01$, R^2=.265; for Women 25–54: b=2.942, SE=.979, $p<.01$, R^2=.233; for Men 18–49: b=1.928, SE=.672, $p<.01$, R^2=.256; for Men 25–54: b=2.698, SE=.769, $p<.001$, R^2=.284; for Rating Retention: b=27.725, SE=12.325, $p<.05$, R^2=.325; n=75 for all estimates.

4 For Household Rating: b=.851, SE=.425, $p<.05$, R^2=.084; for Household Share: b=1.872, SE=.811, $p<.05$, R^2=.104; for Women 18–49: b=.875, SE=.251, $p<.001$, R^2=.169; for Women 25–54: b=.933, SE=.298, $p<.01$, R^2=.137; for Men 18–49: b=.773, SE=.203, $p<.001$, R^2=.176; for Men 25–54: b=.847, SE=.238, $p<.001$, R^2=.162; n=1,290 for all estimates.

5 For Household Rating: b=.324, SE=.131, $p<.05$, R^2=.082; for Household Share: b=.574, SE=.251, $p<.05$, R^2=.101; for Women 18–49: b=.267, SE=.078, $p<.001$, R^2=.162; for Women 25–54: b=.309, SE=.092, $p<.001$, R^2=.132; for Men 18–49: b=.223, SE=.063, $p<.001$, R^2=.168; for Men 25–54: b=.268, SE=.074, $p<.001$, R^2=.156; n=8,197 for all estimates.

6 For Household Rating: b=.552, SE=.198, $p<.01$, R^2=.082; for Household Share: b=1.020, SE=.378, $p<.01$, R^2=.101; for Women 18–49: b=.403, SE=.117, $p<.001$, R^2=.162; for Women 25–54: b=.453, SE=.139, $p<.01$, R^2=.132; for Men 18–49: b=.375, SE=.095, $p<.001$, R^2=.168; for Men 25–54: b=.426, SE=.111, $p<.001$, R^2=.156; n=8,197 for all estimates.

7 For Household Rating: b=.783, SE=.301, $p<.01$, R^2=.089; for Women 18–49: b=.506, SE=.178, $p<.01$, R^2=.169; for Women 25–54: b=.644, SE=.210, $p<.01$, R^2=.141; for Men 18–49: b=.339, SE=.144, $p<.05$, R^2=.172; for Men 25–54: b=.474, SE=.169, $p<.01$, R^2=.163; n=790 for all estimates.

8 See U.S. Department of Justice, Office of Justice Programs, Bureau of Justice Statistics, "Crime Characteristics." Available online at: http://www.ojp.usdoj.gov/bjs/cvict_c.htm.

9 Results for the survey are based on telephone interviews conducted under the direction of Princeton Survey Research Associates among a nationwide sample of 1,005 adults, 18 years of age or older, during the period May 6–16, 2002. Based on the total sample, one can say with 95% confidence that the error attributable to sampling and other random effect is plus or minus 3.5 percentage points. For items on Form A (questions 1–3; n=249), From B (questions 4–6; n=256), From

C (questions 7–9; N=258), or From D (questions 10–12; n=239) the sampling error is plus or minus 7 percentage points.

10 Tom Rosenstiel and Dave Iversen, "Politics and TV Can Mix," *Los Angeles Times*, October 15, 2002.

11 The spike in government and politics coverage in 2000 was due to the increased coverage of election/campaign news that year (9.2% of all stories, compared with 1.7% in other years). Coverage of noncampaign-related government and politics stories remained constant at about 7% per year. In the presidential election year of 2000, coverage of the election got about the same ratings as noncampaign government and politics stories.

12 Stories about law and the judiciary were not coded as political stories. National and local government/politics stories break down somewhat differently on local news. A greater percentage of national stories than local stories are about campaigns and elections. This is not surprising because most of those national stories aired in the presidential election year. Otherwise, national political stories are pretty scarce on local TV news. A significant proportion of local stories are also about campaigns and elections (24%), but a lot of local government/politics stories are about legislative action (19%).

13 For Household Rating: b=2.327, SE=.540, $p<.001$, $R^2=.068$; for Household Share: b=4.385, SE=1.068, $p<.001$, $R^2=.078$; for Women 18–49: b=1.140, SE=.309, $p<.001$, $R^2=.179$; for Women 25–54: b=1.479, SE=.368, $p<.001$, $R^2=.147$; for Men 18–49: b=.976, SE=.257, $p<.001$, $R^2=.190$; for Men 25–54: b=1.147, SE=.299, $p<.001$, $R^2=.171$; n=3,238 for all estimates.

14 Estimates for interview with substantive questioning versus pre-arranged event: for Household Rating: b=2.164, SE=.496, $p<.001$, $R^2=.080$; for Household Share: b=4.324, SE=.982, $p<.001$, $R^2=.091$; for Women 18–49: b=.967, SE=.285, $p<.001$, $R^2=.185$; for Women 25–54: b=1.226, SE=.339, $p<.001$, $R^2=.154$; for Men 18–49: b=.814, SE=.237, $p<.001$, $R^2=.196$; for Men 25–54: b=1.014, SE=.275, $p<.001$, $R^2=.178$; n=1,024 for all estimates (results for substantive questioning generated off of this equation). Estimates for interview with substantive questioning versus wire feed: for Household Rating: b=2.819, SE=.532, $p<.001$, $R^2=.103$; for Household Share: b=5.627, SE=1.053, $p<.001$, $R^2=.115$; for Women 18–49: b=1.277, SE=.307, $p<.001$, $R^2=.198$; for Women 25–54: b=1.665, SE=.364, $p<.001$, $R^2=.171$; for Men 18–49: b=1.030, SE=.255, $p<.001$, $R^2=.207$; for Men 25–54: b=1.266, SE=.297, $p<.001$, $R^2=.191$; n=622 for all estimates. Estimates for interview with substantive questioning versus story attributed to other organization: for Household Rating: b=2.304, SE=1.002, $p<.05$, $R^2=.115$; for Household Share: b=4.001, SE=1.995, $p<.05$, $R^2=.113$; for Women 18–49: b=1.035, SE=.580, $p=.078$, $R^2=.204$; for Women 25–54: b=1.338, SE=.687, $p=.055$, $R^2=.178$; for Men 18–49: b=.865, SE=.482, $p=.076$, $R^2=.215$; for Men 25–54: b=1.121, SE=.558, $p<.05$, $R^2=.203$; n=96 for all estimates.

15 For Household Rating: b=.856, SE=.210, $p<.001$, $R^2=.067$; for Household Share: b=1.774, SE=.416, $p<.001$, $R^2=.079$; for Women 18–49: b=.422, SE=.120, $p<.001$, $R^2=.179$; for Women 25–54: b=.514, SE=.143, $p<.001$, $R^2=.146$; for Men 18–49: b=.391, SE=.100, $p<.001$, $R^2=.190$; for Men 25–54: b=.433, SE=.116, $p<.001$, $R^2=.171$; n=3,238 for all estimates.

16   For Household Rating: b=1.846, SE=.368, $p<.001$, R^2=.070; for Household
     Share: b=4.119, SE=.727, $p<.001$, R^2=.083; for Women 18–49: b=.860,
     SE=.211, $p<.001$, R^2=.180; for Women 25–54: b=1.104, SE=.251, $p<.001$,
     R^2=.148; for Men 18–49: b=.775, SE=.175, $p<.001$, R^2=.191; for Men 25–54:
     b=.863, SE=.204, $p<.001$, R^2=.172; n=3,238 for all estimates.

17   For Household Rating: b=.758, SE=.216, $p<.001$, R^2=.066; for Household Share:
     b=1.680, SE=.427, $p<.001$, R^2=.078; for Women 18–49: b=.490, SE=.123,
     $p<.001$, R^2=.179; for Women 25–54: b=.537, SE=.147, $p<.001$, R^2=.147; for
     Men 18–49: b=.358, SE=.103, $p<.001$, R^2=.190; for Men 25–54: b=.365,
     SE=.119, $p<.01$, R^2=.170; for Rating Retention: b=5.181, SE=2.246, $p<.05$,
     R^2=.225; for Share Retention: b=5.488, SE=2.009, $p<.01$, R^2=.074; n=3,238 for
     all estimates.

18   For Household Rating: b=−1.363, SE=.407, $p<.001$, R^2=.128; for Household
     Share: b=−2.917, SE=.783, $p<.001$, R^2=.136; for Women 18–49: b=−.688,
     SE=.243, $p<.01$, R^2=.261; for Women 25–54: b=−.912, SE=.289, $p<.01$,
     R^2=.227; for Men 18–49: b=−.630, SE=.205, $p<.01$, R^2=.274; for Men 25–54:
     b=−.752, SE=.234, $p<.01$, R^2=.252; for Rating Retention: b=−10.872,
     SE=4.191, $p<.01$, R^2=.179; for Share Retention: b=−9.558, SE=3.897, $p<.05$,
     R^2=.085; n=887 for all estimates.

19   For Household Rating: b=1.327, SE=.625, $p<.05$, R^2=.122; for Household Share:
     b=2.869, SE=1.205, $p<.05$, R^2=.128; for Women 18–49: b=.258, SE=.373,
     $p<.05$, R^2=.258; for Women 25–54: b=1.005, SE=.444, $p<.05$, R^2=.223; for
     Men 18–49: b=.727, SE=.315, $p<.05$, R^2=.270; for Men 25–54: b=.888,
     SE=.358, $p<.05$, R^2=.248; for Rating Retention: b=13.103, SE=6.427, $p<.05$,
     R^2=.176; for Share Retention: b=12.726, SE=5.972, $p<.05$, R^2=.084; n=887 for
     all estimates.

20   For Household Rating: b=.720, SE=.396, p=.069, R^2=.055; for Women 18–49:
     b=.472, SE=.243, p=.052, R^2=.179; for Women 25–54: b=.600, SE=.284, $p<.05$,
     R^2=.152; for Men 18–49: b=.250, SE=.201, p=.213, R^2=.169; for Men 25–54:
     b=.449, SE=.236, p=.057, R^2=.165; n=1,366 for all estimates.

21   For Household Rating: b=.402, SE=.215, p=.062, R^2=.056; for Household Share:
     b=.686, SE=.397, p=.084, R^2=.047; n=1,366 for all estimates.

22   For Household Rating: b=1.979, SE=.799, $p<.05$, R^2=.063; for Household Share:
     b=4.066, SE=1.469, $p<.01$, R^2=.056; for Women 18–49: b=1.614, SE=.488,
     $p<.001$, R^2=.191; for Women 25–54: b=1.888, SE=.571, $p<.01$, R^2=.164; for
     Men 18–49: b=1.281, SE=.403, $p<.01$, R^2=.181; for Men 25–54: b=1.628,
     SE=.473, $p<.001$, R^2=.179; n=616 for all estimates.

23   For Household Rating: b=.744, SE=.282, $p<.01$, R^2=.058; for Household Share:
     b=1.692, SE=.518, $p<.01$, R^2=.052; for Women 18–49: b=.473, SE=.173, $p<.01$,
     R^2=.181; for Women 25–54: b=.549, SE=.202, $p<.01$, R^2=.154; for Men 18–49:
     b=.291, SE=.143, $p<.05$, R^2=.170; for Men 25–54: b=.380, SE=.168, $p<.05$,
     R^2=.166; n=1,366 for all estimates.

24   For Household Rating: b=.004, SE=.001, $p<.01$, R^2=.058; for Household Share:
     b=.006, SE=.003, $p<.05$, R^2=.048; for Women 18–49: b=.002, SE=.001, $p<.05$,
     R^2=.180; for Women 25–54: b=.003, SE=.001, $p<.01$, R^2=.155; for Men 18–49:
     b=.002, SE=.001, $p<.05$, R^2=.170; for Men 25–54: b=.002, SE=.001, $p<.05$,

$R^2=.166$; n=1,366 for all estimates. For the 11–29 second group, the average value of 22.650 was plugged into the equation, for the 100+ second group, the average value of 161.010 was plugged into the equation.

25   For Household Rating: b=2.223, SE=.923, $p<.05$, $R^2=.064$; for Household Share: b=4.628, SE=1.186, $p<.05$, $R^2=.089$; for Women 18–49: b=1.176, SE=.506, $p<.05$, $R^2=.137$; for Women 25–54: b=1.043, SE=.607, $p<.05$, $R^2=.116$; for Men 18–49: b=.940, SE=.412, $p<.05$, $R^2=.155$; for Men 25–54: b=1.100, SE=.484, $p<.05$, $R^2=.143$; n=224 for all estimates.

CHAPTER 7. PUTTING IT ALL INTO ACTION: TECHNIQUES FOR CHANGING NEWSROOM CULTURES

1   Credit for this idea belongs to Newslab, "Resources at Your Fingertips."
2   Knight Foundation, 2002, Newsroom Training Study.
3   Newslab.org.

CHAPTER 8. THE ROAD AHEAD: THE FUTURE OF LOCAL TV NEWS

1   This is fundamentally different than what has occurred in the morning news time period where local TV has been able to tap into a growing audience of early risers by offering a simple menu of overnight news headlines, weather, and traffic reports. In the morning, the primary competition was radio which, in many markets, ceded the air to local TV by de-emphasizing news or eliminating it altogether.

References

Allen, Craig M. 2001. *News Is People: The Rise of Local TV News and the Fall of News from New York*. Ames, Iowa: Iowa State University Press.

Altheide, David L. 2002. *Creating Fear: News and the Construction of Crisis*. New York: Walter de Gruyter.

Bednarski, P. J. 2004. "The Shape of Things to Come." *Broadcasting and Coble*, Jan. 5.

Bennett, W. Lace. 2003. *News: The Politics of Illusion*. 5th ed. New York: Longman.

Boemer, Marilyn Lawrence. 1987. "Correlating Lead-in Show Ratings with Local Television News Ratings." *Journal of Broadcasting & Electronic Media* 31(1): 89–94.

Bryant, Jennings, Rodney A. Carveth, and Dan Brown. 1981. "Television Viewing and Anxiety: An Experimental Examination." *Journal of Communication* 31(1): 106–119.

Cappella, Joseph N., and Kathleen Hall Jamieson. 1997. *Spiral of Cynicism*. New York: Oxford University Press.

Davis, Donald M., and James R. Walker. 1990. "Countering the New Media: The Resurgence of Share Maintenance in Primetime Network Television." *Journal of Broadcasting & Electronic Media* 34(4): 487–493.

Ehrlich, Matthew C. 1995. "The Ethical Dilemma of Television News Sweeps." *Journal of Mass Media Ethics* 10(1): 37–47.

Epstein, Edward Jay. 1973. *News from Nowhere: Television and the News*. New York: Vintage.

Federal Bureau of Investigation. Uniform Crime Reports. Available online at: http://www.fbi.gov/ucr/99cius.htm.

Graber, Doris A. 2001. *Processing Politics: Learning from Television in the Internet Age*. Chicago: University of Chicago Press.

Hamilton, James T. 2004. *All the News That's Fit to Sell: How the Market Transforms Information into News*. Princeton, NJ: Princeton University Press.

Hickey, Neil. 2003. "Cable Wars: In the Desperate Race for Ratings, the Public Falls Behind." *Columbia Journalism Review* 41(5): 12–17.

———. 2001. "Chicago Experiment – Why It Failed." *Columbia Journalism Review* 39(5): 15–19.

Kaniss, Phyllis. 1991. *Making Local News*. Chicago: University of Chicago Press.

Knight Foundation. 2002. Newsroom Training Study. Available online at: http://www.poynter.org/resource/10841/StaffInterviews3.pdf.

Lang, Annie, and Deborah Potter. 2000. "News You Can Remember." Newslab. Available online at: http://research/remember.htm.

McManus, John H. 1994. *Market-driven Journalism: Let the Citizen Beware?* Thousand Oaks, CA: Sage Publications.

Miller, Andrea. 2004. "Me News: What Draws Attention to Breaking News?" Newslab. Available online at: http//www.newslab.org/research/breakingnews.htm.

Moritz, Meg. 1989. "The Ratings 'Sweeps' and How They Make News." In Gary Burns and Robert J. Thompson (eds.), *Television Studies: Textual Analysis*. New York: Praeger.

Newslab. "Resources at Your Fingertips." Available online at: http://www.newslab.org.

————. 2002 "The Savvy Audience for Local TV News: Are Stations Turning Viewers off?" Available online at: http://www.newslab.org/research/savvy audience.htm.

Nielsen Media Research. "Definition of Terms." Available online at: http://www.nielsenmedia.com/ratings101.htm.

————. About "Nielsen Media Research." Available online at: http://www.nielsenmedia.com/about_us.html.

————. "Local Universe Estimates." 2006. Available online at: http://www.nielsenmedia.com/DMAS.html.

Patterson, Thomas. 1994. *Out of Order*. New York: Vintage Books.

Pethokoukis, James M. 2000. "A Dose of Hard News: Chicago's WBBM-TV Fails to Counter Tabloid-Style Local News." *US News and World Report* 129(19): 54.

Pew Research Center for the People and the Press. 2004. "News Audiences Increasingly Politicized," June 8. Survey Report. Available online at: http://people-press.org/reports.

Potter, Deborah. 2001. "From Silly to Shameless: With a Few Exceptions, the Recent TV Sweeps Period Brought out the Worst in News Coverage." *American Journalism Review* 23(4): 72.

Princeton Survey Research Associates. "Why Has TV Stopped Covering Politics?" Survey: May 6–16, 2002. Available online at: http://www.journalism.org/node/172.

Project for Excellence in Journalism. 2005. "Local TV: Audience" In *The State of the News Media 2004*. Available online at: http://www.stateofthemedia.com/2004/narrative_localtv_audience.asp?cat=3&media=6.

Radio and Television News Directors Foundation. 2001. Newsroom Profitability Survey. Available online at: http://www.rtnda.org/research/money/shtml.

————. 2003. *Local Television News Survey of News Directors and the American Public*. "Questionnaire," question 53, p. 81. Available online at: http://www.rtnda.org/ethics/2003 Survey.pdf.

Rosenstiel, Tom, and Dave Iversen "Politics and TV Can Mix," *Los Angeles Times*, October 15, 2002.

Rybak, Deborah Caulfield. "Hubbard Ends Channel 45 9 p.m News: 27 Employees Are Laid Off from KSTP-KSTC Staff." *Minneapolis Star Tribune*. January 7, 2003, p. 4.

Tiedge, James T., and Kenneth J. Ksobiech. 1986. "The 'Lead-In' Strategy for Prime-Time TV: Does It Increase the Audience?" *Journal of Communication* 36 (3): 50–63.

Tuggle, Charlie, Dana Rosengard, and Suzanne Huffman. 2004. "Going Live, As Viewers See It." Newslab. Available online at: http://www.newslab.org/research/liveshot/htm.

U.S. Department of Justice, Office of Justice Programs, Bureau of Justice Statistics. "Crime Characteristics." Available online at: http://www.ojp.usdoj.gov/bjs/cvict_c.htm.

Index